BLINK

BLINK

S.A. JEWELL

Ambassador International
GREENVILLE, SOUTH CAROLINA & BELFAST, NORTHERN IRELAND
www.ambassador-international.com

Blink
©2017 by S.A. Jewell
All rights reserved

ISBN: 978-1-62020-632-4
eISBN: 978-1-62020-164-0

Scripture quotations are taken from the Holy Bible, New International Version®, NIV® Copyright ©1973, 1978, 1984, 2011 by Biblica, Inc.® Used by permission. All rights reserved worldwide.

Cover Design and Page Layout by Hannah Nichols
eBook Conversion by Anna Riebe Raats

AMBASSADOR INTERNATIONAL
Emerald House
411 University Ridge, Suite B14
Greenville, SC 29601, USA
www.ambassador-international.com

AMBASSADOR BOOKS
The Mount
2 Woodstock Link
Belfast, BT6 8DD, Northern Ireland, UK
www.ambassadormedia.co.uk

The colophon is a trademark of Ambassador

I thank the Lord, my God for His mercy, steadfast love, and encouragement,
I thank my husband Steve for his support and love,
And I thank two dear friends, Ginger Cox and Fran Herrick, for their considerable help.

CHAPTER ONE

THE FAMILY

"I CAN'T PRETEND TO KNOW what you're talking about." Jason slurred his words. "I don't really drink wine. And when I do, I can't tell the difference between them except for the color." He swirled his glass, staring at the sloshing liquids.

One of his coworkers laughed. "We'll educate you. You need to be a little more sophisticated if you're going to socialize with CEOs, but at least you can tell the difference between the white from the red. It's a start."

More laughter.

"But then again, he can't tell the difference from box, screw-top, or cork!" someone else said. "So, sip slowly, and let me explain the nuances of fine wine."

"You explain? I think you're as dim as he is." Another drunken friend jerked his head toward Jason, who looked at him in mock offense, then chuckled and smiled sheepishly. "Ah, no offense, boss."

"None taken," Jason answered. He wondered about the dizziness setting in. *I'll have to take a cab home.* Dutifully he took a small sip, which led to another and then another as he listened to his associates babble about how special this particular wine was, its age, and where it came from. When they went through the litany of all the right adjectives to describe it, he thought he heard someone say it was "almost chocolaty." Someone else scoffed. Another said it had just a hint of bark, and everyone at the table roared in laughter. All he knew was the bottle was well over three hundred and fifty dollars, but with the bonus they had all just received, why not? Drunk, he was expansive. Gallantly he ordered not one bottle, but another two.

The waiter brought two bottles and held them up for Jason to inspect.

"Now we're talkin', my man!" his friend said loudly, then poured out a tiny bit in Jason's empty glass for him to sample before pouring out for the rest of the men at the table.

"You're wasting your time," his friend Anthony said. "All he knows is that it's red! Give it to me. I'll sample it."

Dutifully the waiter poured a fresh glass for the man, who was drunk himself. He made an elaborate show of swirling the liquid, sniffing it, then ever so daintily taking a sip. "Superb! Please pour for my friends! This is a fine ending to our celebration!"

The four men at the table lifted their glasses, congratulating each other for a job well done.

The team did an excellent ad campaign for high-end women's jeans, and the design house extended the contract for another three years after getting rave reviews (from men) during the Super Bowl spots. The public couldn't get enough of the near-soft-porn ads. The women they chose to model barely looked sixteen and were exotically alluring posing in skimpy short T-shirts and in the designer's very tight hip-hugging jeans. Even at two hundred dollars a pop, sales for the jeans had rocketed. So who cared how much the wine cost? In the end, the client paid for it anyway.

Sitting at his desk, Jason thought his head was going to explode. He willed the nausea to settle itself quietly in his stomach and ignored the dull pain in his lower belly signaling a soon-to-happen bathroom visit. Why did he have to finish off the last bottle of red wine last night? How stupid. He rarely drank wine, let alone a heady red, but his colleagues teased him into the last glass of that very expensive Cabernet. While enjoying their celebratory dinner at a posh downtown French restaurant, they had already gone through countless bottles of less expensive wines. Then their talk turned to some California vineyard that had won a notable award for their Cabernet. For Jason, it was all downhill from there.

Just thinking of the last gulp sent bile up his throat. Gagging, he closed his eyes to contain the reflex. Oh man, he couldn't remember the last time he was this hungover. College? And how idiotic was it to waste expensive bottles of wine when everyone was too drunk to tell the difference? It was still true. It could have been wine in a box for all he knew, and his colleagues, who bragged they were connoisseurs of fine vintages, slugged it down like water.

Opening his eyes with a deeply controlled breath to settle his stomach, he looked at the three computer screens in front of him begging for attention. There was no way he could concentrate on reading urgent emails, checking the clients' charts from his staff, and keeping up with general business, social media, and competition statistics. Even while sober, managing three screens at once was a challenge. But hungover it was near impossible. To top it off, the incessant buzzing of his phone, which his admin couldn't quite seem to filter, sliced into his brain like a bandsaw. Between the wicked headache and violently sour stomach, he wasn't sure he could function.

The phone beeped again. Angry, he tapped the On button. "Jason here," he snapped.

"Hey, Jason, it's Remy in IT. When can I come by to work on your computers? We're having problems with our servers and I need access to your devices and Becky's. It'll take about a half an hour or so because I have to—"

"Remy, I don't know," Jason said through clenched teeth. "You'll need to check with Becky to see when I won't be in my office. Bye." With effort, he got up, stomped across his office, and threw open the door to the outer office. "Becky. What is wrong with you? You need to start screening my calls. I can't be interrupted for your administrative work! Call Remy in IT and have him make an appointment." Before she could defend herself, he turned back to his office, slamming his door.

Dizziness overcame him and he staggered. He steadied himself against the door and taking deep breaths, he managed to quell his vertigo and nausea caused by his outburst, but his lower belly pain grew worse. He sprinted into his private bathroom. He wasn't sure whether to throw up or sit down. The pain reminded him to sit down.

Feeling a little relieved, he washed his hands, splashed cool water on his face, and went to his desk, where he picked up his coffee cup and calmed himself by looking out the floor-to-ceiling window that gave an imposing view of the city. His interior decorator had done a magnificent job on his office. The furnishings and floor coverings were designed to calm, to enable thinking without bold colors and designs to distract. The view had an uncanny peaceful effect. Although this was a high-paced advertising agency that demanded unique and clever solutions, Jason wanted his office to be a haven for deep thought.

But he couldn't think much this morning. Remembering breathing techniques from a long ago yoga class he took with his wife when they were into spirituality, he inhaled deeply for three counts and exhaled for three counts. He did this three times and found himself a bit steadier. He needed coffee. No point in asking Becky to get it. She could screw up even a black cup of coffee. Exiting his retreat, he barged past his administrative assistant and headed to the elevator going down to the lounge on the second floor.

The hallway to the lounge was thickly carpeted and beautiful Turkish wall hangings lined both walls in between private offices and conference rooms. The company did not believe in bullpen configurations or cubicles, so each employee and administrator on all three floors of the building had an office of his or her own, although there was distinction between the worker bees and the senior managers, who were all located on the third floor.

Jason rarely came downstairs because, quite frankly, it was way below his status of vice president of sales and marketing. Today, however, the executive lounge was closed due to remodeling, and he was making the exception because he badly needed a jolt of caffeine; here he could find a variety of steamy hot Starbucks coffees and teas, cold juices, soft drinks, and ice water. The shot of black coffee might level his nerves. He had to start feeling better soon. Tonight he had to meet a potential client for dinner and drinks (yet again!) and he had to be alert, charming, and sharp, but the thought of more alcohol made his stomach flip. The client company, Luna International, had three large resorts in the Caribbean, and the CEO wanted to interview Jason's firm to manage their advertising and marketing efforts. Although Jason's company, Word Expanse, was a small boutique advertising agency, it was extremely successful due in large part to Jason and the creative team he assembled. Word Expanse was also choosey in the clients they represented. Only successful companies with solid sales who were open to unusual marketing approaches were accepted, like the erotic jean campaign during the Super Bowl. That campaign was edgy, a little on the inappropriate side, but it had immediate impact. It beat out the Clydesdales.

As he entered the break room, he glanced at five people, casually dressed and slumped on couches and cushioned chairs, their eyes glued to their cell phones while their thumbs tapped away. He smirked knowingly. People, except maybe old people, rarely watched TV, read newspapers, or bought books. Critical thinking was limited to a sentence or two on Twitter or any of the other popular social platforms. If you didn't capture the attention of a person in eight seconds, you lost them.

Lilly (he couldn't remember her last name) was the only person not holding a cell phone. Surprisingly, she was quaintly reading a very thick book, while sipping a can of Coke. As he entered, she looked up and teased, "Hi, Jason. How goes life at the top?"

"Okay, I guess." He smiled feebly and went to the coffee counter. As he reached for an insulated cup, he knocked the short stack to the floor. They popped apart and scattered under Lilly's chair.

The five workers on break briefly looked up from their phones and in unison mumbled, "Hey, Jason," before diverting their eyes back to video or messaging.

Jason responded with a wave of his hand and looked at the cups rolling on the floor.

Lilly popped up from her chair to help. "I'll get them. I don't think anyone will mind if I just restack them." She gathered the dozen or so up. "It's the five-second rule. Besides, the floor looks very clean and no one looks beyond eye level anyway."

Jason leaned against the counter, fearing if he bent down, he would either be overcome with faintness trying to straighten up or never be able to get up—period. He'd just lie back on the very clean floor and sleep. It was inviting. No one would see him. No one looks beyond eye level particularly if they have a phone in their hand.

"Thanks, Lilly. I appreciate it." He blinked twice to focus his eyes.

"You okay? You look pale." Lilly was an average-looking woman with beautiful eyes. He didn't know her personally, but she was always pleasant, had a good professional reputation in the company, and worked well with others.

"I'm not feeling great this morning. I just need some coffee," he explained. With a shaking hand, he took a cup from her, poured a large serving of strong black coffee, said a weak good-bye, and walked out. He hoped he'd rally by five o'clock so he would be quick-witted when he met his new client. He would have to ask Becky to go out and get him some Alka-Seltzer—if she could handle it—and then he would take a nap on his office couch.

The next morning, as he parked his new BMW 5 Series in the parking garage, Jason went over the previous night's success. He did feel measurably better by five o'clock last evening and when he met with Mr. Nathan Kurtz of Luna International. He managed to cautiously sip a vodka on ice and later enjoy a glass of white wine with dinner. (He was off red forever.) He also managed to convince his potential client to come on board with Word Expanse. After extensive discussion, Kurtz agreed to work with Jason and said, "Set up a meeting next week to talk contract, marketing, and sales strategies."

Jason smiled as he replayed his reply. "Mr. Kurtz, I can assure you Word Expanse will dramatically break open the international tourism market for your properties with impressive and equally quick results." With a nod of his head, he added, "I already have my most seasoned team in place to take your success to the next level."

"My own team has done due diligence researching your company, and although your firm is small, you've had striking success. I like your creative approaches. A little avant-garde, but that's what's needed to stand out in this oversaturated market," Kurtz conceded. "I wanted to meet you personally and of course hear your pitch. I've met with a number of other agencies too, but at this point, I can give a verbal agreement on us doing business together. Have your legal pull together a contract and I want to meet your team next week."

Jason went home that night hugely satisfied with himself, but his happiness was sidetracked by his teenage daughter, who was arguing with her mom for—of all things—the designer jeans of Super Bowl success.

"Mom, I need those jeans. Cripe, Dad was the one that made them popular. Why can't I have a pair? All the girls at school already have them. I'm the only one not wearing them."

"Because they cost two hundred dollars! Don't you think that's a bit pricey for a pair of jeans? And don't you think they're just a little too sexy for a girl your age?"

"My age? Mom," she whined, "I'm almost sixteen and all the girls my age are wearing them. They're the most popular designer jeans! And heck, if you said I could get a new BMW SUV for my sixteenth birthday next month, then why would you argue over jeans that cost a measly two hundred dollars?"

From the family room, they stopped arguing and looked up from the oversized leather couch where they were sitting to see Jason, tall, thin, and sauntering through the hallway, obviously pleased with himself. He tossed his car keys on the counter and smiled at them. His wife, Allie, a stunning woman of cover girl quality, was dressed in designer clothing herself: a lightweight cashmere T-shirt, tailored linen pants, and delicate leather handmade sandals on her tanned feet. She popped off the sofa and greeted him with a hug. While she was asking how his meeting went, Sabrina ran up and grabbed his arm. "Dad, I want those jeans! Mom is being mean!"

Allie stepped back and rolled her eyes. "Hardly."

"Ah, Allie, why not? If she wants them, let her have them. We don't want our baby girl unhappy. "Got to keep up her maintenance," he teased. "And I did make every woman and girl on the planet want a pair." He cocked his head and grinned hugely.

"Hooray, Dad!" Sabrina screeched and ran to her bedroom to order them online.

Allied sighed. "Yes, and all those women and girls think they are going to look like those sultry buxom teenagers modeling them." She picked at a piece of lint caught in her diamond-and-ruby bracelet and turned to sit on the couch.

"Sabrina fits the image," Jason mumbled as he looked through the mail. He had to admit, they were all caught up in a spending frenzy as he scanned one bill after another. He recently purchased a new BMW for himself, and he was planning on getting the 3 Series Beemer for his daughter for her birthday. His wife drove a new mid-sized Mercedes. Both women had untold numbers of handbags stowed away in their closets that were well into the hundreds of dollars—for each—not to mention salon treatments, pedicures, manicures, accessories, and designer clothes.

Allie sighed again breaking into his thoughts. "I just don't want her getting ahead of herself. She gets just about everything she wants."

"True, yet you just gave her diamond earrings."

Allie groused. "Yes, I did, my darling. But lest you forget, I am the primo jewelry designer for Henry Sotheby. My daughter must have diamond earrings, especially if I designed them. I know we're getting her the car, but I wanted her to have them too. Sweet sixteen and all." As an afterthought she said, "By the way, Henry wants you to represent his business."

This announcement surprised Jason and he put down the stack of letters. "I thought he did well enough through word of mouth with wealthy heiresses, dowagers, and trust fund babies and didn't need big budget advertising."

"He's changed his mind. He now says you can never have enough success or money. Why not reach out to the masses?"

"Well, that is good news!" Jason was elated. Henry Sotheby's was a catch and he didn't have to pitch anyone. His reputation for clever success was even influencing the elite. Smiling broadly, he crowed, "I have more good news. My meeting with Nathan Kurtz of Luna International went really well. I got the contract."

"Wonderful!" Allie said with wide-eyed enthusiasm. "Now we can redo the kitchen!"

Thinking back over last night, Jason smiled again, gathered his laptop bag, and walked to the elevator in the parking garage. For feeling as lousy as he did yesterday, he had a very successful day and evening. He clinched the deal with Luna International and now Henry Sotheby, world renowned jeweler for the rich and famous, wanted his company to represent him.

In his office he sent update emails to senior management and his team regarding a number of issues to include his new conquests. He next called the marketing director.

"Keith, I want your best mind in helping me conceptualize strategy for Luna International. I know you're taking off for a few days and I need help now, so your second in command will do. Also, Henry Sotheby—yes, the jewelry guy—said he wants us to work with him. I know, huh? What a great couple of days. Anyway, we'll deal with Henry later. I'll call him today for next steps, but in the meanwhile Nathan Kurtz wants a meeting with us next week. I need a compelling presentation laying the strategic groundwork before bringing the entire team together to brainstorm some campaigns to present to Kurtz. So I want your best strategist to work with me for a few days. Can do?"

Half an hour later, there was a knock on the door. In stepped Lilly, the book reader.

"Lilly, thanks for joining me," Jason said. "You familiar with Luna International and Nathan Kurtz?"

"Yes, a bit," she answered as she sat down in front of his desk. "But I need to research more. I understand the hotel properties are successful and Kurtz himself is quite an interesting guy from what little I found out between the time Keith called and now. Did you know that he has a stable of Arabian horses that he shows? He's well-known in the equestrian world and has a very important equestrian center in the Carolinas. It's a hobby."

"No, I didn't know that. When I met him, we spent time focusing on business rather than personal conversation." It took Jason a moment to recognize that most of the meetings he had with clients he rarely entered into conversation about their personal lives. In retrospect, no one ever asked him about his personal life either. "My meetings are usually about business. Sure, there are always comments about sports or golf, but conversation never much morphs into much more than casual banter." He paused. "Okay, do more research and give me details of the company, their financials, the chief executive officers, their trends, their likes, and their style . . . "

"I know the drill. How soon do you want it?"

"Let's circle back here about 4:45 with what you've got. We'll work for about an hour."

Lilly arrived at Jason's office right on time. She carried her tablet, a handful of manila folders, her purse, and the big book she was reading the day before in the break room.

"Let's go into the conference room and layout any material you might have." Jason gathered his tablet and phone.

As they entered the conference room, he tilted his head at the book she was carrying. "What're you reading? I can't remember the last time I saw anyone with a book. Well, except my daughter, but those were schoolbooks and few at that." He grimaced. Sabrina hardly ever cracked open a book. "I guess they do most of their work on tablets."

"It's my Bible." When she put her things on the large polished table, her purse dropped to the floor. Taking a seat, she drew a book from her pile of work and slid it over to him.

He sat down and read the cover with a frown on his face. "A Bible? Are you kidding? Who reads a Bible?" He put a hand on it. "I honestly don't know of one single person who reads a Bible—in fact I've never even seen a real one." He casually flipped a few pages and then slid it back to her. "Well, that's not entirely true. I've seen them in hotel rooms in the side tables by the bed or in the desk drawer, but I've never opened one."

"I have Bible study tonight, and I'm leaving from here," she said casually. She looked directly at him as if to make a point. "I try to study during my break and, to be frank, I read it in the break room on purpose, so I can pique the interest of any of our employees."

Jason looked annoyed.

She smiled as she held up her hand. "Don't worry, Jason. I don't proselyte unless someone asks. And you know, in fairness, we have a number of Muslims here who have the freedom to pray two to three times a day, without interruption. I would like that same freedom to practice my own beliefs," she said simply. "And reading during my break doesn't interfere with my work."

"You could read in the privacy of your office during break," he said indignantly while thinking, *Oh no, not another religious fanatic.*

"Yes, I could, but I guess I really don't want work to interfere with my study. You know, phones ringing, people popping in . . ."

"Then close the door!" Jason countered. "Don't answer the phone!"

"What's wrong using the break room? I'm not preaching, for goodness sake. I'm just reading and besides, no one yet has shown any interest in what I'm reading anyway."

"I'm not complaining, Lilly," Jason said testily. "I just think this whole religion thing has gotten way out of hand. It has no place at work. Besides, with the exception of the Muslims, who even believes in God anymore?" he said defensively. "Look around. I can't say I know of anyone who goes to church. It's all myth and fantasy, and unfortunately, a lot a people have died because of it. Just look at any news story. Daily—and I mean daily—Islam extremists are slaughtering people who don't believe in their version of Islam and Allah. Who wants a God like that? You don't even hear 'moderate' Muslims denouncing the slaughter."

"My God is not Allah," Lilly said quietly but firmly.

"What's the difference? God, Allah? Those names are someone's 'God.'" Jason said, finger-quoting. "It's all myth," he concluded with a dismissive wave of his hand.

"Jason, I'm sorry to say, but you're wrong. It's not myth. How can you speak with authority if you have never read the Bible? It's like trying to write a book report if you've never read the book."

Jason sputtered a moment. "Well, it's common knowledge among people who are thinkers, scientists, scholars."

"Why would you take the word of other people that God is a myth, without finding out for yourself? Do you think because someone is considered a 'thinker'"—she, too, finger-quoted—"that they're smarter and have more wisdom than anyone else?"

"Well, of course! They're educated professionals!" Jason argued. Lilly didn't reason further, just shrugged, and turned to her tablet to begin their meeting, but he wasn't letting it go. He leaned across the table, pointing a finger at her. "Look, you're bright, and I respect you. That's why you were recommended to me by Keith. He considers you his best, and I'm looking forward to working with you. Don't misunderstand me; I like people who argue with me. Can't stand pushovers. But for all your talents, it surprises me you'd be caught up in . . . " He jerked back as if zapped by a cattle prod. Involuntarily his eyes flew open wide in utter disbelief. In a nanosecond, panic enveloped him so completely he nearly blacked out. Fighting for consciousness, his heart lurched against his ribs and his lungs burned for air. Automatically he sucked in a stabbing shallow breath. Sweat tickled down his armpits and back. He could smell his own rancid fear. With white fingers, he gripped the table for a sense of reality. He was disoriented, confused, and terrified.

Lilly had disappeared.

He couldn't move. Seconds ticked by. He looked up at the wall clock. It was a few minutes after five. Then panic gave way to uncontrollable trembling. "I must calm myself, I must calm myself," he muttered.

Pulling in great deep breaths of air, he was able to regain a sense of self but still shaking, he got up from the table and went to the door and into the hallway. He was in a fog of confusion. He needed a drink of water. He had to get away from that room. What had just happened there? Did he hallucinate? Was she still there, or worse yet, was she *ever* there? Was he imagining all this? He stopped for a moment thinking about going back into the room.

"Jason, what's up, ma man?" It was Ron Perelman, the company's attorney leaving for the day with briefcase in hand, coat over his arm, and cell phone in his other hand. He stopped when he was abreast of Jason. "Whoa there, friend. You don't look so good. Everything alright? Do you need to sit down?"

Jason looked at him in confusion. For the first time in his life, he didn't have a word in his mouth. He couldn't possibly tell Ron he had just had a hallucination. No, no, no!

Ron grabbed his arm and steered him to a small alcove with two chairs and sat him down. "Stay here. Let me get you some water."

When Ron came back, he handed Jason a cold bottle of water. After Jason gulped down nearly half the bottle, he was able to pull himself together enough to be coherent and apologetic. "Ron, I'm sorry, man. Didn't mean to frighten you. I took some allergy medication earlier and just had an awful reaction to it. I . . . I think I'm okay," he lied and took another long swig and felt the water flow down his throat, pooling cold in his belly. He was beginning to get a grip. He was feeling better. Water was reality. He was going to be okay. Whatever happened he would deal with it.

Ron looked at him closely. "You sure? Want me to call your wife to come and get you? Or I can drive you home."

"No, no. I'm good. Really. Thanks. It's just that crazy prescription medicine," he lied again. "Seriously, if I don't feel better I'll call Allie to come and get me. I still have more work to do."

"Okay, Jason. Call me if you need me."

After Ron left, Jason realized he had to go back to the conference room. Face his fear. Face the fact that he had a hallucination. Maybe he was drinking too much. Maybe he even had a ministroke. Who knew? He went back in.

Jason sat down heavily on the cushioned mahogany chair. "She's gone, disappeared, evaporated into thin air. I'm not imagining this," he said out loud. "Her purse and Bible are still here." In shock, he reached out his hand and slid the book toward him, idly holding it. "What's happened? Is this some kind of alien attack?" he asked of no one and looked out the window into the sky. Not expecting to see anything, he whispered, "I've got to get out of here," and ran back to his office and grabbed his jacket and keys. Becky wasn't at her desk, but it was after five. She often left before the hour.

In the hallway and on the elevator down to the first floor, he didn't encounter anyone in the company until he came to the lobby, where he saw the security guard staring at the monitors, crying in disbelief. Steeped in fear, the man looked from the screen to Jason as he stepped through the elevator doors and walked toward him.

"What's wrong, Ralph?" What's wrong?" But Jason knew what was wrong.

"Jason, I don't believe what I just saw. I was watching all the monitors and saw Linda and Leo on the second floor. I know I'm not crazy, but they were walking down the hallway talking and Linda just disappeared beside him. I couldn't believe my eyes. I thought there was a video glitch, but Leo went crazy. He saw what I saw!" Ralph flipped on the audio.

Jason peered at the monitor. Leo indeed was going crazy, he was running up and down the hall, screaming Linda's name, twirling around as if he was in an acid-fueled dance. A few people came out of their offices, demanding to know what was going on. Leo fell to his knees crying, babbling, trying to explain. They crowded around him when a woman came screaming out of her office toward them, saying her assistant had disappeared before her eyes.

"Susan's gone! She . . . she . . . just disappeared!" She, too, fell against the wall crying, unable to be consoled by a man who put his arm around her shoulder.

"What do we do?" Ralph turned to Jason in horror.

"Go home," advised Jason. "Check on your family!"

Jason was on the move. He made it to the garage and clicked his fob. Lights momentarily flashed, a beep sounded, then he yanked open the door to his BMW and threw in his coat. To his surprise he realized he still had Lilly's Bible in his hands. He tossed it on the front seat, then pushed the start button with a shaking finger. The engine roared and the radio blasted on.

The broadcaster was trying to make sense of what was going on in the city. "Disappearances are being reported throughout the community. The police and emergency personnel are advising all to stay indoors." He couldn't say more, because he didn't know more, but some people had reportedly evaporated into thin air. His voice was cracking.

Jason threw the car into reverse and sped from the garage to the usually busy side street. It had been busy, but two fresh car crashes blocked the one-way street. Not stopping to check on the occupants, he made a U-turn, drove onto the sidewalk to get around a stalled car, and raced to the main artery. His ride home was normally a thirty-minute drive; tonight it took close to an hour. Sirens blared as ambulances, cop cars, and fire trucks weaved in and out of traffic, trying to reach those crashed on the roadways and against guardrails. Smoke was seen in the distance. Jason surfed station after station on the radio. All were in the same mode, high alert, and no one knew what was happening except to advise that everyone stay home.

"We're trying to get home!" Jason screamed at an announcer. "Just tell us what's going on!" When he finally made it to his house, he jammed the car in park, then ran in through the kitchen to the family room. To his great relief he found Allie collapsed on the couch, a pillow on her chest, watching TV.

No Sabrina. Where is Sabrina?

Before he could ask out loud, Allie jumped up and said, "You're here! Oh, thank goodness you're here and alright! I tried calling you, but you didn't answer! I was frantic!" She ran to him, but he stopped her and grabbed her arms.

"Where's Sabrina, Allie?" Jason whispered urgently.

"Don't worry, Jason. Sabrina's okay. She called. She's on her way home now. I came home early because I didn't feel well," she babbled. "Your mom called and said your brother's missing and she wanted to know where you were. I tried calling you," she repeated, "but I couldn't get through! My mom and dad are okay, but they can't find my grandma!" She was wailing now. Her grandmother was a wonderful woman who lived alone in an old home on her farm that had once been a working small farm, but all that her grandmother had now was five chickens, her pride and joy. She spent many hours tending to her small flock and her garden, but she always had her cell phone with her in case of emergency. Always. She wasn't answering. "Jason, what is going on? I don't understand it!"

"Baby, I don't know. We'll call the rest of the family. Maybe someone can check on her." He turned his attention to the newscaster just as Sabrina came in with tears streaming down her cheeks.

She threw her coat and books on the counter and barreled into the family room. "Mom, Dad? What's happened? Laurie and Jenny were sitting beside me at the library. They literally disappeared! It happened so quickly! One minute we were all laughing, the next they were gone! I could hear other people in the library screaming and crying because other people disappeared too!" She leaned into her mother, sobbing. "I'm so scared. I thought Dad was gone too! What's happened?"

"No one knows yet." Jason held his two girls, then steered them to the couch all the while silently hoping it wasn't an alien attack. But what else could it be? The newscaster announced that the president of the United States would be speaking to the country at ten o'clock. Until then, he advised his listeners to stay tuned to the channel for ongoing updates and warnings. An explanation would be forthcoming, but the announcer emphasized that an unidentified spokesperson confirmed it was not an alien or terrorist attack and believed it to be a one-time event.

Letting go of his wife and daughter, Jason walked over to the liquor cabinet and with trembling hands opened it and took down two Waterford crystal goblets. He poured a stiff scotch for Allie and himself and sunk down deep in the couch. It was all too much to assimilate. The terror was real, but he had to hold it together for his family. His girls snuggled him and sobbed and talked about what could have happened as they waited for President Foster's speech. Sabrina leaned into her mom, shivering and crying. All three, in their own stricken world, waited through commentators, talking heads, and newscasters until the president made her appearance.

With little introduction, the president's upper body filled the screen. "The United States and the world has experienced what our scientists believe is a one-time event. As devastating as this is, we believe that there has been an electro-cosmic interaction with some people's commonality of DNA segments, and this commonality has caused what is seemingly a large group to be vaporized. At this time, we are confident that this is not a terrorist attack in any form. As soon as we gain more information, we will inform you. In the meantime, please stay calm."

The family listened to her explanation with rapt attention.

The president continued, "Before I introduce our spokesperson to explain the basic theory of this heartrending but concluded event, I would like to add that this situation, though catastrophic, will not set the country back, and America will rise from this heartbreak stronger than ever! My condolences to all who have missing loved ones. In three days hence we plan an official day of mourning for all those who were lost, not only in the United States, but in the world."

Although it all sounded plausible, it still seemed incomprehensible that a physio-cosmic interaction caused some people to be instantly vaporized. However, Jason, his family, and millions of Americans, as well as the world, were buying into it. Jason hugged his daughter tighter that night, and he and Allie slept closely but fitfully. The president's speech was being aired hourly, giving commentators little time to work their spin of the events into a frenzy, which was promised to come.

CHAPTER TWO

THE UNITED STATES

BEFORE THE OCCURRENCE OF THE devastating disappearances, the secretary of defense, secretary of state, chief of staff, deputy vice president of national security, and others of high rank were seated around the oak and glass table in the Situation Room in the West Wing of the White House. It was a little before five o'clock in the late afternoon. They were impatiently waiting for the arrival of Madam President Foster and her two closest advisors, Chet Henley and Jorge Rivera. Those standing, the directors of the National Security Agency (NSA) and National Intelligence Agency (NIA), were quietly conferring by the coffee pot. The discussion at hand was about another planned fanatic Islamic attack—and this time on the Roman Catholic Church. The energy in the room was tense and foreboding.

Madam President entered looking tired, but still attractive and imposing, considering her age and work load. Many would not vote for her because she was a woman, regardless of her party. Many believed she would never live up to her campaign promises, yet she was strong enough to carry the electoral college—although not the majority people's vote. While her tenure so far was politically turbulent, she was steady and firm.

The biggest complaint against her was that she was not addressing terrorism in the manner the United States intelligence and military community thought she should. They criticized her for not being aggressive enough toward radical Islam as in past administrations, who let the threat of extremism get far too close to home. Four mass terrorist episodes had occurred in the United States in the past two years—all suicide bombers, and all occurring at large public gatherings. The last being derailed just before the Super Bowl, but it should never have gotten that far. Never.

No one in the room was certain how she would respond to this latest intel, but they had already agreed they would push her to take a stand, particularly NIA Director Paul Storey. He was going to give the highly sensitive briefing to the president and the rest of those gathered in the room.

After short and formal greetings to the president and her advisors, all sat down while Storey turned on the ultra-high resolution 62-inch monitor for his briefing. Without preamble, he got to the heart of the matter.

"For months, we've been collecting data on various terror cells in Europe and, of course, elsewhere. Chatter has been collated, analyzed, and tracked to a sleeper cell in the Vatican itself, where we found three operatives or 'priests' who have been groomed since boyhood in Ireland by a very sophisticated Islamic extremist group named Kingdom of Islam. KOI for short. This group is a splinter group of Islamic State of Iraq and Syria, also known as ISIS. It is far more educated and organized. Although smaller than what we know of ISIS it is lavishly funded via high-level Saudi Arabians. The organization is powerful."

A layout of the Vatican offices flashed on the screen.

Turning, he looked directly at the president. "Proving once again the unusual reach of Islamic extremism, this particular multinational and stateless group is highly strategic. Imagine grooming young men in Ireland in the Roman Catholic Church. It underscores how dedicated and forward thinking their international *jihad* is. The three young men were ordained as *priests* and now they're working within a few hallways of the Holy Roman See's office." Turning from her, he pointed his laser at the offices where the terrorists worked and showed the proximity to the pope's offices. All eyes were expectantly on Storey as he turned back to his leader and forcefully advised, "Madam President, we cannot, I emphasize we cannot, deny the impact this would have on—"

The president and her staff collectively gasped. Some whispered expletives in horror; others were mute in their terror. All were stunned. An awful silence descended on the room. The only sound that could be heard was the pounding of their hearts in their ears and a light and distant whirring of internal fans cooling banks of electronic equiprime ministerent. Grasping for sanity through their alarm, they nearly collided with one another as they staggered to their feet to get to the president who was still sitting in abject horror.

Paul Storey had simply disappeared.

Someone finally shouted, "Where did he go?"

"He just disappeared," Isabelle, an aide, responded frantically as she jumped up to open a door to an adjacent office to see if somehow he was miraculously there. All looked at her expectantly. "There's no one there," she said barely audibly.

Chet Henley, President Foster's chief advisor, had the presence of mind to adhere to protocol and hit the silent alarm. Moments after his finger depressed the button, three armed marines stormed the room and made their way to a stunned and confused president. As they grabbed her by the arms to muscle her out of the room, the secretary of state screamed, "Where is the rest of the security team?"

"Gone, sir. Gone. Just evaporated," a shaken marine answered. "Air Force One is standing by, but the chief pilot is gone too; his number two is waiting. The chopper is ready now. Let's go. We'll evacuate President Foster, her family, and you and the others from the White House grounds to the Cottage."

"Cottage" was the code name for an obscure retreat in Indiana where the president along with family, senior decision makers, and other high-level officers were sequestered in the event of a catastrophic occurrence that could jeopardize national security and the decision making arm of the government. The design of the Cottage allowed the president, high-level staff, and advisors to maintain command and control of US forces throughout the world. It was equipped with a secure, advanced infrastructure that allowed the president to conduct secure communications with leaders worldwide.

"Where's Jorge?" Henley shouted, wildly looking around.

President Foster, being hustled by three huge marines, squirmed to look back over her shoulder. Wide-eyed, she shouted, "He's not here with us? Where is he?"

"He disappeared too," Isabelle whispered.

"This is crazy," moaned a security officer as he followed the entourage through the secure exits.

In the short period of time that the president was being evacuated from the Situation Room and boarding Air Force One, secure communications alerted that many people all over the country were disappearing. Hundreds of airplanes had crashed, vehicular accidents were unprecedented, and the devastation was escalating. Confusion and fear were building at airports, fire and police stations, as well as at municipal emergency response agencies. Homeland Security was scrambling for intelligence.

After takeoff, the president and her entourage gathered around the conference table.

"It's clear we have to contain this," Henley said desperately. His shirt was soaked with sweat and he could smell his own fear. "We need to give some spin to the American public. We're being bombarded with ongoing reports of people who have vanished in the presence of witnesses. If we don't contain this, there'll be chaos."

"There already is chaos," President Foster quietly said. "This has happened globally." Her eyes scanned page after page of reports she swiped on her secure tablet.

The secretary of defense looked up from his tablet. "This event happened at precisely 5:02 in the late afternoon Eastern Standard Time. The event, for want of a better word, lasted less than one third of a second."

"The blink of the eye," the secretary of state pointed out. "Literally."

Looking at a printout, the secretary of defense added, "We don't know what happened and we're not sure the threat is over, but all of our intelligence agencies are working to find out what happened."

"We've got to get you on TV as soon as possible. This needs to be addressed immediately," Chet Henley, her chief adviser told President Foster.

"But what can I possibly say? What . . . what?" she stammered.

"We also need you to speak to world leaders, the secretary-general and president of the General Assembly of the UN after your TV appearance," Henley interrupted, thinking they had to control this incredible disaster. He knew his president was focused, and he didn't want her to dwell on this illogical and terrible situation. He had to keep the ball rolling. "I've contacted our media studio at the Cottage. They're waiting for you and I've directed an aide to alert the leaders to be ready for a conference call after your TV appearance."

"You're not hearing me, Chet. I understand the logistics, but what on earth would you have me say? My concern is what actually happened!" Fear and apprehension were enveloping the president's heart and mind. Her coolness and strength were slowly melting under the heat of a catastrophe that could throw the world into mayhem. "Because right now," she continued, "we haven't any idea what happened. We don't know if this is an isolated event, or if it will be reoccurring. We don't know if this is an attack of some sort or if it's some natural incident. We don't know who is being targeted. We haven't a clue!"

"Madam President, we've got the finest minds and resources available in the world working on this as we speak. We'll make something up if we don't get answers in three to four hours—which I know is not enough time, but we might get lucky," a grim secretary of defense responded.

"What is foremost in our strategy is to calm everyone down nationally. And once you've made your appearance, you'll speak with the world leaders who will work with us, the UN, which is powerless but has to be included, and the European Parliament President. He can coordinate with his members. You will also personally reach out to Russia, China, Saudi Arabia, and Israel. This has to be simple for starters. We take the lead over and above all nations," Chet Henley explained to his president.

"Agreed," said the secretary of state. "Whatever we come up with in the next few hours, we'll give them all the same spin. We can't have the world in panic, and the United States must be the leader and spokesnation."

Chet Henley looked at President Foster, who nodded in agreement to everyone seated around Air Force One's conference table.

"This is how we'll approach it," the deputy vice president of national security outlined. "We'll alert the press you'll be making a television emergency broadcast to assure the American public of their safety and of the nation's safety. This will give us the upper hand."

President Foster gained control of her mind and emotions. Speaking like the leader she was known to be, she took command. "Okay, stop for the moment. Again, we know the logistics of what needs to be done, but what we need is content," she demanded. "Listen to me now. No multitasking. I want your undivided attention." Immediately, they put aside their electronic devices, pens, and papers. All eyes were on the president. "Here's my view. Yes, we've got to assure the nation of its safety and give the people a reason for what happened, letting them know we have it under control, and that there is no cause for panic . . . then the rest of the world needs to agree." She stopped for a moment and eyed her team, who waited expectantly for her to continue. "So, let's consider a few scenarios that are plausible to the public. One, it could have been a space alien attack—"

Someone at the end of the table snickered.

"Don't!" the president angrily pointed at the culprit. "There will be no sarcasm at this table—and by the way, you never snicker at the president! Never!" Continuing she said, "But it could have happened. We don't know if there is other intelligence out there and certainly can't disregard that if there is life in space, they might have sophisticated *Star Trek*-like transporters to capture hostages or enemies. Or have weapons that can penetrate our defenses and vaporize whom they choose."

No one said a word.

The president paused for a sip of water. Putting the glass firmly down on a presidential coaster, she looked around the table, holding the attention of all. "Another thought is a virus that attacks or attacked only certain people with a certain genetic makeup, causing that person to literally be vaporized. This is a little trickier, but it's a scenario. Or, it could be a natural occurrence. Something in the atmosphere or beyond that had some kind of impact on certain types of people. Lastly, we could view it as a terrorist attack, but if it was, the perpetrators have amazing capabilities. But whatever direction we take, people will be fearful it could be ongoing and that fear will be crippling."

"As a sidebar," the director of the NSA interjected, "we have absolutely no data on terrorists having any kind of virus that can cause vaporization, so we can rule out a viral terrorist attack."

"Doesn't mean it couldn't have happened," someone mumbled.

The director shot back, "As I said, we have absolutely no data of a virus that can cause vaporization!"

"Good," President Foster said. "So let's go back to the atmosphere. Perhaps some biological, electrical, cosmic mishap occurred—and I'm no scientist—that caused this to happen and only certain people were affected."

The deputy vice president of national security spoke up. "Madam President, all of your ideas are thought provoking," he said patronizingly.

"But an alien attack, while a possibility, is something we don't want the public to remotely consider. It would cause untold fear."

"Our military personnel are working on this now, so this is not a joking matter," the secretary of defense added as he looked pointedly at the staffer who snickered. "I also don't believe we should talk virus unless we say can say it's contained. Remember the panic about Ebola and Zika." He paused for effect. "What could be safe is your third scenario: An explanation about some type of cosmic atmospheric interference that interacted electrically and physiologically with certain bodies to cause them to vaporize, if you will."

"With all due respect, Mr. Secretary, how can we prove they were *vaporized*? They disappeared in less than a blink of an eye," said a staffer, Joanna Wright, to his left. "I don't know of any scientific data on human vaporization."

"Are you a scientist?" someone sarcastically asked.

"No, of course not, but . . . "

"We stick to a vaporization theory," the secretary of defense said. "It's as good an explanation as we have."

"Why can't we wait until we get some facts?" Joanna persisted.

"We can't wait! We need to control this immediately!" the secretary snapped, then reopened his tablet and tapped a few times. "Let's see. Ah, here it's explained simply. Wikipedia says, "A flux of so many gamma ray, X-ray, ultraviolet and heat photons strikes matter in such a brief amount of time, that is, a great number of high-energy photons, some overlapping in the same physical space, that all molecules lose their atomic bonds and 'fly apart.' There. You have it. Vaporized. The answer."

"From Wikipedia?" Joanna asked incredulously. "Are you serious? If you want to be that inane, how about considering the rapture?"

The secretary of defense asked, "What do you mean, the rapture?"

"It's a God thing," the director of the NIA said disparagingly, waving his hand.

"Explain, Joanna, please, for all of us who are not familiar with the term," demanded the president.

Joanna paused. *The rapture did seem unbelievable, but it could be as good as any explanation so far.* She had read it about it when she was a kid going to a Southern Baptist church in South Carolina. It was really quite fascinating teaching, but like so many so-called Christians, she went to college, fell away from the church, and quite honestly didn't really believe God existed anymore much less the rapture. Although it was intriguing at this time.

"The short version, Joanna," the president demanded. "Speak. We need something prepared soon and we need all ideas."

"Okay. Christians believe that they will be raptured, or taken off the earth in the blink of an eye to be with Jesus just before the great tribulation begins."

"What tribulation?" asked one of the deputies disbelievingly.

"Let her explain without interruption. Ask your questions later," the president said wearily.

Joanna continued, "Let me back up a moment. Christians believe in a triune God, that is, one God with three essences or persons. I know, it's complicated," she agreed as she looked at the confused faces around the table. "The Father, the Son, whom you all know as Jesus, and the Holy Spirit. Once the Christians are gone or raptured, the Holy Spirit, who lives in them, will leave the earth too, and evil will no longer be held in check. Then the tribulation will start—seven years of escalating grief, horror, pain, and suffering. Natural and unnatural disasters, war, famine, and disease will occur. Early in that seven-year period a visionary, charismatic leader will rise and many countries will look to him to manage the confusion and turmoil; he will become the anointed world leader. He is known in Christendom as the Antichrist."

The secretary of defense threw his pen on the table in disgust. The president glared at his behavior and then stared steadily at Joanna, nodding at her to continue.

"At first he'll be adored by many nations, but then his real intention will be made known: a quest for world domination through evil and treachery. Once in great power shortly after the rapture, he'll create a peace treaty with Israel, even allowing the Jews to rebuild the temple which was—as you might or might not know—the center of worship from ancient times until 70 CE. As a little background, the Jews rebelled against the Romans in the year 66, but by 70, the Roman legions surrounded the city and destroyed the Jews' temple of worship."

"Thanks for the history lesson," mumbled the secretary of defense.

"His plan is to break the treaty with Israel with the intent to crush and annihilate her. He'll team up with a false prophet who'll help him gain notoriety by performing miracles." She paused to take a breath and think. Continuing, she explained, "He'll be preempted in his attack—other countries attempt to attack Israel, but fail. Yet later he will march to Jerusalem, and the false prophet will set up a statue of the Antichrist in the temple, where it will speak and move miraculously. The Antichrist will become godlike and worshipped. Satan will give supernatural powers to both men." She sat back, arms wrapped across her chest, preparing her next words carefully.

Some at the table were deathly quiet, thinking, maybe remembering their past Bible studies. Others were smirking and sighing in exasperation.

Then Joanna bore on, "All people will have to have the mark of the beast, as he is called in the Bible, on their heads or hands. The mark itself could be a tattoo of sorts that will be identified as the number 666. There will probably be a chip imbedded in their hands or foreheads, because only those with the mark will be able to buy or sell. Those who don't take it will suffer terribly. If anyone converts to Christianity, they will be slaughtered. Many will be beheaded."

More than half of the people around the conference table were shaking their heads in utter disbelief. The secretary of defense spoke up. "Madam President, we are wasting valuable time!"

"Sir," she responded. "Shut up. I want to hear the complete story. And Joanna, get to the point!"

"During the tribulation there will be two witnesses of God in Jerusalem who will be calling for repentance and who will preach the gospel. Some people will believe, but many won't. The witnesses will ultimately be murdered by the Antichrist and left for dead in the streets of the city for three and a half days, but then they will rise, to the terror of the spectators. An earthquake will decimate much of the city and kill many people. Chaos will follow, but still the people will not turn to God and the Antichrist will rule. There will also be 144,000 Jews who will be protected by God from the Antichrist's persecution, who will not take the mark, and who will evangelize the gospel to all who will listen. Anyone who becomes Christian during that time will suffer greatly at the hands of the Antichrist."

"And get beheaded." A staffer sighed. "Sort of like what the Islamist extremists do," he added.

Joanna was surprising herself that she remembered all of this from her Bible-study days, particularly the book of Daniel and Revelation. It was as if words of remembrance were being put in her mouth. She stopped for a sip of water.

The president gave her a silent glare to get on with it.

"War will be made against the Antichrist too, because of his deceitfulness. Possibly Russia, maybe some African nations, and other countries will come against him, but he will persevere until the war to end all wars, Armageddon, which will happen at the end of the seven years of tribulation, when Jesus will come back for the final battle with the Antichrist and win." She paused. "Then—"

"Oh my word, Madam President, I have heard *enough*!" Turning to Joanna, the secretary of defense asked, "What kind of weed are you smoking? You think vaporization is off the wall? What kind of crazy story are you spinning?"

The president shot him a glare.

The secretary of defense persisted in questioning Joanna. "We are going to have a world leader soon after this 'rapture' has happened?" Holding up a finger to make his point, he argued, "Who, one, is a tool of Satan, no less, and called the Antichrist? And two"—he flipped a second finger—"that the United States will no longer be a democracy? It will be absorbed into a new world order?"

He dramatically looked around the table with an incredulous look, erupting audible divisive noises around the table. Many shook their heads in absolute rejection of such notions. The president sat quietly, her chin leaning on her hand.

"The Bible doesn't speak of the United States so I don't know the future of the country," Joanna responded testily. "You asked for an explanation of the rapture and so I gave it," she said, pointedly looking at the president. Turning her head, she spoke directly to the secretary of defense. "It doesn't mean I necessarily believe it, but maybe we should find out if any Christians were taken?"

Madam President was shaken by Joanna's story but would not show nor admit it to anyone at the table. She had heard of the rapture in a vague way, and she knew of Jesus, and while she didn't believe He was the Son of God, because she was agnostic, she did think that there was something out there that pulled humanity together; she just wasn't sure what it was. Nevertheless, the story struck a chord of irrational fear in her heart, but she had to show professional strength and logic. She brusquely acquiesced. "It is a bizarre story, but no more bizarre than anything else we discussed here today. Find out if those who disappeared were Christians. Someone. And let us know. In the meanwhile, we'll develop the vaporization theory and run with that but I want to get to the bottom of this, and I want the best scientists on this *now*!"

The captain came over the speakers and said, "Please prepare to land. Return to your seats and fasten your seatbelts."

As they moved to their seats, each pondered that such an event that just happened without cause or notice was beyond comprehension. For something so catastrophic to occur not only in the United States, but worldwide, was inconceivable. Yet it happened. As the movers and shakers of the world, as strategists, and world policy makers, in this instant, all of them were reduced to mere mortals. They had lost control. They could make up answers and reasons, but how close to the truth was it? And without true knowledge, the real deep-seated question was how to rationally proceed? Would the country and the world believe a concocted explanation if a truthful one wasn't uncovered? Many quietly talked among themselves; others frantically tapped their tablets for updates. Some stared out the windows.

President Foster checked her watch. "We'll be at the Cottage soon. Chet, put together some talking points and get the writers to polish my speech. As soon as we get some scientific input, I want to present the scenario of the 'event' to the country in a plausible but oversimplified way."

"I'm on it, Madam President."

She sighed deeply. She had to admit, while the "Vaporization" was the way to go public, she was shaken by Joanna's story. Very shaken.

In the nation and the countries where those that had the ability to watch TV were able to hear the president of the United States speak, all were in a state of shock as they listened intently, holding onto the reasonable explanation of 'Vaporization.' Each one listening had lost family, friends, and neighbors. Fearful and heartbroken, they grasped for hope. It was imperative that in each person's heart and mind, this was to be a onetime occurrence. Reactions and consequences were moving quickly, too quickly for leaders and the general population alike to understand and manage.

"Madam President, good job on the message," Chet Henley said to his president as he ushered her into the situation room beside the TV studio in the Cottage. "Truly, I think you calmed the situation although we still need an awful lot of backfill for this story to play out true, but we are working on it now. In the meanwhile, we have your speech televised on the hour throughout the night and tomorrow through noon. All the social media and print news outlets have videos or copies of the speech."

"I realize it's still early, but did you get at least a sample of the religion of those who disappeared?" she asked as she sat down and reached for a hot cup of coffee. "I'd like to discount the rapture," she said sardonically.

Chet turned to the secretary of national security who looked extremely perplexed as he read the stats on his tablet. He cleared his voice, spoke softly, but clearly. Everyone stopped their work to hear him. "Madam President," he paused and looked around at those who stopped delving into reams of reports and reading multiple e-files on their monitors. "What we are able to ascertain this early in the event, is that, yes, the population that disappeared was all Christian . . ."

Someone else spoke up, "I beg to differ. I have information here that says there are a number of pastors and priests still around."

Another said, "And I see here," as she read from her report, "that there are a number of Jews who were taken too. So it can't be a Christian thing."

"Wait." Joanna Wright sighed. "Just because you call yourself a Christian doesn't necessarily make you a Christian. You can go to church, you can give generously, you can attend potlucks, you can even be a priest or pastor, but if you don't have true faith, then it doesn't mean anything. It's a charade. And I bet if you found out what type of Jews those were that are gone, you'd find that they were Messianic, meaning that they believed in Jesus Christ. Same would hold true for Muslims if they were frightened and hid the fact that they really held to Christian beliefs about Jesus and no longer believed the Muslim doctrine. The evidence points to an overwhelming population of Christians that are gone."

"And Paul Storey and Jorge Rivera were Christian," the secretary of state offered. He scanned another report and looked up. "The pope's gone too." Swiping the page again with his finger he continued, "And it looks like there was little impact on huge nations such as India and China. It's too early to tell in Europe. Most are in bed." He swiped again. "The Middle East is basically intact. Some African nations are reporting large populations disappearing, but it appears that the greatest hit taken was here—in the United States and the Americas."

Everyone in the room quieted for a brief moment, then pulled out their own cells and started checking on families and loved ones. Stunned reactions filled the room; some were of despair and grief, other reactions of joy.

Madam President sat back, closed her eyes, and said to her chief of staff, "Whatever actually caused this to happen, has changed the world. It will never be the same again."

He sighed. "The loss of so many talented people. We don't even know the count yet, but it is now, pretty significant." He wondered about his own family and fumbled for his phone.

President Foster thought of the vast labor force consisting of blue-, gray-, and white-collar jobs. So many businesses, institutions, and sectors of commerce would be slammed with loss of key personnel. The American people still around would suffer. There was no question that the country was dramatically weakened. The US' position in the world was now parallel with so many others who would be battling loss of everyday normalcy. The country's might, power, and position would be gone forever.

She took out her own cell and began calling family members.

CHAPTER THREE

THE EUROPEAN UNION

DAG LITZ, EUROPEAN PARLIAMENT PRESIDENT, left his office in Brussels after nine o'clock in the evening to go home only to do more work in his home office, hours before the catastrophic disappearances. Consequently, he didn't get to bed until a little before eleven o'clock. He had an exhausting day; they were in concurrent negotiations with two Slavic countries that hopefully would be added to the EU's roster that was shrinking. One country was digging in her heels, but Litz believed his team would eventually overcome her dissension. Although, since a number of countries had left the EU, it was beginning to be a challenge to get new members.

The EU, at one time, was strong in influence and power. That was before Britain left. Once her people voted her out, a few other nations followed but for those who remained, the organization intertwined a unified political and economic platform that enabled its members to more easily trade with one another due to the standardized system of laws that allowed for a single market practice. Yet interestingly, multilingualism—over twenty-three languages—was elemental to the EU's cultural multiplicity. The EU employed a staff of over 1,700 linguists and more than 600 support staff. The EU was pushing its potential members hard to accept and adopt the single standard currency, the Euro2, a next generation Euro, as the Union's legal tender. This was, in the case of some countries, a hard sell, but in the overall economic management for all the countries who belonged, one currency made critical sense. By the creation of a single market and standard currency, the EU, though embattled, was still maintaining a chief trading authority.

Currently, it held its economic growth by investments in transport, energy, and research. It also sustained itself by taking a percentage of each member nation's gross national income, as well as from import duties on products from outside the EU. Moreover, it gained a percentage of the value-added tax imposed by each country. The EU had a keen eye for managing and enhancing its own economic prowess.

The EU had its struggles, but with solidarity of its members, under the direction of its three main institutions, Parliament, Council, and Commission, it was able to better control the collective economy, environment, and social challenges of a large group of nations.

After taking a hot shower, then a shot of an antacid medication to settle his stomach, Dag Litz sat at the side of his bed. It was eleven o'clock. Quietly, in order not to wake his wife, he prayed, "Dear Lord, please bless the European Union, according to Your will, to show strength and harmony not only for trade practices, but also strength to uphold and sustain the millions who are struggling in all our member nations."

With over 500 million people in the member countries, many were living in poverty. Several years back, the Nobel Peace Prize was awarded to the EU for the advancement of peace, reconciliation, democracy, and human rights. It was quite an achievement. At the time, Litz remembered the then president of the European Council,

Herman Van Rompuy, say, "The award recognized the European Union as the biggest peacemaker in history."

Although many people prayed to themselves, he liked to pray out loud because he felt he was having a conversation with his God. Yet he didn't want to disturb his wife, so he whispered, "I humbly ask that Your hand of peace be upon our efforts and I pray for wisdom in—"

His wife, who was asleep when he came home, groggily woke up hearing him whisper. Listening to him from her side, she put a gentle hand of encouragement on his arm. She didn't pray, didn't believe in God, but she indulged her kind husband. What could it hurt? He was one of the few in their social and political circle who ever went to church. Those who did either attended a funeral or perhaps a wedding, but church attendance was becoming less common. The Muslims in their political sphere still held fast to their beliefs and in her husband's position, he made a point of respecting all beliefs. He had a talent for keeping people together for the cause of unity regardless of faith or ethnicity.

As she gently squeezed his arm, it evaporated at her touch. She reached again, but pawed only air. Startled, she opened her eyes. The clock glowed a couple of minutes after eleven. He wasn't there. "Dag? *Liebling*? Where are you?"

Throwing off the covers she hurried to the bathroom. It was impossible he could have been speaking one moment and she touching him, and the next moment he could have left the room. She could have sworn that as she touched his arm she suddenly felt nothing. Empty space. The bathroom was empty. Staring at herself in the mirror she reasoned she must have been dreaming that he was praying. After all he did so each night. She pulled her robe from the hook on the door and quickly went downstairs. Poking her head into his office, she saw he wasn't there, and as she advanced further into the suite, she looked in the adjacent rooms including his library, private bath, but they, too, were empty. Going back to his office she stopped. There was indication he had come home because his briefcase was on his desk, open, and his jacket, the one he was wearing when he left this morning, thrown over his chair. She wasn't dreaming. He had come home. She called his name out loudly. No answer. She went into the kitchen. Empty. She called his name again. No answer. She tried both front and back doors. Both were locked from the inside. Horror-struck, she hurried to his office and dialed security at the EU offices.

"Hello, this is Mrs. Litz. I'm looking for my husband. When did he leave the office?" Her heart was beating rapidly, and her hands were shaking.

"Why, Mrs. Litz, his driver took him home a little after nine o'clock. You're saying he is not home?"

"No," she whimpered.

"We'll be right there!"

Marcus Junius, who had just fallen asleep, was startled awake by the jarring ring of the phone by his bedside. Then his cell phone vibrated. Instinctively he reckoned for bad news as he groped the handset, while punching a code in his cell phone to shut off the high alert terror app.

"Mr. Junius. We are sending a driver to pick you up immediately. We have in issue in the Parliament president's office. Code Ice."

"What issue?" Marcus sat up and swung his feet to the floor. Code Ice was dire. It meant that the president of Parliament was kidnapped. It was unbelievable. He had just left Litz's office; they were working on negotiations and proposals for two potential new members. "This is a secure phone. Answer me, man. What is going on?" Marcus headed for his dressing room.

The security officer on the other end of the line was momentarily tongue-tied. Finding his words, he carefully said, "There has been a catastrophic event of disappearances across the globe and President Litz is gone."

"Gone? Like how is he gone? Kidnapped?" Marcus asked frantically. What was the guard talking about 'catastrophic disappearances'? "What on earth do you mean?" Marcus was on high alert. This was disastrous.

"Sir, I don't know. A driver will be there shortly. We're assembling the others."

Marcus Junius was the president of the European Commission, one of the main institutions of the European Union. Each member nation had its own commissioner who was led by the president of the Commission. As president of the Commission, he managed the EU's budget and funding, enforced the EU law, and proposed new laws to Parliament and the Council. The Parliament, on the other hand, had the sole power to dismiss the Commission. The appointments of the president of the Commission and the commissioners were subject to approval by Parliament; thus the Commission was accountable to Parliament. High priority at the moment was to work closely with Litz on a number of items, including dealing with issues concerning some member nations' desire to withdraw from the Union.

Italian by birth, Marcus had been educated at the University of Cambridge, majoring in economics and later received his higher degrees at Harvard University. Shortly after graduation, he went back to Italy, where he worked as a chief advisor to a deputy of the Chamber of Deputies, the Parliament's lower house. Later, he worked in the Senate, the upper house of Parliament. Through his networking, hard work, and high profile, he was nominated to the position of commissioner to the European Union, where he immediately made a name for himself as a well-rounded politician, economist, and diplomat. Eventually, he was voted in as president of the European Commission, a segment of the EU. He was respected by Dag Litz and the rest of the Parliament hierarchy, who heavily depended on his sharp negotiating skills and intelligence. Sadly, he was not able to convince Britain's commissioner to stay in the EU. The people had voted, and he had little influence on the populace. Later, a few other countries followed suit and left the union, but he was able to keep the block from breaking apart when he continually pointed out how the mavericks were struggling economically.

Thus, he was able to maintain control and influence over most of the other the member countries regardless of their diversity in government and social structure. The common denominator was financial power. He knew economics and politics and was able to blend these two strengths for his and the EU's advantage. It helped, too, that he was fluent in several languages. This made him all the more valuable and powerful because he was comfortable switching from one language to another and thus had immense sway in direct conversations.

It was well after midnight when Marcus entered the EU offices. Security, aides, and other staffers met him at the door.

An aide explained, "Because most of the European nations are six hours or more ahead of Eastern Standard Time, the initial discovery of missing people has been slow," he said as he hurried to keep pace with Marcus. "Many are sleeping through the disappearances. Most people don't know what's going on, but we're getting reports in from different agencies locally and globally. It seems to have happened all at the same time, a little after eleven."

"Two minutes past, to be exact," someone clarified from the crowd.

Marcus stopped walking and stared at the man. "All at the same time?"

"That's what we're getting in, sir."

Marcus went into the situation room with a trail of aides and advisors following him.

Another staffer held up a printout. "There have been horrendous air and vehicular crashes. Hospitals and clinics have been alerted, but they're dealing with their own disappearances of staff. Police and fire departments are thinned too, and won't be able to fully respond once the morning comes! It will be a matter of hours before the full impact of this hits Europe. It's like a domino effect and it's happening as we speak."

"We haven't been able to reach the deputy director," a frazzled staffer said to Marcus as he sat down amid people, monitors, and computers. The deputy was under the president of Parliament. "She didn't respond to calls or the alert app. We went to her apartment and her husband said he had been frantically searching for her. Yet she had come home from work earlier. They had a late dinner. He thought she was working in her study, but when he looked for her before going to bed, she was nowhere to be found. He called family and friends to see if she went out to visit, but it all seemed strange because it was so late at night. No one had seen her. Clearly, he was beside himself with fear and worry."

"She's probably gone too. Don't worry about her," Marcus said dismissively. "For the time being we can't be focused on those that have disappeared. We need to get a grip on governing and managing what we have." Just as he finished the sentence, his administrative assistant, Roberto Pertucci, flew through the door, smoothing his hair and tossing his coat on a chair.

"Good news, everyone. Roberto is still here," Marcus said humorlessly. "Roberto, get all the commissioners and the Council on secure communications now. And any staff here in Brussels, bring them in immediately," Marcus ordered, determined to control the calamity.

Forty-five minutes later, Roberto came back to the room where Marcus was going through screens of updated data on the disappearances. He had classified access to all the member nations' emergency disaster response activities and was stunned by the sheer magnitude of the disappearances. Multitasking, he was also reading intelligence reports that pointed to no known reason for the disappearances. But strangely, it had all happened at the same time. In about a third of a second. Unbelievable.

"We were just informed President Foster will address the US at ten o'clock EST. After her televised speech she has scheduled a call with us, as well as other nations outside the EU," Roberto said anxiously.

Marcus sat quietly, thinking. Trust the United States to have a handle on this. They never wasted any time in taking control, wrong or not, and getting in front of their people and the world. But to their credit it had happened at their so called "rush hour," so they had the jump on it. Marcus would have been disappointed if they hadn't moved quickly.

He was impatient to hear what the president had to say. *It seems inhumanly possible for this to be a terrorist attack,* Marcus thought. He turned to Roberto, who was dabbing his brow with a crumpled tissue. "When is the televised speech and the call?"

"Four a.m. our time for the speech and five for the call," Roberto replied.

"Doesn't give us much time to get it together ourselves," grumbled an aide, tapping data into a spreadsheet.

"Time is critical," Marcus said to all within earshot. "In times of terror, you don't have the luxury of taking your time assessing the situation. You act!"

As the night wore on towards dawn, those that were still around began trickling into the situation room; their faces were sober in fear and confusion. Crowding into the work space, they collated statistics and scrutinized data coming in on monitors and phone lines. Although immersed in activity and conversations, they all counted on the United States to provide some answers.

At four in the morning, the anxious souls of the European Union's staff and hierarchy listened to the American president's explanation for the disappearance of millions of people. At the conclusion of the telecast, murmurs of incredulity peppered the air. Marcus mulled over the president's speech while the room grew in volume of discordant conversations. Could it be possible? Was there some type of cosmic explanation for all of this?

To set his own mind and his organization at ease, Marcus stood and held up his hand for quiet. The room hushed. "I want a team put together to research her explanation and look at other possibilities. Roberto, coordinate the task. I want it done quickly and I mean quickly. In the next three hours I want either corroboration of the vaporization theory or other possibilities—including terrorism. And I want the rest of you to keep collating the data coming in. I want an update on the hour of any pertinent information to this event." The group went back to work trying to make sense of the data now streaming in on the vast array of electronics.

"President Foster will be communicating with us in less than a half an hour, Mr. Junius," a staffer interrupted.

Marcus left the aides to work, and took his senior management in for the call. Dutifully the people found their seats while apprehensively talking among themselves, and resisting the urge to check on family and friends. Marcus took out a small pad of paper for notes and questions. He still relied on pen and paper.

As in her televised speech, President Foster's upper body filled the monitor as she sat at her desk in a makeshift Oval Office. The Cottage had a set that perfectly mimicked the room in the White House. Viewers would think she never left Washington. Protocol normally would be that she would speak first, then anyone who wished to speak had to log into the queue via a secure communications intranet. A moderator managed the conference call.

The president of the United States was calm, yet Marcus could see the anxiety in her eyes, read the tension in her body language and even makeup couldn't conceal the deep lines around her eyes and mouth. Her story of what occurred was somewhat plausible, and due to the gravity of the situation, the world had to perceive that her explanation was true and a onetime occurrence. But it was interesting that nations like India, China, the Middle East, and Israel had few citizens who disappeared.

"At this time it is critical we stand behind this explanation to our citizens," she stated. "If we move together in accord and offer a unified confidence that this is what did in fact happen, then all nations will be able to control the rising confusion among the populations—which, if not contained, will result in disorder, mayhem, anarchy, and ultimately war. The very existence of our nations is at stake."

"I certainly concur with your evaluation," Marcus said, breaking in and breaking protocol. "As it stands, we know a number of our people are gone to include our president of Parliament, Dag Litz."

President Foster was momentarily shocked. Litz was a strong and fair leader. What would the EU become without him? It was imperative that they hold their nations together and subdue any panic. A number of his own commissioners broke in, but the moderator muted any comments and concerns.

"Colleagues, please. We have leadership under control," Marcus firmly stated before he could be muted. "As soon as we assess our losses in governance positions, we will fill those positions and make it public as I'm sure all countries will do the same." *Unlikely*, thought Marcus. None of the attending countries of China, Russia, Israel, and the Middle East nations would ever come clean. They will call any losses a "reorganization," and those people who disappeared would never be referred to again.

"Please, Madam President, continue," the moderator asked.

"All attending countries are to immediately create a point of contact person three days hence. The secretary of state will be the point person for the United States and he will expect all contact information for your POC.

"And for near term, the United States will take the lead to schedule meetings with the POCs, including the UN, but, in the very near future, a committee must be formed to take over any administrative functions to keep all countries duly informed of any activities that threaten any country's security or economy.

"The POCs will obviously disseminate any communal information according to each country's structure of emergency/catastrophic management, government, and trade. More information will be forthcoming regarding the United States' own losses and any pertinent reorganization that would directly affect our relationship with the world.

"I realize that this is short notice for such an important communication, so I request that any questions and concerns that you have you pass through to your appointed POC to be addressed at our next scheduled call. This will give us more time to assess our damages."

Although China and Russia bristled at the United States taking the lead in managing the catastrophe, action had to be taken, and the US was in the best organizational position to pull together a superficial, temporary plan. Marcus realized this. For the time being, let the US do the administrative heavy lifting.

After the call ended, Marcus advised the members and staff, "For now, unless something dramatically changes, we go along with the scenario the US has put forth: 'Vaporization' due to an extraordinary and abnormal cosmic-physiological event, but we will do our own investigating of the matter as I'm sure all other countries will do. Concurrently, we will ascertain among our member nations what percentage of upper-level people have disappeared and what type of work they performed, and what their capacities were." Standing before his staff, Marcus continued, "I am inclined to agree it is a onetime occurrence. Roberto informed me earlier that our Science and Intelligence Departments will look into the president's rationalization of vaporization." He looked to a science committee member, who nodded confirmation. "So then, until we get other information, let's consent to the vaporization theory. In the interim, we must move forward in solidarity. We have a tremendous amount of work to do under these dire circumstances. Do we all agree?"

There was no disagreement and little discussion. They were preoccupied multiprocessing their immediate problems. Foremost in every commissioner's mind was to keep his own citizens calm at all costs and to determine how many people disappeared.

"Unless anyone fervently disagrees," Marcus continued, "I suggest that under the circumstances I take over as president of Parliament because—"

"But Marcus," a commissioner interrupted in alarm, "we truly need you now, more than ever, as president of the Commission! You realize we are in a state of disarray and without a leader, this traumatic situation could fracture more of the EU!" referring to the recent defects of some nations.

Before Marcus could answer, the president of the Council stood. "As you know, the Council, as well as holding other responsibilities, passes EU laws and signs agreements between other countries. I believe that under these wholly unusual and serious circumstances, we should enhance the powers of the president of Parliament to include overseeing the Commission and I would like to propose a vote to elect Marcus Junius to a position that would blend the two. All in favor?"

Those who were unable to make the meeting in person were on secure communications monitors and spoke in unified agreement.

"I agree. At this point, we need to maintain continuity and structure," the commissioner from Spain said.

Others voiced similar opinions. Those that were present agreed too, except for a few.

"Shouldn't we discuss this before we vote?" one argued.

"We don't have time for discussions! They could go on for days. We need action, and we need it now! Marcus has the most experience of all of us and has been working with all bodies of the EU closely, as well as with nations outside our organization. If we had the luxury of pouring over every candidate's curricula vitae, I would say yes, we should discuss. But this is an unprecedented emergency!" The rattled Council President nearly shouted.

Arguments broke out among members in the room, on the speakers, and on the monitors. Some who initially agreed now weren't sure.

"Ladies and gentlemen. Enough! I will accept the position," Marcus said. "We will call it the 'president of the EU,' and I will offer to have my position revisited in six months. This will enable us to take swift action and make policy now. Later we can debate any other issues that occur. This will satisfy those who want to digest this more thoroughly. Will you agree to this course of action?"

After a long discussion and finally a vote, the Parliament, the Commission, and the Council agreed. Marcus Junius was elected president of the EU.

Ensconced in his office, Marcus laid out the strategy for moving forward in containing the turmoil and handed the simple, clearly worded documents to Roberto, who had been elevated to chief of staff and EU point of contact: "Get these out to all the commissioners and to the Council members. Send them by secure servers, and keep the hard copies in the vault. Post this"—he handed another document to Roberto—"on our website. The world needs to know how we are now structured at the top. And this is my revised reporting system for the member nations. Give it to all staff as well. Under these circumstances, I want strict adherence to my authority." As Roberto walked out to give the work to an aide, Marcus called, "Set up separate meetings with the Central Bank, the Economic and Social Committee, and the Data Protection Supervisor as soon as possible."

Roberto turned. "What about the Court of Justice?"

"Send them a classified email. We'll set up a meeting after I speak with the other groups."

Marcus was feeling powerful and totally in control. Immensely sure of himself and prideful in the fact that so many talented, intelligent, politically savvy men and women looked to him to calm the storm. It was amazing how a disaster could bring out weaknesses in so many perceived strong. He had a lot of work to do. He still needed to control the Council of the EU. An important responsibility of that body was synchronizing teamwork between police forces and judicial systems of member countries. This was indeed going to be required, and he had to have the ability to implement and make final decisions if the EU was to keep this disaster under control and maybe even use it to its benefit. Britain would regret leaving. He would work with Roberto to take control of the Council to keep the EU together.

When Roberto came back, Marcus asked, "By population, did you see who the majority was that disappeared?"

"Vaporized," Roberto corrected, holding a folder of reports.

Marcus smiled indulgently. "Ah, yes, *vaporized*."

"The buzz is that Christians made up the vast majority. Most were United States and South American citizens. And that Israel, the Middle East and other largely non-Christian groups remained."

"Fascinating," Marcus murmured. "Is there any hysteria about it being the rapture?"

"Rapture? I really don't think so, because, while the vast majority were Christian, there are pastors and priests that are still here. Even the famed Cardinal Giovanni is still at the Vatican. It's all in the reports." He laid down a sheaf of papers.

"Yes, but are he and the others truly Christian?"

Roberto shrugged. "If they got that far in their careers, I would think so." He paused in thought then concluded, "So, I don't think the rapture works."

In the weeks to come, Marcus Junius would show unusual fortitude managing numerous meetings, calls, policy creation, document reviews, and all the vast amount of coordination, appointment setting, staff relocating, and discussions with world leaders. He would be focused and single-minded. He would congratulate himself on his mental and physical strength. A lesser man would have ultimately succumbed to exhaustion and stress, but Marcus would will himself to keep moving on. And he would have the Council under his control. Truly, it was the only logical way to keep the EU cohesive and strong. And while it was interesting that the nations of the EU lost substantial amounts of people in the mysterious cosmic vaporization, the Americas were hit the hardest.

CHAPTER FOUR

ISRAEL

"ON MAY 14, 1948, THE United States recognized Israel as a new nation. Israel, a tiny country no bigger than New Jersey with a population of better than seven million, is hated bitterly by Arab Islamic countries that are 640 times her size."

Israeli Prime Minister Moshe Ben-Zion was reading to his eight-year-old granddaughter Sarah, who'd had a bad dream and wanted to be comforted. She had awoken crying and shivering. She couldn't remember her dream, but she said she it was very scary.

"Why?" Sarah asked.

"It started a very long time ago. God promised to bless Abraham, the father of the Jews, in many ways. God promised to make Abraham a great nation, meaning that from one man, a boundless nation would be created. That means we are all descendants of Abraham and God promised to show him a land that would belong to his descendants forever. This is the land of Israel, and it now belongs to us, although there is more that also belongs to us. However, it is called the Holy Land because it really belongs to God."

"How come they hate us so much?" she asked softly.

"It started way back when God promised the land to the descendants of Abraham. Abraham and his wife Sarah couldn't have a baby, so Sarah said Abraham could make a baby with Sarah's maid Hagar."

"Yeeew! That's not nice!"

"Well, in those days they had to have children, so in the event the father died, an heir would take care of the family and all they owned. So if one woman couldn't have a child, then another had to help out and have a child. So Hagar had a little boy, Ishmael. Then later, Sarah had a little boy too, and named him Isaac. God said Isaac would be the favored son who would inherit the blessings of Abraham. You know what that meant?" he asked his granddaughter.

"Yes, it meant Isaac would get the land!"

"That's right. I'll continue. Then Hagar and Ishmael made fun of Isaac, and Sarah got angry. She told Abraham to send them away. They went away into the wilderness."

"Oh, was Hagar sad and scared?"

"Yes, she was, but God sent an angel to help her. The angel told Hagar that Ishmael would be the father of a great nation too. So one nation, we Jews, descended from Isaac, and the other, the Arab nation, came from Ishmael. Ever since then there has been animosity between the two groups of people. Do you know what animosity means?"

"Um, no."

"It means hostility or anger, because Isaac received God's promise of land and Ishmael was left out. But there is more. Before Israel was given back her land in 1948, the British ruled it. The majority of the people living in Israel then were Arabs. Only about one third were Jews. So you can imagine how they felt when the Jews were given back the land they claimed was theirs."

"Really angry. Still, it belongs to us. God says so."

"Yes, He does."

The prime minister doted on his granddaughter, who lived with him in the large fortified home, Beit Rosh HaMemshala, in Jerusalem. He spent time there when he wasn't in Tel Aviv. The home had an interesting history. In 1941, the King of Yugoslavia lived in it, and during the 1948 war between the Israelis and Arabs it was a hospital for the National Military Organization in the Land of Israel, an armed underground Zionist paramilitary group. It was of block construction and covered in Jerusalem stone, a limestone that was used even in ancient times.

The reason Sarah was living with her grandfather was that both Sarah's parents and the prime minister's wife died in an aircraft terrorist attack as they flew to Italy three years ago. At that time, Sarah and her grandfather had stayed in Tel Aviv while the rest of the family went to Italy to tour the Vatican. Sarah was only five at the time and at the last minute her mother decided it best if she stayed home. She was too young to appreciate the art and history. Moshe didn't mind staying with her. As prime minister of Israel he was far too busy for any vacation time and gladly stayed behind. Intelligence on the terrorists had not been updated—they targeted the private jet thinking that the prime minister was aboard.

As Moshe droned on with his story of independence, Sarah finally fell asleep. While pulling up her blankets, he heard a discreet yet insistent knock on the door.

"Prime Minister Ben-Zion, we have urgent news," his security guard said, poking his head through the doorway. "We need to get you and Sarah underground to Beit El now."

Beit El, or House of God, was a code name for a protected underground command and control center in Israel north of Jerusalem. Whenever Moshe heard the referenced named, he inwardly acknowledged the importance of the name. While most Jews were now secular, he was not. He was a Reformed Jew, one who believes and affirms God, the Torah, and Israel. He believed that Jews were made in the image of God and that they were partners with God in peace. Beit El was appropriately named, one way or the other depending upon your perspective. Prime Minister Moshe Ben-Zion longed for peace, but he was not going to succumb to terrorists.

The prime minister scooped up his startled granddaughter, who had just fallen back to sleep, and handed her to his security detail. She whimpered in surprise and reached out for him. "Sarah, we've been over this many times. You must be brave. Go with your friends, and I will be with you shortly."

Quickly, he went to his private office, grabbed his laptop, tablet, and phones, which he handed to his two aides. In moments they were out in the street, racing down the narrow roads of Jerusalem in a four-car armored caravan.

"Brief me." The prime minister strapped on his seatbelt.

His aide could only give him the short story, for that was all he had. "Mossad and the Ministry of Defense report instant disappearances of people globally. It happened shortly after midnight." He checked his phone. "It looks like 12:02 tonight. Two minutes after five, Eastern Standard Time."

The prime minister gaped at his two aides. "What of Israel? Is this an Islamic terrorist attack? What . . . " He was unable to articulate his questions and thoughts.

"We hope to have more answers when the staff gathers at Beit El."

As the SUVs flew through the streets to the main highway, there was evidence of a few vehicular accidents: cars rear-ended, some crashed into guard rails or crumpled in the medians. Sirens were sounding in the distance, both medical and police, but there was no foot traffic because most people were sleeping. Prime Minister Ben-Zion listened as his aides updated him on the status of disappearances coming in on their cell phones and stared out the window of the vehicle looking for anything unusual. Other than the vehicle crashes caused by drivers who were no longer in control of their cars, there was nothing out of the ordinary. But then again, driverless cars were not ordinary.

"It appears that this is a worldwide phenomenon. Reports aren't clear as to who has disappeared or how many, but as far as we can tell so far, most nations are reporting losses," his aide said, looking at the prime minister, who was clearly astonished.

The prime minister's phone rang.

"Moshe, Moshe! Are you and Sarah safe?" Levi Gur, his chief of staff, was shouting.

"Yes, yes, we are on our way."

"I am too. This event seems to have occurred in a moment, but we are researching how this transpired and if it will happen again. We have not ruled out terrorism."

"Levi, I don't think it is. It is far too widespread. This has occurred across the globe at the same time. No group is that well-coordinated. It's impossible! But I will see you shortly."

In the compound, the minister of defense, the chief of staff, the head of Mossad, and other high-level officials, including the cabinet, were gathered around a large conference table poring over intelligence from around the world. Screens were alive with data, concurrent briefings were taking place as analysts took notes, asked questions, and compiled reports.

"The president of the United States will be speaking at five o'clock!" an agitated administrator announced, holding a handset.

Moshe sat beside his chief of staff and good friend, Levi, who had been his chief of staff as well as longtime colleague. The man was doing his best to synopsize the many reports coming in continually. Aides hovered by, checking their cell phones and scanning the screens that were alive with changing data. The frantic voices of analysts, politicians, and staffers filled the room. It was mayhem.

"Quiet, please. The president of the United States will be speaking," a young woman commanded, and President Foster's face filled the array of monitors stationed throughout the room.

As voices died down, all the great men and women, with immense experience in terrorism, politics, war, hatred, and persecution, sat numbly watching the monitors.

"What has just happened?" whispered a frightened staffer more to himself than anybody in particular. It was one thing knowing your enemy, no matter how powerful, but it was quite another not knowing who he was and how he was able to perform such an astounding feat.

The president's speech didn't calm anyone, but it did put the disaster in perspective. According to US intelligence and NASA, it appeared to be a onetime natural occurrence and, to the fragile relief of all in the room, terrorism was not implicated.

At President Foster's conclusion, and before they could get organized in their thoughts and discussion, the same young woman announced, "There will be a coordinated conference call between the European Union, Russia, China, the UN country representatives, the Middle Eastern nations, and us. Globally, all nations would be on the call, on speakers, on monitors, or other secure communications in one hour."

"Yes, we will be on the call, but I need information on the status of our people!" The prime minister turned to his chief. "Will we be the only country who doesn't know if our people are safe? I want information now, Levi!"

The room exploded again in desperate activity. Aides scrambled to gather the information, reading screens, and answering phones, and swiping tablets. No one precisely knew the status of the Israeli people, because reports were ongoing of disappearances and emergency management response. It appeared that the activity was nowhere near the level of the guesstimates of other countries, particularly the Americas.

"People are still sleeping and not out and about yet," an aide explained, her ear glued to a cell phone as she took notes.

"Discoveries are only starting to trickle in, but they are few compared to the other countries," another responded.

"Keep on it. Use whatever resources you need, but I want an account of who has disappeared!"

Minister of Defense Abba Elon took a long sip of coffee and eyed the prime minister with scrutiny. "Do you agree with this cosmic vaporization theory?"

"I don't know," the prime minister replied, running a hand through his thinning hair. "It's a convenient explanation, but it would be incomprehensible if it was connected to any terrorist group. And if it was an act of terrorism, we would be the first country targeted so I'm leaning to a onetime 'cosmic' occurrence, as the president explained. But I want it verified. I'm not taking the US' explanation for it alone. We have our own people working on it."

As information was raging back and forth, the prime minister corralled his inner governing circle and senior staff. "Come. Let's move into the conference room. Let the analysts work. After we review their reports we will address our own nation."

As the cabinet and his senior staff settled into chairs in the secure meeting room, Prime Minister Ben-Zion stood and spread his hands wide. "As the United States President said, we must investigate for ourselves, but at the moment I will agree with her. We cannot show weakness, confusion, or diversity," he said slowly, worrying about the Israeli people. "It's unlikely the terrorists have this kind of weaponry or virus, and as I said to our Abba Elon, Minister of Defense, terrorists could not possibly have the capabilities of coordinating such an encompassing event at precisely the same moment globally."

"Prime Minister Moshe Ben-Zion," the head of Mossad addressed him formally. "I agree. For the moment. As you said, we must investigate for ourselves, but at this time, all of our intelligence indicates that the terrorists do *not* have the capability of vaporizing people. Also, we are still here," he dryly added.

"But what of our people out there?" The prime minister pointed angrily to the walls.

"It's very early to tell, but it appears there have been fewer reports of disappearances than in the US so far. We might have dodged the bullet on this one." Levi, his chief of staff, sighed, shuffling through documents.

"And yet the United States, South America, Mexico, Europe, and some African countries are reporting huge losses," the prime minister said in confusion. "And the Arab states are still with us."

"Perhaps it really was a cosmic event," his chief responded. "But we are still gathering information. Hopefully we will know soon enough. In the interim, we will pull together a speech for you to address the people. We'll go with the 'Vaporization' storyline. It's the best we can do for now and we, as I'm sure you all agree, must keep the nation stable."

Throughout the day, amidst the reports of chaos and commotion, the staffers and cabinet ministers continued to research, strategize, and pull together the necessary government officials and resources to control uncertainty, fear, and confusion among the populace and within their own agencies. Collectively, they believed the immediate threat was under control, and hopefully over, but historically, the Jews were always suspect of their Arab neighbors regardless of Mossad's opinion of their inability to vaporize humans on such a large scale. The first directive was security. The Israeli's ramped up surveillance both in the air and on the ground. The military was on high alert.

Days later, the reports of the onetime event were being studied. Although early in the research stage, the analysts and scientists agreed that a vaporization of sorts was possible, negating thoughts on possible terrorism. The conundrum was why certain people were vaporized.

The prime minister pondered over the data on the monitors arranged around his desk on the walls. "The largest group to have disappeared strangely comes from the US, Mexico, and Brazil," he said to Levi.

"Equally strange is that India, China, the Middle East, and our country were barely affected," Levi added as he looked over the demographics in puzzlement.

Prime Minister Ben-Zion shook his head. "Who actually disappeared? Was it any particular ethnic, religious, or age group? Was there any commonality?"

Minister of Defense Elon entered the room. Hearing the question directed at Levi he answered for him. "This is what we have so far." He slapped a report on the desk and pointed at the papers. "The discussions between the different intelligence organizations show that an overwhelming majority was Christian. Hence, nations like ours, the Middle East, India, China, and a number of others were not nearly as affected as the Americas. But, there is also indication that some very high-profile Christians are still here. The pope is gone, but some of his cardinals are still at the Vatican, including Cardinal Giovanni who, as you know, is a very powerful presence at the Vatican. Curiously. Some Jews are gone, but we are discovering that all so far were Messianic."

The prime minister nodded as he sat with his hands steepled in front of his mouth, deep in thought. "You know what this means, of course? The United States has been radically debilitated in a blink. We'll know over time just how bad, but as our strongest ally, I'm not sure where her attention will be directed for some time to come. More likely internally."

Levi and the prime minister followed the minister of defense to the common work table. They sat down amid monitors blinking and scrolling, stacks of printouts and folders. Minister Elon directed their attention to the large screen on the wall as an aide manipulated the many windows that appeared across the monitor.

"The guesstimate," began the minister, pointing a laser at the statistics on the monitor, "is that there are more than two billion Christians in the world. While world population has increased, anecdotally Christianity has been on the decrease. However, of those two billion who call themselves Christian, some might be only in name."

Levi nodded. "The evidence overwhelmingly points to Christians with exceptions. And yes, I've heard the reports of high-level Christians that are still here, including Cardinal Giovanni. Those so-called Christians that are still here might be, as you say, Minister, Christians only in name, yet others of uncertain religion and even some calling themselves Muslims are gone.

"There is talk of the Christian belief of the so-called rapture, when their Jesus descends from heaven with a shout and a trumpet call. All Christians who believe in Him will be snatched up to 'meet Him in the air.' It's a little far-fetched, but just read the Torah. That has some overreaching stories as well," Levi concluded.

"Gentlemen, I discount the theory of the rapture," Abba said, shaking his head. "But I'm a secular Jew. My way of thinking is logical, scientific, strategic. For the Christian Jesus to become active is mythical. Even Cardinal Giovanni, the pope's closest adviser is still here! What does that tell you? It can't be the Christian rapture. Yet I will concede—and this is problematic—that the majority of Christians are in fact gone and, while Europe has a good percentage of this faith, the majority who disappeared is in the Americas." Taking a pause to adjust his glasses, he added, "But our main concern is the disappearance of those that were strongly pro-Israel: the US."

"Yes." The prime minister frowned. "The disappearance of such a large group who openly supported Israel means that we lose backing and will be regarded as an unimportant distraction under the circumstances. They will have enough serious concerns to manage; we will not be a priority. Additionally, their economy will be greatly impacted, along with their armed forces. They'll be scrambling to hold the government, economy, and homeland defense forces together. I'm not sure of their appetite to embroil themselves in our defense should the Arab world arise."

The minister of defense was silent. Thinking. He could visualize the impact of losing a strong, influential ally from at least two standpoints: military and diplomatic.

The prime minister realized they must meet with the Israeli Security Cabinet to rearrange strategies. The Israeli Cabinet had twenty-two members that oversaw a number of government segments, but this smaller group of inner cabinet members was put in place to implement defense policy and make quick, educated decisions in times of crisis and war. "Levi, schedule a meeting with the Security Council in three days. The agenda will address the Arab threat that will escalate now that the United States is dealing with their own turmoil and—"

An alarm went off and all three men turned to the overhead monitor.

"And so it has already begun," Abba interrupted, looking up at a screen that just flashed a high alert. Hamas in the Gaza strip had lobbed an air assault on Israel. "It's a good thing we have practice, gentlemen," he said contemptuously, getting up to leave. "But remember Operation Protective Edge. We crushed them."

"Operation Protective Edge" was a combination of rocket attacks and ground fighting between Israel and the Palestinians in the recent past. Nearly 2,200 people were killed, mostly the people of Gaza. Hamas had launched over 4,500 rockets against Israel, but Israel dropped nearly 20,000 tons of explosives on the tiny strip of Gaza.

"Abba, I'm moving the meeting up today," the worried prime minister called to Elon's back. "We can't waste a moment. This could start a chain reaction from all of our enemies."

"Yes, yes, call me," Abba instructed as he hastily made his way toward the door.

"Prime Minister, look!" shouted Levi. The screen alerted another series of rockets launched, this time from Syria. As the men's eyes trained on their track, the rockets were blasted out of the sky by Israel's Iron Dome.

The Iron Dome, a mobile missile defense system developed by Israel and jointly funded by the United States, had been in use since 2011. It was originally put in place to protect the country from short- and medium-range rockets fired by Lebanon's Hezbollah Islamist group and by rocket attacks carried out by Hamas in Gaza. It had a record of destroying some 15 rockets fired simultaneously by Hamas. Immediately the screen showed Israeli's firing back rockets into Syria's Quneitra governorate, a province that bordered the Israeli-controlled Golan Heights, Lebanon, and Jordan.

"The Islamic State is attacking us!" Levi shook his head in wonder. "The Vaporization was only last week and now ISIS is striking. The chaos in Syria has allowed them to steadily move through the country to the southern end." He pointed to the screen that showed a series of blips. "They are strategically positioned!"

"Jordan has attacked them numerous times since they burned one of their pilots alive in the cage, but they haven't been able to contain or stop their spread into new territory," the prime minister said almost conversationally, but this was severely threatening. "They are known to have about fifty thousand militants—and growing. We know how capable and dangerous they are. Levi, we've got to get everyone together as soon as possible."

Hours later, the Security Cabinet was sequestered in the Israeli version of the White House's Situation Room. Intelligence was coming in fast and furious of Arab countries and Islamic military groups flexing their muscles.

"While not all the twenty-two Arab nations are openly talking aggression, they constitute a population 60 times Israel's size and 640 times her land mass," the minister of defense stated. "And you know that all by heart. Those stats are not new."

"Just last night I told my granddaughter the same thing," the prime minister said sadly. "Who knew it would be repeated again and under these circumstances? Without protection, defense, and offense, it might just be a matter of time before Israel could be annihilated. But in the meanwhile, my friends, Israel is retaliating and pummeling ISIS and Hamas, pushing them back and putting an end to the attacks—at least for the short term."

CHAPTER FIVE

THE FAMILY

THE ENSUING WEEKS BROUGHT MORE information on the networks and the internet about the disappearances, including the Christian belief of the rapture, which was roundly discounted due to the fact that a number of Christians, and prominent ones at that, were still on the earth, decrying that the catastrophic event couldn't possibly be the rapture. Otherwise they, too, would be gone.

To be clear, the Vatican went public via television, the internet, and social media. Cardinal Giovanni, now spokesperson for the Vatican, underscored his dedication to his faith and his God.

"I am a man of God. My faith is unshakeable and I have been dedicated to the Church for over forty years. Many others like I am are still here to proclaim the gospel and help our countries heal. Although our beloved pope and others have disappeared, we believe, as do other world and religious leaders, that this was a tragic and unexpected physio-cosmic event. If this was the rapture, I, along with my colleagues and many others, would be gone. I am here. We are still here!" the Cardinal firmly stated.

To the agnostics, atheists, and other religious groups, this was a compelling argument. So much for the rapture. The world was accepting the horrific disappearance of so many by reason of a cosmic interference with the physiological makeup of those individuals. It couldn't be proved or disproved because there were no bodies to autopsy, only scientific theory. The world was going with the event officially called "Vaporization."

The force on business as usual was extremely problematic. Everyone across the Americas and Europe was shorthanded but, in the United States, it was more apparent. Lawmakers, healthcare workers, teachers, farmers . . . the list went on. In many cases, there were people who were able to step into the vacated key positions and although those people were instrumental in keeping the fabric of the country together, there were many holes, runs, tears, and a constant unraveling. The fabric was stretched and weakened.

"Jason," Allie said, "you're barely doing any real work. This 'working from home' thing has got to stop. You sit around all day moping and reading that book; you're doing nothing constructive. You've got to get back to your office and real life. It's been nearly two months since the Vaporization. Sabrina is back at school, and I'm back at work. You can't go on like this."

Jason looked at his wife standing defiantly at the door of the study, with hands on her hips. "I've been trying to work, Allie, but with all that's happened, I just can't get into it."

"No surprise there, Jason. That's why I want you to be around your colleagues who are working on their careers and finding excitement and challenge in new contracts, and not being holed up at home like some old man with an ancient, outdated book!"

Jason ignored the jibe and said, "Becky called and said my conquest of Nathan Kurtz from Luna International is gone. He disappeared too. Their company is in turmoil and can't move forward with the contract. Other companies that we had in our portfolio are in a mess. I have to start all over again, finding more key accounts my boss is clamoring for. I'm just so tired." He rubbed his eyes and sighed forlornly as he leaned back in his chair. "I've lost my heart for all of this striving. It's not going to make any difference."

"Yes, it will! We still have bills to pay and that's a reason why you've got to get out of this funk, and get back to work. You need to pay attention to your job, career, and family. Whatever you're reading on the side, it's time to put the book down and get back to reality. Life goes on. There is still excitement and success out there."

He could only gaze at her. His entire outlook on life had changed. Hers had not. Did he ever think that they would find themselves so fractured in their viewpoints?

With authority she stated, "While things look bleak, they're not really. It's actually a blessing in disguise, except for losing my grandmother and your brother whom you never talked to anyway." She stopped and dabbed the corner of her eyes with her fingers. Composing herself she asked, "Do you know that the greatest percent of Europeans and Americans that were spared from the Vaporization are among the richest and most powerful of the world? Do you know what that means to Henry Sotheby's Jewelry Incorporated? We still have our customer base. And you do realize that because of this I was promoted to fill the chief designer's position. And you, too, have benefited."

He looked at her in surprise. "How have I benefited?"

"You might have lost Luna International but"—she pointed at him—"but *you* now have the most prestigious jewelry designer account on the planet. This means that every business in the world that sells high-end products will want your company to represent them, all because of me and Henry Sotheby." She paused in quiet irritation, seeing he wasn't getting it. "Honey, we're in the big league now," she insisted. "The world is our very rich oyster! We're going to make tons of money! So don't worry about Luna International or the other accounts, that, by the way, you haven't lost. They just need to be reorganized. You do have a prime account and it was handed to you without any work: Henry Sotheby."

"Your grandmother was a devout Christian and so was my brother," Jason stated, not impressed with his new account or their new status of working with the rich and famous. He looked at her expectantly, hoping she might understand. The point was the loss of people, not the gaining of contracts.

"Get over it!" She flounced out of the study, slamming the door.

Jason looked at Lilly's book, her study Bible. It had touched his curiosity and he couldn't bring himself to ignore it or toss it away. His mind and heart were in turmoil. How could his wife think that what had happened to so many people was good for those still here? He wanted to explain to her that money and status meant nothing now. How many people simply ceased to exist in a moment, and what was the real reason? He so wanted to confide in her that he had lost his resiliency, his quest for corporate recognition and power. He couldn't go on with a business as usual attitude. His world had changed.

After she left, he tried to concentrate on work, but couldn't. His eyes kept sliding to the closed black book to his right. The Bible was now a challenge to him; he couldn't put it down. Yes, it was difficult reading sometimes, particularly when he was originally predisposed to the Bible as myth. Yet he worked on reading the Scriptures objectively and was aided by the study notes. So as he plugged on he was seeing that it wasn't myth. There were too many similar accounts that were covered in other parts of the Bible by other writers. The Gospels of the New Testament were starting to flow and connect. Jesus seemed real. He had emotions, had physical needs, and was faced with temptations.

He opened the book of Matthew, the first book of the New Testament, with the Bible being composed of the Old and New Testaments. He was at the part where Jesus' disciples were asking Him about what signs could they expect to see at the end times, or life as Jason was now knowing it.

Jason read that Jesus liked to go to the Mount of Olives, sometimes referred to as Olivet, or as "mount facing Jerusalem," to teach His disciples. It was one of three peaks of a mountain ridge, east of the Old City of Jerusalem. The slopes of the mountain held great ancient Jewish history. This was where King David, ancient king of Israel and Judah, escaped the uprising of his son Absalom, and where Jesus' well-known Sermon on the Mount was preached.

In the current age, the outcome of the Israeli-Arab war in 1948 resulted in Jordan occupying the West Bank, taking control of the mountain range, along with other areas: Jericho, Bethlehem, Nablus, and Hebron. By 1950, Jordan had formally annexed the land. In 1967 Israel captured the area in the Six Day War fighting Jordan, Egypt, and Syria.

So while Jesus sat on its slopes so many thousands of years ago, He answered His apostles' request for how they would know when the end times were near. Jason poured over the book of Matthew and started reading chapter 24, verse 4:

> Jesus answered, "See that no one leads you astray. For many will come in my name, saying, 'I am the Christ,' and they will lead many astray. And you will hear of wars and rumors of wars. See that you are not alarmed, for this must take place, but the end is not yet. For nation will rise against nation, and kingdom against kingdom, and there will be famines and earthquakes in various places. All these are but the beginning of the birth pains."

Jason stopped reading and sat quietly, twirling a pencil in his hand, the one he used to take notes when not tapping on his computer. In addition to work folders, on his desk were scattered paper notebooks, loose sheets of paper, a coffee mug, an open bag of chips, and various electronic devices: tablet, cell phone, and laptop. He leaned back in his chair, not seeing his mess, or thinking about his conversation with his wife. Instead, he was thinking what Jesus said was going to happen and escalate. The key word being *escalate.* Jason recalled the recent wars, the constant terrorist attacks, the famine that seemed to be ongoing in many African nations, earthquakes that caused devastation, tidal waves, unearthly tornadoes, cyclones, and hurricanes. And what about last winter with the record breaking amounts of snow that fell in the Northeast? And the horrible drought in California and Texas? The decimating fires in California? The tornadoes sweeping through houses, farms, and businesses? Many, many people perished.

It was also true that he frequently heard or read about some kind of savageness or brutality. People were abusing their kids, themselves, and animals. And flagrant sex was everywhere. He certainly used it to his advantage for the jean campaign and what a success that was! But, he realized, not only he, but so many others were desensitized to blatant sexuality and cruelty. Who complained? It was mainstream. Watch any TV show or movie and it's in your face. Any person who did complain was called an intolerant religious fanatic.

He saw a reference note scribbled on the side of the passage by Lilly. *See 1 Thessalonians 4:16-17.* He figured it must be another part of the Bible, so he went to the index and saw that it was a book called 1 Thessalonians in the New Testament. He flipped to the page and read: *For the Lord himself will come down from heaven, with a loud command, with the voice of the archangel and with the trumpet call of God, and the dead in Christ will rise first. After that, we who are still alive and are left will be caught up together with them in the clouds to meet the Lord in the air. And so we will be with the Lord forever.*

He saw another note on the side of the verses she had written. *See 1 Corinthians 15:51-52.* Again he went to the index, saw the book was in the New Testament. *We will not all sleep, but we will all be changed—in a flash, in the twinkling of an eye, at the last trumpet. For the trumpet will sound, the dead will be raised imperishable, and we will be changed.*

Another clue was given at the side of this passage: *See Matthew 24:40-41.* Jason went back to Matthew where he read: *"Two men will be in the field; one will be taken and the other left. Two women will be grinding with a hand mill; one will be taken and the other left."*

It didn't take a rocket scientist to figure this out. Vaporization? No way. This was the rapture! He had no doubt in his mind. He fired up his computer and started the research. If what he believed was true, he needed more information.

Let's get back to basics, Jason told himself. He Googled: *What makes a person a true Christian?* After reading for hours, it seemed pretty simple, but it took faith to believe it. A Christian was one who believed in Jesus, that Jesus was the Son of God, and that He died for the people's sins on the cross. He came back to life again—*rose from the dead* was the terminology used most frequently—three days after He was buried in a tomb. A person had to have faith that the sacrifice Jesus made was real. Another thing, God was three essences in one: God the Father, God the Son, and God the Holy Spirit. He was called the Holy Trinity. It seemed once a person believed in the work of Jesus, the third person of the triune God, the Holy Spirit, came to live in that person's heart. The Holy Spirit helped counsel, encourage, and convict a person of his sins. Although it is impossible to keep from all sin while on earth, by confessing and repenting of those sins, a person grows in his relationship with God. By declaration, the person gets baptized. It is a symbol of renewal, rebirth, and cleansing.

Jason began to furiously scribble notes and an outline. Once he was satisfied with what he discovered, he would share the news with his family.

At dinner, Jason announced simply, "I'm going back to work."

"Finally," exclaimed his wife in barely disguised annoyance.

Hoping his announcement would make her happy and open to discussion, he decided to plug on anyway. Ignoring her attitude, he said, "Girls, it's fascinating and makes logical sense. Look, I have it all right here in this outline and in my notes. God—"

Allie interrupted him. "Sorry, Jason. I don't believe in God. I think there might be some energy out there that we all become part of when we die." She whirled her hand in the air. "But, God? No."

"I agree with Mom," Sabrina added, playing with her food and looking at her iPhone.

"Wait, listen, hear me out." Jason put down his papers and folded his hands on his lap and eagerly leaned forward. "Sabrina, put the phone down for a minute. Pay attention. Okay, you don't believe in God, but let's say you *do* believe in God for the sake of the argument. So then, if you do, you know that God can't tolerate sin—even the tiniest sin, like a 'white lie.'" He shot a look at Sabrina, who was shooting looks at her phone. Undaunted, he picked up his notes. "Because God is perfect and holy, He can't let sin go unpunished. No matter how small the sin is, it's still sin. And punishment for sin is death. That's God's rule. So the ancient Jews sacrificed animals for their sins, but it was ongoing because, like us, they were always sinning. And by the way, they had to kill an animal that was unblemished."

"Ewwww," complained his daughter, finally looking up from her phone. "Do we have to talk about this at the dinner table?"

Ignoring her, he asked, "So how to solve this ongoing sacrifice problem once and for all?" He looked at both expectantly. Neither responded. They looked at him blankly. "I'll tell you. Jesus, the Son of God, who was without sin or 'blemish,' became the perfect sacrifice. Jesus made the sin payment, one time, for all of us by His death on the cross and subsequent resurrection. Sabrina, do you know what resurrection means?"

"Dad, I'm not a moron! Yes. He supposedly came back to life." She rolled her eyes.

"Right! So do you get it? Those that believed in Him would be accepted into God's presence with Him in heaven because He was and is the sacrifice for our sins. It makes sense and it is so logical, right?" he said excitedly. "And it's so simple!"

"Seriously, enough," Allie said ominously. "I have to listen to this foolishness at work too. Next you'll be saying the Vaporization was really the rapture." She threw down her napkin. "Oh, pleeeze. It's 'Jesus this and Jesus that. We need to believe in Jesus to be saved!' Well, I don't. If there is a God and heaven, then all good people will go to heaven anyway."

"Allie, you don't understand. Think about it. How good do you have to be to go to heaven? What you think is good might not be considered good by someone else and vice versa. I mean, what is the defining level of how good is good enough? How many good things do you have to do?"

"Dad, this is getting boring. Who cares? We're here, and although I miss some of my friends, I'm getting over it. It was scary for a while, but it's getting to be the new normal." Sabrina went back to her phone. Under her breath she said, "Move on."

"But, Allie, Sabrina, this is critically important," Jason insisted. "I also read that those of us who were not taken will suffer terrible hardship; there's going to be great trouble. It's called the great tribulation, and for the next seven years—"

"Didn't you hear us? We don't want to talk about this idiocy." Allie got up to clear the table. "You're making us uncomfortable, ruining our dinner hour, and sounding like a religious fanatic! And if you don't go back to your job soon, you'll lose it!"

"Mom, there's this new purse I want. All the girls have it, but the one I want is . . . " Sabrina followed her mother into the kitchen.

Jason stopped listening. Dully he finished his dinner. They had no idea what was in store for them, and he had no idea how he could convince them. The things that were important to them had nothing to do with the spiritual realm. He prayed it wasn't too late for himself and that he wasn't truly left behind. He never had felt so alone and scared.

The next morning, dreading work, Jason went to the office anyway. He had no more interest in life as his family knew it. Work and career were inconsequential. Something was happening in the world and that something was judgment. By absorbing a tremendous amount of Biblical prophecy at what seemed like warp speed, Jason was convinced this was a true life-and-death situation and one, he mourned, his beloved family just didn't grasp.

"Good morning, Becky, how goes?" he asked sincerely as he stood in front of her desk, thinking, *I wonder what will become of her?*

Becky seemed surprised that Jason was actually being nice to her. "I'm okay, I guess. Lost some of my family, which is hard, but at least my husband and I are still here. Did you see the internet this morning? Another suicide bomber in New York City. This makes three since the Vaporization. The Arab nations are still rattling their sabers against Israel and everybody else it seems, street crime has exploded, and food prices are skyrocketing. It seems like all hell has broken loose. One awful thing after another. And you don't even want to go to the stock market page. Horrendous. So, other than that, another day."

"Well, when all the good guys are gone, stuff happens. And it's only going to get worse. Thanks, Becky. I'll be in my office for the morning, but I have an appointment at lunch."

"Sure. Whatever," Becky called to him and turned back to her computer screen.

Jason sat down at his desk and turned on his laptop. Sure enough, all that Becky was telling him was screaming from the various news websites as it had been since the Vaporization, which was now a proper noun. It was horrifying that in just a short period of time, only months, really, the United States and the world seemed to be imploding. Commotion and fear were growing worse by the day, but Jason knew why. It wasn't just because a chunk of the world population was gone. There were enough people left to pick up the pieces, and as his daughter said so aptly, it was the new normal. Yet he wasn't kidding in what he said to Becky about how "stuff happened" when the good guys left.

Now all one had to do was scroll through any number of news websites to see what was going on. Evil and calamity were running rampant. If it wasn't so dire, it would be ironic: sports teams were still in the news, fashion was still on the runways, leaders of industry were still making money and pontificating, and because Hollywood was still in place, a new sci-fi movie was being crafted based on the Vaporization.

His boss greeted him stiffly. "Glad to see you're finally here. Working from home doesn't cut it in this business. The company has suffered a lot of lost accounts and creative people. We've got to get back on track. I'm not kidding, Jason. It's essential you are at your best. I know you have to catch up with your staff, but let's get together in the afternoon. We have a lot to discuss." The boss glared at him.

Jason nodded. "Sure. I understand." He'd fake it for the time being, but he wasn't ready to jump back into the corporate world of wheeling and dealing. His life had changed. Truly, nothing on this earth mattered anymore. It was all going to end in seven short years.

Yes, he'd go through the motions for a while until he could come up with a plan.

At noon, Jason hurried down a subdued hallway, got on the elevator, and went down to the lobby.

Ralph looked up from the receptionist counter and smiled sadly. "Lost my wife and half my family, Jason. I can't believe this has happened." Without warning he began to cry. "I'm sorry. I just didn't expect anything like this to happen!"

"I'm sorry too." Jason hesitated for a moment wanting to encourage him. He believed there was still time for those that were still on earth to turn to God. He decided to take a chance. "Ralph, ever thought of God? Maybe everything that's happened is God's wake-up call for those of us that are still here?" He looked inquiringly at the grief-stricken man.

Ralph was silent for a moment, wiping his nose with an oversized handkerchief. "I . . ." He hesitated for a moment collecting himself. "I have thought of God," he admitted. Fat tears rolled down his cheeks.

"I don't have all the answers. I'm just realizing the errors and stupidity of my own life in ignoring God." Jason paused, letting the reality of his unbelief sink in. Shaking his head at his own foolishness, he begged, "Ralph, seriously, turn to God. Ask for forgiveness for all the wrong things you've done in your life. Get yourself a Bible and start reading." He thought for a moment. He was such a newbie in faith himself. "Start with the book of Matthew. That's what I did. It's in the New Testament."

With a shaking hand, Ralph reached under the receptionist counter and pulled out a black book and held it up. "It's my wife's. She had it beside her bedside table and read from it every night. I never paid attention or cared. Never went to church with her; never listened to how she thanked God for her 'many blessings.' I just didn't care. Now, I do. I'm going to start right away," Ralph answered.

Jason didn't know what else to say. He waved and went to the street. His destination was only a couple of city blocks away, so he could walk. As he walked, he thought. It was important to be surrounded by like-minded people. This meeting would be a start. He had to find answers and look for direction; otherwise he just didn't know how to cope.

A worn wood-constructed church sat on a small lot on a quiet side street surrounded by a parking lot and chain-link fence. He had found the group on Facebook. They were open-minded in believing that the Vaporization was really the rapture. Not only had his Bible given him comfort, but this small group would, he hoped, bolster his convictions. Jason realized how important it was to have people who cared about his well-being and who could clarify what certainly was sometimes confusing in Scripture, especially for a new believer.

The door opened before Jason could reach the handle. "Ah, Jason, I presume?"

Jason nodded.

"Glad you could make it." The scruffy young pastor reached for Jason's arm. "There are a number of us already in the sanctuary. C'mon."

Jason sat with over a dozen people, some of whom were holding Bibles and tentatively smiling encouragement at one another. Jason got the feeling that no one knew each other. He sat down and thought of Ralph. How many people were struggling in believing the

Vaporization explanation? How many people were taking another look at their lives and their beliefs? Ralph obviously did. Jason's mind flew to his family. How could they not just give him the time to explain what he discovered? What was the harm in listening to another side of the story?

His attention was drawn to the young pastor, who was still greeting latecomers. Jason looked them over. Some were old, some young, all had a variety of looks. Some looked well-off, others not so much. But who was he to judge? They were here for the same reason. They were scared and realized something powerful had happened and were questioning their beliefs. They had choices to make. There was still time.

Looking at his watch, the pastor said, "Well, I guess Facebook and Twitter are good for some things. I've had the opportunity of connecting with you online, and our forum has been helpful to all of us. Then, seeing so many of you had questions and were local, I thought it would be good for us to meet. I realize some of you are here on your lunch hour, so we'll begin."

"Yes," an older woman said. "I really need some support and help with all that has happened. Thank you for letting us meet."

The pastor half smiled and nodded in acknowledgement as he stood before the small group. "As most of you know, I'm Pastor James. I normally would ask each of you to introduce yourselves, but for now, I want to keep that information private. Some of you will stay for our meetings, some of you will leave. I understand and accept it. We don't know what's in store for us, so for the time being we'll keep our identity to ourselves. Having said that, I'm shutting down our Facebook group, and suggest caution when discussing anything contrary to Vaporization on your personal Facebook accounts."

There was a little commotion within the group, but the pastor held up his hand for quiet. The room became still and tense. "You, that is we, need to take this seriously. We are discussing things that go against government dogma. We don't know where their propaganda can lead and social media is a hunting ground for those entities that might find our way of thinking a threat."

That was a sobering thought, Jason agreed. Worldview was changing. Caution was priority now. Security was high priority. Little by little it was becoming evident that many groups were now being questioned and watched. He saw it every day on social media and the news.

"So let's get to it. Truly, I'm glad you're all here for our first meeting and I'm delighted that you've taken the initiative to seek out answers to your questions. What really happened out there to many of our family, friends, and strangers?" he asked as he pointed outside the church. "I'm convinced that what we experienced was not a vaporization as the government would lead us to believe. I believe it was, based on Scripture, the rapture."

Many squirmed in their seats. A few whispered to one another. Jason sat stoically.

The older woman, Mary, as she introduced herself, said softly, "I agree."

Standing beside the pulpit, the pastor continued, "It's time to take action for our inaction. It's time to be honest about who we were and who we are now. The purpose of this group is to keep each other strong, and to understand who our God is, what he's done for us, and what we need to do. It's all about confessing our sinful ways, changing those ways, and strengthening our faith. Some of you will believe. As I said earlier, others may not and will fall away from our group. But for those of you who do stay, we will study Scripture, we will come to believe our God, confess our sins, and try—with the help of our Lord—to find a way through the upcoming judgements, called the tribulation, which will come on the heels of the rapture. It will last seven years until the end."

The group looked at one another and whispered among themselves. One person got up and left. Jason leaned forward and said barely audibly, "My family. What will become of my family?"

"So to you, I need to confess my situation, and why I have been 'left behind.' I didn't believe. I played the game, was the youth pastor, had a great time with the kids, but I was living a lie. When nearly my entire congregation disappeared, I knew exactly what happened and wasn't going to fool myself into thinking otherwise. I fell on my face to God to confess my faithless heart and prayed He would give me grace to believe. He gave me that chance and I do believe. By His grace, I'm getting a second chance. And it's not too late for any of you either; but if you choose to follow Jesus and stay with this group, it's going to be really hard. We'll be persecuted, we'll be deserted by our loved ones, some of us will be forced to go on the run, and some of us will be killed. Yes, killed. Judgments are going to be handed down to all on the face of this earth. These judgments, God's anger, will affect people, land, water, fish, animals, and the heavens."

He bowed his head for a moment, then said, "I'm praying that if you choose to stay, God will give you the strength to keep strong. So strap yourselves in folks. We're entering into the tribulation."

CHAPTER SIX

THE UNITED STATES

PRESIDENT FOSTER AND HER CABINET met in a room adjacent to the Oval Office. All were seated around the elliptical mahogany table, a gift from President Nixon back in the 1970s. They had met each week in the last several months since the Vaporization for updates on the effect of personnel losses and how each department was being impacted and how issues were being resolved. After greetings, President Foster expected briefings from each secretary. Those with pertinent ones were to go first.

The secretary of homeland security cleared his voice and looked at his notes. "We have many issues, but I will identify a few you all need to be aware of. Our borders are still being inundated with illegals from Mexico and South America. Our staff has been drastically reduced, and the flow of illegals has surged. California and Texas are hardest hit of course, because that's where they are coming across. But what is happening is that once they get through the border, many are moving on from Texas and dispersing in record numbers. However, many in California have been staying. The flow is enhanced by the 'network effect,' meaning many of the illegals already have friends and family residing in the US. It makes it easier for them to find shelter and support, at least in the beginning. Yet, we've discovered the gang element beefing up their kingdoms with the people who don't have anyone to go to and are so poor and desperate to escape the poverty, they are willing to believe anyone if there's something better on the horizon. So the gangs are taking many of these unsuspecting refugees and recruiting them to their strongholds in the major cities of Los Angeles, Chicago, Miami, and New York."

The secretary paused for a drink of water. His mouth was dry. He had a blinding headache from little sleep and too much stress. There was no light at the end of this tunnel. For years, illegal immigration had been a problem, but liberal politicians never drew a line in the sand. Consequently, millions and millions had already crossed over the borders. Several years ago, tens of thousands of women with children as well as thousands of unaccompanied children from Central America easily crossed the Rio Grande. They turned themselves into the Border Patrol, knowing that the US made special provisions for children and would take the children in. And now it was worse and there was no way to ebb the flow. In his heart, under these present circumstances of reduced staff and money, there would never be a solution. The tide would still come in, but never go out.

He continued, "The tentacles of gang influence are rapidly spreading throughout the entire country. Human trafficking, a subset of gang activity, is especially concerning. We're finding innumerable male and female victims purposely hooked on drugs by these gangs, then sold into the sex trade. We simply can't keep up with their activities and, I'll be honest, it will be out of control unless we can get more staff." He knew there was no hope for that either, but he had to let everyone know that the DHS needed funding.

"Go on." The president nodded.

The secretary of homeland security looked at his notes. "Moving on, while we have contained a number of terrorist cells throughout the country, we're finding many of our own citizens joining, aiding, and abetting the Islamic jihadists, making it even more difficult for us to ferret out these cells. Our so-called citizens, who are sympathetic to their cause, are converting in record numbers to Islam. Once the extremists imbed themselves in the community, the culture grows, and anyone who is considered a moderate Muslim is silenced through intimidation and threats. Moderate Muslims have no voice. No influence. They too, are afraid. So we can't rely on their influence."

Sighing loudly, he added, "The terrorists are picking up the pace of attacks. We all know about the recent suicide bombers and, even now as I speak, the FBI is currently investigating chatter of bomb threats against the airlines. Flights have been dramatically curtailed pending the outcome of these investigations."

The secretary of homeland security continued another thirty minutes. He could have filled their ears for days on the failed efforts of containing crime and terrorism in the country, for the gangs and other organized crime groups were proving too strong and one step ahead of the DHS, whose numbers had been drastically reduced in the Vaporization.

"DHS is making every effort to recruit more employees, but all federal and state departments and organizations are recruiting across the country too, and it's only a matter of time before funding will dry up, further hampering any efforts to shore up the department to where it once was," he said. "As you all know, funding is so tight that we're prohibited from entering into contracts, or incurring other expenses, unless previously appropriated in the budget . . . if the funds are still available. It's a tough situation. You all have been briefed on a possible federal lapse in appropriations would cause DHS to cease many of its functions that are considered nonexempt or nonessential," he added.

"Everyone here has budgetary problems," the president put in. "But people expect to be paid and supplies have to be purchased. The government recognizes the necessity to protect life and property, only specific mission-critical functions are approved for additional monies."

"And this leaves a huge gap in the overall continuity of DHS operations," the secretary complained. After he spoke, the secretary of state gave updates on ISIS, Al Qaeda, Boko Haram, Hamas, Hezbollah, the Muslim Brotherhood, the Taliban, and other groups with ongoing terrorist campaigns. All at the table were desensitized over the brutality of their attacks and campaigns. Outrage was reduced to a few weary shakes of the head. Beheadings, crucifixions, live burials, and stonings were not uncommon in the extremist's quest to conquer and decimate anyone not adhering to their interpretation of Islam. "The unrest in Syria, Iran, Iraq, and other Arab nations is bubbling to the top; we are going to get scalded in this altered state of affairs," the secretary of state cautioned. "The Middle East is a cauldron about to boil and spill over. We have been advised that the extremists believe that the time to strike is soon—starting with Israel. The Islamic State and Hamas have already sent rockets into Israel's territory as you know. She responded quickly and accurately. They have pulled back, but it will only be a matter of time before they resume. And it's possible that other Muslim nations will join the extremists against her."

The secretary of defense spoke up. "We don't have the funds or personnel to defend Israel should any of the Arab or Islamic States decide a full assault on her. I never thought the United States would find herself in such a position, but we cannot at this time of extreme unrest in our own country engage in a war that is certain to further impact us in this critically damaged socioeconomic time. Israel is going to have to look for another knight in shining armor. We don't have the resources, Madam President."

"We all understand, Secretary. We can only work diplomatically. Let's take a fifteen-minute break," she said and got up to get coffee while others filtered out of the room to check messages and take a bathroom break.

The DHS secretary stood beside her, pouring his own cup. "This is unlike any situation in the past, so we have no history to draw from. No lessons learned, no cautionary tales of strategies."

"This is true," she answered. "It's unchartered territory, and the fear in everyone's gut is real and won't be eased by political pander. But as far as Israel is concerned, we can only assist through diplomatic negotiations."

"I believe words have little power with extremists, Madam President, but that's all we have to offer now," the secretary of defense said.

When they reconvened, alarm and dread only intensified as all cabinet members gave overviews of their problems, challenges, and outright failures their departments were experiencing. Without money and people, solutions were unattainable. The United States was unravelling.

Back in her office after the meeting, the president took a moment to have a discussion with her advisors. "The Great Depression was a worldwide economic depression that lasted, I don't know, about ten years?"

Her advisors nodded, and Chet said, "From Black Tuesday, October 29, 1930, when the stock market collapsed, through 1939 or early '40. It was the worst economic depression of the century. I believe the worldwide monetary value of all the finished goods and services dropped fifteen percent. International trade dropped fifty percent. Some areas in the United States, like Harlem, had fifty percent unemployment. On the whole, unemployment in the US hovered around twenty-five percent. It was overwhelming and devastating. So many people committed suicide."

"Yes, and I recall reading some trivia that forty percent of the farms in Mississippi were slated to be auctioned on FDR's inauguration day," she added.

"And don't forget the Dust Bowl," her other advisor, Anne, reminded them. "The dust storms that damaged so much of the US farmland during 1934, '36, and '39? The storms damaged nearly a hundred million acres. Talk about devastation! Between the Great Depression and the Dust Bowl, it was a horrific time for the country."

"The Great Depression lasted ten years, and look at the heights America has achieved since then," Chet said encouragingly.

The room was silent for a moment.

"I don't know if we are going to rise out of this," the president said quietly. "Because this is different. While this similarly has widespread appalling economic impact, our country also has lost innumerable influential people, from grade school teachers to scientists. Those people were shaping our country with a strong conscience. They had a compass for right and wrong and had morals that weren't subjective, as ours are now as we lean on political correctness, Hollywood influence, and popular trends. Those religious types, while narrow-minded, had convictions. It seemed they had a handle on personal behavior unlike what we are seeing now. Maybe their belief in God had merit."

"God? Madam President, that's very noble, and true to a degree, but there have also been plenty of so-called religious evildoers. They've been around throughout history. And while not everyone believes in God, there are some very good people still here. I like to think of myself as one."

"Yes, of course, you are and that's why you're here, including the fact that you're brilliant." She smiled. "But my fear is the dramatic rise in global transgression. We're briefed on it daily, and it's not just the Islamic extremists. We're seeing it right here in the United States. There's a wave, a surge in crime that we have never seen before. And it appears that the average American doesn't care as long as it doesn't directly affect him or her."

Chet conceded, nodding his head. "I mean, it's only been a short time since the Vaporization, but there's a definite change in the population's attitude. It's back to the 'Me Generation.' They think only of themselves and not the greater good."

Anne chimed in. "Well, it's not about self-fulfillment or self-realization, typical of the 'Me Generation.' I attribute it to post-traumatic stress of the Vaporization. I think while everyone is trying to move on, there is an underlying animal sense of survival. They need to keep moving forward and don't want to get sidetracked. So although they don't necessarily condone crime and ill behavior, they have other things on their minds."

"You may be right," the president concurred. "But to be candid, our country is in dire straits. You heard all the cabinet members speak of their problems, and the solutions offered were few because we simply need money and people. The economy is tanking. We can all agree on that. We can all agree on the rise in crime, but if we can't hire and pay employees to help battle the crime, where does that leave us? We're seeing an unprecedented rise in offenses from petty misdemeanors to felonies. The worst is coming out in people and no one is willing to take the higher ground. Pick up any newspaper, go online to the various right- and left-wing news sites, and you'll see the same reports. People are edgy and hardened." The president went behind her desk and sat down. "Give me about twenty minutes, Chet and Anne. I need some quiet time."

After they closed the door, she slid open the top drawer of her desk, reached in, and took out a book. A thick book. Placing it in front of her she opened it. The Bible.

Joanna Wright, the staffer that suggested they consider the Christian rapture, had placed a seed of concern in her heart and curiosity in her mind. Unlike most of her staff, she didn't readily dismiss Wright's explanation of the rapture, although she appeared to dismiss it at the time. In truth, Joanna's explanation of the seven-year tribulation aroused grave concern. What if? What if what she was saying was true? The president set out to find out for herself. This was a time when one didn't rely on a staffer's synopsis.

Piqued with the theory of rapture and the tribulation, she had her husband, a staunch atheist, get her two study Bibles.

"There are many translations but, I've opted for a couple of the literal translations instead of the dynamic equivalents of the literal." Handing them to her, he had said, "Just understand. I don't agree with the Bible or any other religion. It's myth, stories, fables, and traditions. And I'd be happy to argue with you if you become swayed. You're the president of the United States. You need to be clear headed, logical. Don't get caught up in unsubstantiated dogma." He shrugged. "But if you're considering the disappearances are a result of the Christian rapture, you'll get push back from your own party."

She did pull her husband into a later discussion, and his arguments while intriguing, were not compelling. He was a successful and talented researcher and would not consider anything based on "faith." She continued the exploration on her own.

She opened to Mark, the second book in the Bible in the New Testament, and flipped to verses 3 through 8 in chapter 13. Her online research had pointed her to one of many passages concerning end times and she didn't get a chance to read this last night. Now in this break time she read,

> As Jesus was sitting on the Mount of Olives opposite the temple, Peter, James, John and Andrew asked him privately, "Tell us, when will these things happen? And what will be the sign that they are all about to be fulfilled?" Jesus said to them: "Watch out that no one deceives you. Many will come in my name, claiming, 'I am he!' and will deceive many. When you hear of wars and rumors of wars, do not be alarmed. Such things must happen, but the end is still to come. Nation will rise against nation, and kingdom against kingdom. There will be earthquakes in various places, and famines. These are the beginning of the birth pains.

In a footnote, she saw that it was almost identical to 24:3–8 in the book of Matthew. She flipped to Matthew. Sure enough, it was. She then went back to Mark 13:32–36 and continued to read,

> "But about that day or hour no one knows, not even the angels in heaven, nor the Son, but only the Father. Be on guard! Be alert! You do not know when that time will come. It's like a man going away: He leaves his house and puts his servants in charge, each with their assigned task, and tells the one at the door to keep watch.
>
> "Therefore keep watch because you do not know when the owner of the house will come back—whether in the evening, or at midnight, or when the rooster crows, or at dawn. If he comes suddenly, do not let him find you sleeping."

She took off her reading glasses and carefully wiped under her eyes so as not to smear the mascara. Was she found asleep? Was what she was reading true? She put her glasses back on. The notes at the bottom of the page referenced the book of Luke too, the next book after Mark. She had to hurry; her advisors would be back shortly. She could digest this more tonight. Flipping to Luke 21:11, she read where Jesus foretells the destruction of the Jewish temple, wars, persecution and then another—pestilences: *"There will be great earthquakes, famines and pestilences in various places, and fearful terrors and great signs from heaven."*

An insistent rap snapped her out of her amazement. She slid the book into the top drawer. "Come in."

Chet and Anne, along with two other aides, entered her office. Without preamble Chet said, "Madam President, we just got word of a thunderous set of tornadoes ripping through Tornado Alley—Texas, Oklahoma, Kansas, Nebraska. The intensity, damage, and loss of life are astronomical! The Enhanced Fujita Scale is a five! Winds are guesstimated at over two hundred miles an hour per three-second gust!"

The president was momentarily dazed, remembering Jesus' other words: "And there will be terrors and great signs from heaven." What could be more of a terror than an EFS 5 tornado? "Brief me on the status of the response—FEMA is going to be taxed beyond measure after what we heard from the secretary of homeland security at the cabinet meeting." Inwardly, she was reeling. More mayhem and as the day progressed, the news of death and destruction was demoralizing.

"Hundreds upon hundreds of homes are leveled and hundreds of people are killed or missing. Many more are homeless," Chet said grimly, coming back to her office in the late afternoon.

Anne trailed behind him with notes in her hand.

Looking at printouts, Chet said, "The land was ripped apart and all that's left in the tornadoes' paths are snapped timber, twisted metal, and rubble. No semblance of neighborhoods or even towns. If we think FEMA was in trouble before, they'll never be able to keep pace with the need now."

"State emergency response and recovery teams had been greatly reduced as well. We have to do the best with what we have of EM teams and the National Guard," Anne explained with clear worry in her tone.

"That's all we can do. Our best. We're limited, but we can only try," the president said. "Keep me updated." She waited on her next scheduled appointment as her staff went out.

At the end of an extremely weary and disheartening day, and after another late night meal, she kissed her husband good night.

"Al, I'm going to do a bit more reading," President Foster said as she walked to her study.

"Mona." Al gently he caught her arm. "I know that you're going through untold stress. But I caution you. Immersing yourself in the Bible, trying to make sense of their so-called rapture will only make you more confused." She opened her mouth to protest, but he hastily explained. "Don't misunderstand me. I'm not saying you can't understand it, but none of it has been substantiated. These stories were written thousands of years ago under the historic belief that the Holy Spirit inspired the writers. The 'Holy Spirit,' Mona. It used to be called the Holy Ghost in years past. What does that tell you?"

"Al, just because the majority of people bought into the spin of Vaporization, doesn't make the rapture less real. And so far, no clear scientific evidence had been presented explaining the Vaporization. Propaganda, yes. Validating evidence, no. The American people and those worldwide were comforted by a supposedly onetime cosmic physiological occurrence. It was partially my idea. Even I bought into it once we polished the presentation . . . and then I sold it to the people. Al, understand, the explanation was reassuring because they could continue with their lives."

"Mona, how do you think the people will deal with the godly force of the rapture? It will be a living nightmare!"

She shuttered to think of the people's reaction. "I know you don't agree, but . . . "

"Of course I don't!" he heatedly broke in. "It's a dangerous and ludicrous option! Think of the confusion and even terror you'll create. And you can't even prove it!"

"I can tell the people what I've read and give proof with Scripture written through the centuries," she argued.

"Mona, please, they'll tear your thesis apart," he reasoned. "Consider this, if Cardinal Giovanni is still at the Vatican, then the rapture never happened. There is no statesperson of the Catholic Church more recognized and highly thought of than he, other than the pope. And plenty others are still here too. Yes, the pope disappeared, but many religious people—and well-known ones at that—are still in the pulpits, preaching and teaching. It's politically perilous to talk about the rapture. It's Christian myth at its best and don't even talk to me about the great tribulation! Mona, listen to me," he insisted. "It's all bunk. It's no different than Greek mythology. Seriously. You're the president of the United States. Start thinking like a president."

She gazed at his worried handsome features, wishing he would open his mind, but she could see no amount of her own reasoning would convince him. It was useless. "Al, thank you for your concern, but I need to research this myself."

In her study, Mona pulled out the Bible and went back to the book of Matthew. She couldn't let it go, contrary to what her husband believed. She was reasonably convinced the rapture was a real event and it happened. Now she must learn more about the "great tribulation." Finding the passage in Matthew 24:21–22 she read, *"For then there will be great distress, unequaled from the beginning of the world until now—and never to be equaled again. If those days had not been cut short, no one would survive, but for the sake of the elect those days will be shortened."*

A note at the bottom of the page referenced Daniel 12:1-3, "The Time of Trouble." Quickly she looked in the index and found this was a book in the Old Testament.

> At that time Michael, the great prince who protects your people, will arise. There will be a time of distress such as has not happened from the beginning of nations until then. But at that time your people—everyone whose name is found written in the book—will be delivered. Multitudes who sleep in the dust of the earth will awake: some to everlasting life, others to shame and everlasting contempt. Those who are wise will shine like the brightness of the heavens, and those who lead many to righteousness, like the stars forever and ever.

She followed the other references of prophecies in the Old Testament: the book of Jeremiah 30:4-6 where he speaks of "Jacob's Trouble," the book of Ezekiel 26:34 when Israel will "Pass under the Rod," and then still Ezekiel 22:19-21, where she read how God would cast Israel into His "Melting Pot." Hours went by as she continued to read.

But what of the United States she wondered? Where was the reference to seven years of tribulation? She went online again for a quick search and was directed to Daniel 9:24-27:

> Seventy weeks are decreed about your people and your holy city, to finish the transgression, to put an end to sin, and to atone for iniquity, to bring in everlasting righteousness, to seal both vision and prophet, and to anoint a most holy place. Know therefore and understand that from the going out of the word to restore and build Jerusalem to the coming of an anointed one, a prince, there shall be seven weeks. Then for sixty-two weeks it shall be built again with squares and moat, but in a troubled time. And after the sixty-two

weeks, an anointed one shall be cut off and shall have nothing. And the people of the prince who is to come shall destroy the city and the sanctuary. Its end shall come with a flood, and to the end there shall be war. Desolations are decreed. And he shall make a strong covenant with many for one week, and for half of the week he shall put an end to sacrifice and offering. And on the wing of abominations shall come one who makes desolate, until the decreed end is poured out on the desolator.

She was tired and emotionally drained. The tribulation would last seven years, and then the end would come. She couldn't think anymore. Her day had been pure stress and now her night was pure fear. Walking into their bedroom, she so wanted to shake her husband awake and warn him of the suffering and pain that was going to come, but looking at him sleeping soundly, she let him be.

Undressing in the dim light, she asked herself, *Maybe I better think about saving myself. What must I do to be saved from the tribulation?* She pulled her robe on and went back into her study. She was drawn back to her Bible, but didn't know where to look. She went to her computer and googled "How can I be saved by God?" Many commentaries popped up as well as referenced verses. She was directed to what Jesus did for sinners and began by reading a portion of the New Testament, 1 Corinthians 15:3, in which the apostle Paul wrote: *"For what I received I passed on to you as of first importance: that Christ died for our sins according to the Scriptures."*

Scrolling through the commentary, she came to the reference of Mark 10:45: *"For even the Son of Man did not come to be served, but to serve, and to give his life as a ransom for many."*

Jesus, known also as the Son of Man.

Why did He have to die for our sins? Why were we "ransomed"?

As she continued through the commentator's explanations, Mona was amazed that Jesus' death atoned for sins and reconciled humanity with God. The writer noted, in Romans 5:10, *For if, while we were God's enemies, we were reconciled to him through the death of his Son, how much more, having been reconciled, shall we be saved through his life!*

As she continued to read and search, the underlying theme was that Jesus was crucified for the sins of the world and rose three days later from death. Those that confessed their sins and believed in Him were given salvation.

It was nearly three in the morning when she grasped that it was all so simple, really. Tears blurred her vision, as she read from John 3:16: *"For God so loved the world that he gave his one and only Son, that whoever believes in him shall not perish but have eternal life."*

She shut off her computer, closed her Bible, and went to bed.

The following morning, the president was anxious to share her thoughts on the rapture and tribulation with Chet and Anne. She wanted to speak with her husband as well, but she would tackle that problem tonight after dinner. In the meanwhile, Chet and Anne would help her formulate a plan to soft sell this critical information to her staff, then eventually to the cabinet, Congress, and the American people. It would be an immense challenge. So many were clinging to the Vaporization theory. Mentally, she argued the direction most would take. The safe route was the Vaporization theory allowing them to believe that there was light at the end of the tunnel. Life could get back on track with fewer people, but nonetheless, life would go on. The frightening route was acknowledging the tribulation and the impending consequences of pain, terror, the Antichrist's rule, and Christ's return to reclaim the world.

Convincing her advisors that the rapture was real, and the upcoming tribulation imminent, was going to be equally challenging because of Chet's lack of belief. He was keenly intelligent, and from past experience she knew he had no time for religious discussions that he believed, like her husband, were myth. He simply was not a believer in God. He didn't like the term *atheist*, but it was what best described him. She was not certain about Anne, although the woman had a sense of "otherness" about her. It was difficult to describe. She was intensely bright, but there was also a foreboding air about her that was somewhat unsettling. Did she believe the rapture could be true? If so, she would know of the looming tribulation, hence her controlled anxiety. Yet, she was always businesslike and rarely spoke of her personal opinions or thoughts. She kept focused on her job and she did it well.

The president's other concern, assuming Chet would listen and might consider the possibility, and Anne might believe as well, was that her senior staff would not believe, or that some would believe and others would not. How would that further divide the country? The government already was in gridlock on solutions to the country's many problems, let alone implementation. The rift between the Democrats and the Republicans was bewildering, astonishing, and getting worse. It was always an issue first of money and then ideology, which segued into who was most successful in flexing their political muscles. This was a time when both parties needed to be working together in a bipartisan manner, yet they were more polarized than ever. They were more concerned for the party line and jockeying for position in power than for the good of the country and people. Their tunnel vision and obvious power plays were stultifying logical solutions to the problems now at hand. Would they even want to consider a situation that was truly beyond their control? Would they dare consider God in this state of affairs?

She understood the risk and realized if she didn't get the majority of support, she would be impeached. While she might not save their lives or country, she could save her own soul. The people had to know the truth, whether they chose to believe or not. She would accept the outcome of their choice. And what of her husband? The thought crushed her. He had stood by her through so many ups and downs and was always supportive, yet she knew he would never change his stand on his nonbelief. He might not try to dissuade her from Jesus, but he would logically lay out for her the consequences of such a move. His heart was hardened. But she decided. She must do this. He might or might not be willing to reconsider, but even if he didn't she was moving forward.

Calmly waiting for her morning meeting with her advisors, she prayed for strength, direction, and perseverance.

"Chet, you look so tired!" The president said, genuinely concerned as he entered right on time for their meeting.

Usually so sharply dressed and coifed, today he looked rumpled. His hair needed a trim and it looked like he used a dull razor. "You look tired too," he countered and poured himself a cup of coffee from the sideboard in her office. "With all of this chaos going on, I don't think I've had one decent night's sleep."

"Me, neither. Where's Anne?"

"She said she would be running a few minutes late," he answered, adding sugar and cream.

"By the way, I haven't seen Joanna Wright around. I'd like her to join us for the last part of our meeting."

"She left us about a week ago. I don't know where she went. She just left. No notice."

"Oh," the president said, disappointed. She had counted on Joanna to help brainstorm the course of action.

Taking a deep breath, she got up from her desk to join Chet in the chairs arranged at each side of the square coffee table. In her hand was a folder listing various Scriptures, commentaries, and timelines. He looked distracted and when he took a sip from his coffee his hand shook. Slowly, he put the cup down and focused on her. "I don't know what's taking Anne so long, but you have appointments back to back and I don't want to disrupt your schedule. Do you want to get started anyway?"

"Yes. Let's start. We can catch her up. Chet, I know that you don't believe in God, but I have some startling and compelling information I would like to share. This business about the rapture and the tribulation—I believe it to be true." She held up her hand. "Please, just listen to me, without interruption."

"I wouldn't think of it," he smiled crookedly. From his pocket, he leveled a small caliber pistol at her face and shot her through her eye. Then, he turned the gun on himself.

CHAPTER SEVEN

THE FEDERATION

MARCUS TOOK A SHORT BREAK from his work. "Ladies, gentlemen, I need a moment. Let's regroup in a half an hour, but Roberto, stay a moment." The staff filed out of the office. Once they were alone, he put his feet up on his desk, sipped from a cold bottle of water, and opened a package of peanut butter crackers. Offering one to Roberto, he said, "The days are long, but we're making great headway."

Roberto concurred. "So far, the majority of member countries back your policies and decisions. Under the circumstances, it's been a remarkably smooth transition."

"They squirmed a little under my new authority and I know there's some grumbling, but the decision to empower me is proving correct."

"Absolutely. All that you set out to do in the short term has succeeded so quickly," Roberto admitted, admiring how effortlessly Marcus' governing was proceeding with little dissension, for Marcus already had the Council in his pocket. Under his authority and direction, the EU was creating and implementing policies, decrees, and regulations internationally to control the rapid downturn in the EU's collective economies. "Any decisions on international agreements needed fifty-five percent of the votes of the member countries, but it's proving to be no problem. You have the backing of all but a few countries." After swallowing his cracker, he continued, "And I think your master economic plan that includes not only EU members, but those countries that trade with the EU has been gratefully embraced."

"Yes," Marcus agreed. "Mainly because they didn't have to spend time hammering out the details when they all have so many of issues of their own."

"Still, they recognized that you enabled the mutual economy to start moving again, even with the obstacles we face because of the Vaporization."

"Yes, and even now, Roberto, what are we seeing? Because of our political, economic, and social successes, potential members are beginning to knock at the door to join the Union. We haven't seen this interest in years. We're gathering renewed strength. Even Great Britain is making noise to rejoin."

"And with reason," Roberto replied. "Nations are suffering deeply. The blow of losing so many people and the great losses in the United States has the world reeling. Her economy has had a dire economic domino effect on everyone. It makes sense that world leaders are looking at how the European Union is bouncing back."

"Here, look at this headline." Marcus tossed a newspaper to him.

Roberto read out loud. "Junius' leadership surpasses that of any current leader. He's proving to the world that he has unquestionable strength and unparalleled creativity. His vision embraces worldwide economic and social unity."

"As we move forward in our global recovery, we'll continue to emphasize how these unusual circumstances call for world unity and focused creativity," Marcus said, pointing at the newspaper.

The thought was echoed around the globe as nations struggled to maintain order and control economic disaster. Many nations readily accepted Marcus' plans of recovery with little resistance on directives that appeared questionable or debatable, if in the short term there were positive results.

Roberto said, "And look how easy it was to move headquarters. Even though our members were shocked, they were elated. The move gives greater prominence and visibility to the organization."

Marcus smiled at the very recent memory. Without discussion or permission, Marcus moved the EU headquarters from the Berlaymont Building in Brussels to his own country, Italy. There was little resistance for that directive too. It was a dramatic jaw-dropping moment for the Parliament, Council, and Commission when Marcus announced the move. "Frankly, it made sense, Roberto. We had the golden opportunity of moving to Rome. Let's face it, because of the disorder in the Catholic Church due to the pope, many of the clergy, and lay workers disappearing, most of the Vatican was vacant," he reasoned. "So why not take advantage of the situation?"

He thought back to when he announced it to the assembly. The members could only gape at Marcus in awe. The confidence and accomplishments of this man were astonishing. To have the EU's headquarters in the most well-known landmark in the world was astounding. Most of the members were delighted beyond measure. What power and distinguishability the EU would have throughout the world! With Marcus leading, they could not fail to achieve their goals of bringing the EU and their countries beyond where they were before the cataclysmic event of the Vaporization.

"At first there was polite resistance from some of the Vatican personnel." Marcus remembered when he approached Cardinal Giovanni of the idea. "But when I made my case, the remaining clergy was happy to have a prestigious organization such as the EU take up some of the vast expanses of the Vatican. Funds in the Catholic Church were and are decreasing, particularly since so few contributions are coming from their churches. And although the Church has a huge cache of art, artifacts, and priceless documents, they do little good when there's not a market for such things—or when there aren't any tourists to pay to see such things. I negotiated a better rate than what we are paying now. Who can complain about offices in a palace?"

"Well done, Marcus. Bravo." Roberto laughed. He certainly wouldn't complain. He was Italian too, he would be closer to home, and his office would be in the most beautiful palace in the world.

Marcus smiled with pride, remembering when he had announced his coup for the Vatican. The members had cried, "Excellent decision, perfect opportunity!" The crescendo of applause was deafening as members came to their feet, honoring Marcus as he smiled charmingly and bowed in humility. Clapping one another on the back at the wonderful news, the buzz in the room was that Marcus was well chosen to lead the Union. He was a true leader who, out of ashes, brought the organization to the top, like a phoenix rising. The world would now see the power and the fortitude of the European Union. It was reborn and regenerated into a premier authority of the world. "A new Roman Empire led by the EU," some joked.

Although few openly questioned why Marcus went ahead without conferring with the two other branches to discuss the move, there were those members who talked quietly among themselves. They formed a secret partnership on their own to monitor Marcus' moves.

A clandestine meeting was recently held where the chairman of the group said, "We're in agreement that we don't believe in Marcus' altruistic motives. Some other member countries, while not in our group, have mumbled that they, too, aren't entirely satisfied with his grab of power which is resulting in ultimate authority in decision making. However, they readily admitted that on the surface his policies and directives were logical and successful. These members are torn between allowing someone an essential dictatorship that is seemingly economically successful, versus a democracy, which could drag out economic recovery. However, they are seeing an ominous pattern developing of decisions being made without vote."

Another group member added, "A quiet arrogance is developing, hidden behind false humility." They all nodded and murmured in agreement.

"Historically," someone added, "unchallenged power can change what appears to be benevolent and impartial rule, into brutal tyranny."

"So the question, ladies and gentlemen, is where is this going to lead, and what can we, as a small group, do about it?"

None knew how to go about controlling the power of Marcus. They adjourned until their next meeting. Perhaps someone would have a plan.

"I get there is a quiet pool of unrest," Marcus admitted, "and we must monitor it." He was working his way into a position that defied questioning because he was proving to the world he, and only he, could solve problems economically and socially. He crumpled the package of empty crackers and threw it into the wastebasket. Thinking about his detractors, he turned to Roberto, "What are your thoughts about the dissension of my rule among a few of our members?"

"I have heard about this group. You can't keep secrets in the Federation. As you suggest, we'll monitor them. Maybe put in a mole," Roberto advised. "We don't want them to gain any strength or negative momentum."

"My track record of successes is my testimony," Marcus argued. "If any complain, it's only because of the manner in which I make my decisions. And so far, I've been always right."

"You have no argument with the majority of the members. They can't possibly find fault with your achievements, because, let's face it, everything you do, is for the common good. Rest assured they're grateful as long as they still can eat!"

Marcus agreed. "The dissenters had better watch themselves, because if they're looking for democracy, they aren't going to get it. I have worked too hard to let the EU slip into stifling bureaucracy and democracy." His goal was to be viewed as a benevolent dictator. It was the only way to keep the growth, power, and trade momentum of the EU. While he was establishing his position, he would monitor his detractors closely. It would happen that he would strike when the time came. It was the only way to maintain success in this new world order and he needed to be constantly updated on the economic, political, and social state of the US. He did not want his goals to be thwarted by a country that considered itself a global enforcer. "Let's move on. Brief me on the status of the US."

As Roberto shuffled his folders for the synopsis, his cell phone buzzed. A look of awful surprise crossed his face as he listened at length to the speaker. After finally hanging up, he looked at Marcus. "We have a serious issue in the Middle East. Reports of rockets fired to and from Israel. Israel intercepted rockets from the Islamic State in Syria and Hamas in Gaza. Hezbollah in Lebanon is looking for trouble with Israel too. The Jews aren't taking the diplomatic route, not that you would expect it; they're firing back with a vengeance and it looks like they've stopped the aggressors, but they're teaching them a lesson in the process. We need to get a handle on this, Marcus."

"What about the US?" Marcus demanded as he dropped his feet to the floor. "From what I was told, they are taking the diplomatic route of talking, but we don't know the details yet. What we do know is that shortly after the Vaporization they made it clear they would only be willing to help negotiate should a conflict arise. *Help* being the operative word, not *lead*," mused Marcus. "They are worrying about their own security."

"And while we are speaking of the US, there's more," Roberto said, pointing to the reports on Marcus' desk. "America is in a more weakened state overall than we thought. I'll give you the short version. The country is gravely concerned about the economy and the influx of illegal aliens, which is causing a spike in crime. And their healthcare system, which has been troubled for years now, has the challenge of caring for millions of sick people. Some diseases they thought were eradicated years ago are now infecting the population at such a swift rate, they don't have enough medication or vaccination serums to keep up."

"What is their government doing? It sounds like the US is imploding."

"The Democrats and the Republicans are squabbling on how to halt the tail spin of their economy, how to shore up the military, and how to control social issues. From our reports, we see little bipartisan cooperation—only arguments, stalemates, and vetoes." Roberto took a breath. "President Foster can't even lead her own party. It's a mess."

"Hmm. And you didn't even mention homeland terrorist attacks," Marcus added as he moved to look out the window. "They've had at least three suicide bombers who took out hundreds of people attending sports and music events just since the Vaporization."

"I was getting to terrorism, because it's a part of the equation of instability and weakness in the US we can't ignore," responded Roberto. "The president herself doesn't speak out against what is really going on! Like her predecessor, she avoids using the term 'radical Islamic terrorism.' Instead she uses 'violent extremism' addressing attacks and threats from very real radical Islamists."

"The Muslim discussion is difficult," Marcus conceded. "The problem of terrorism and most of the solution rests with the leaders of Islam, but at the moment, we have an attack on Israel by Islamic extremists and the US is watching and talking."

"They'll never get into a military confrontation with the extremists over Israel. They're trying to protect themselves from their own internal chaos."

"It was just a matter of time, wasn't it?" Marcus asked as he finished off his bottled water, turning from the view of Brussels. "A super power brought low through broken down borders, ponderous bureaucracy, too many wars, negligent spending, and, for want of a better description, political correctness. It's no wonder the great protector can no longer be mama bear to her cub Israel."

An aide rapped on the door frame and poked her head into the office. Her face was grim. "I have terrible news. The president of the United States has just been assassinated."

Marcus and Roberto looked at the woman blankly. "How?" they both asked in unison.

"Apparently she was having a meeting with her long-time trusted adviser Chet Henley in the Oval Office. They were alone, and he pulled out a small pistol and shot her in the head. He then shot himself. So far, they have not determined a motive and the story going out from the White House press secretary is that this was an isolated event, not connected to terrorism. But you know how those stories go. The truth isn't necessarily what we all get to hear. And, her other advisor, Anne Rich, was found dead in her office and stuffed in a closet, purportedly shot by the same gun."

"How did he get a gun in the White House?" Roberto asked, surprised.

"I don't know. The authorities surmise that he shot Anne first because they both were supposed to be in the meeting with the president."

Marcus reflected on the shift of power and shook his head. "Vice President Sarratt won't be able to pull the country out of its decline. He is another politically correct administrator and clearly inexperienced."

"True, but in all fairness, everyone is inexperienced in these cataclysmic times," Roberto pointed out.

Except me, thought Marcus. He went still for a moment, thinking of the vice president, soon to be Mr. President. He had met him, and knew that although he was charming, he was also an opportunist. He was more interested in the pomp and circumstance of his position in the political theatre than actually involving himself in anything of true substance. He could be useful in the near term, Marcus considered, and turned his thoughts to the problem at hand.

"For certain the United States is in no position to come to the aid of Israel. All the Arab nations will know this. Any war now will be devastating to the world." Marcus turned to his monitor. "The intelligence that we're now getting in looks like Israel is holding her own against the attackers. At least for now."

"So what is our, that is *your*, next move?" Roberto asked.

Marcus paused rooted in deliberation. This was a time to exert control. No ideological war was going to disrupt his long-term plans. Looking at Roberto, he firmly said, "We must schedule an emergency meeting with our members to address a number of issues: Israel made her point. Now she must back off attacking the Islamic State in Syria, and Hamas in Gaza. Second, we must control Hezbollah in Lebanon. Third, we must acknowledge the condition of the United States, thusly implementing a world security strategy. And lastly, we must take a look at the impact the US will have on global financial systems. Our current gains in manipulating the EU economy will quickly deteriorate if we don't take a proactive stand and implement a tactic now."

"That's a lot to cover," Roberto groaned. He stood to go, but Marcus stopped him.

"Wait. Here's another thought, Roberto. The fireworks with Israel could segue into a nuclear war if Russia and Iran get involved. Keep in mind that in the near past the Russian Defense Minister and the Iranian Defense Minister signed a mutual agreement and 'multifaceted military' cooperation between both countries. Iran could get into the fray with Israel and why wouldn't they? They detest the Jews.

Russia could easily become involved too. They have no love for the Jews either. The implications of any joint effort between them would be devastating. With the US out of the picture, Russia and Tehran could control a huge swath of the globe."

"Your plan?"

Marcus paused, then pointed to Roberto. "I want the North Atlantic Treaty Organization a part of this discussion too, chiefly since many of our member countries are also members of that organization."

"Yes," Roberto agreed, tapping out notes on his tablet.

"Because NATO was created as a political and military alliance focusing on communal defense and crisis management, we can be assured that if Israel gets into a war with a variety of Arab groups, and in all likelihood loses, it will be a matter of time until other countries in our alliances could be attacked by Russia, Iran, or any number of Muslim terrorist organizations or Arab countries."

"Agreed. We've already been witnessing the Islamic military groups launching organized attacks and takeovers." Roberto nodded.

"To your point, consider the African continent. Take a look at what just happened in Somalia, Ethiopia, Cameroon, and in Nigeria, where some thirteen thousand people alone have been slaughtered by the *jihadist* group Boko Haram who, incidentally, has ties to Al Qaeda and the Islamic State. They are overrunning northern Nigeria. The group aspires to create a caliphate in the city, based on hardline Islamic law."

"And an Islamic State affiliate attacked the north Sinai and the Suez, killing hundreds of people and scores were killed in a blast in Cairo, again by an ISIS affiliate. We could be caught in a vise by any number of foes coming from the north and south," Roberto added.

Marcus paused as he went to his computer files for information. Finding what he needed, he looked up at Roberto. "We should include the continent of Africa's Joint Multinational Force because we need to bring in all stakeholders."

"What about the UN?"

"Forget the UN for now. I want to establish a core group of like-minded nations with the focus on controlling any attack on Israel that goes beyond the members of the EU. Because, Roberto, Israel is pivotal. She is a key component to our side of the world's security and power. We must protect Israel and form an alliance of NATO, EU, and Africa's Joint Multinational Force committee. Given the United States' current situation, I'm sure she will be agreeable for the creation of a coalition of diverse ethnic nations to help protect Israel, and contain radical Islamists."

"Do you think Africa's Force will care about Israel when their plates are so full?"

"It's all about the possibility of radical Islam running amok. If Israel gets wiped out, it will be a free-for-all among the extremists. Or—and here is where it will be equally shattering—if Russia and Iran team up with their nuclear powers, they would end up with all the spoils of war."

He stopped speaking. Surprised. Suddenly it was all so clear! All these many months of constant chaos. This was his moment of realization. This was what was mapped out for him before he was born. One act could make him a hero to all countries. Nations would be grateful to him for his prescience and visualization of a secure world. How could they not be fearful of their own security if threatened by the Islamic extremists? Worse, if nuclear weapons were used, a third world war would develop and to what result? He would offer a way to gain control of the impending chaos without going to war. He would now have the resources of the Federation (the name he wanted for this new organization) and, with strength in numbers, he had the ability to gain control. And control meant heady power.

"Roberto, we will architecturally form a federation of the stakeholders of which the EU will be a part. We'll work on its structure immediately. I will lead the group. The meeting will address the issues we've discussed. There is a component I want to present as a solution. We need to create a very important historical document." His pulse quickened in excitement. "I am going to make a treaty with Israel to ensure her peace and protection."

"What?" Roberto asked dumbfounded.

"A treaty. It's a workable solution. A treaty between Israel and our newly formed Federation. Lest there be complaints, it will only be for a short time." Marcus paused. "Let's say, seven years."

He smiled.

CHAPTER EIGHT

ISRAEL

"THE JEWS HAVE BEEN PERSECUTED and her land occupied for nearly twenty centuries. It's amazing we are still in existence," Chief of Staff Levi Gur said to his prime minister, "when I think of all the displacements our people have had to suffer and all the empires that have ruled our land."

"Even now, we still don't have all of the land we were promised through our patriarch Abraham. We should be occupying one hundred miles north of Damascus and one hundred miles south of Jerusalem. We should own Lebanon, the West Bank of Jordan, and large parts of Syria, Iraq, and Saudi Arabia," the prime minister added. "Indeed, but the twenty-five hundred-year-old prophesy was fulfilled, wasn't it? We have our own state; even if it's abbreviated."

Chief of Staff Levi Gur and Prime Minister Ben-Zion reminisced about God's promises to the Jews. The prime minister believed that God would fulfill His covenant with Israel, maybe not in his lifetime, but someday. He believed the words of the prophet Isaiah: *A remnant will return, a remnant of Jacob will return to the Mighty God* (Isaiah 10: 21).

Levi said, "Remember the promise of Ezekiel's prophecy in chapter 36, verse 24? *'For I will take you out of the nations; I will gather you from all the countries and bring you into your own land.'*"

"*Your land,*" the prime minister repeated. "Genesis 15:18–20: '*On that day the Lord made a covenant with Abram and said, "To your descendants I give this land, from the Wadi of Egypt to the great river, the Euphrates."'* I believe we'll get it all back," he said, looking at not only his chief of staff but close friend.

"I do too, but it's not going to happen in the near term. We're continually threatened with our very existence. If we defend ourselves without help, our people will face mass destruction."

For a moment, the prime minister thought of all the times the Jews looked to other countries to help them. It was well documented throughout Jewish history. When they stopped depending on God for protection, seeking nations to stand for them, they were slaughtered and captured. So was the country repeating history once again by depending on other countries to protect them rather than trusting in God's protection?

Prime Minister Moshe Ben-Zion and Levi Gur had great memories when it came to the history of the Hebrews or their Bible. The Torah, the first five books of the Bible also called the Pentateuch, was the book of law; the second section was the Nevi'im, the book of the prophets; and last was the K'tuvim, the book of writings. Quoting facts and Scripture was an integral part of their friendship. Each had incredible memorization capabilities and both respected each other's knowledge of Judaism. Often they had long fruitful discussions to ease the stress of government and politics. They would meet at either the prime minister's residence or at Levi's apartment and talk well into the night. Their friendship was strong.

A verse popped into the prime minister's head from Isaiah 20:5. *Those who trusted in Cush and boasted in Egypt will be dismayed and put to shame.* He thought about it. The Jews had looked to Cush and Egypt for aid, only to see those nations' authority overtaken by Assyria, a powerful empire that invaded those nations and led as captives. The Jews had depended on the wrong source for help. They had turned from their God and were ultimately led captive themselves.

He turned to his chief of staff. "Levi, you know the history of the Jews better than anyone I know. Will God or Marcus Junius protect Israel?"

"Between 1939 and 1945, six million Jews were slaughtered." Levi sighed. "If we have war with the Islamic State, Hamas, and probably Hezbollah, and who knows who else will jump in—perhaps Iran with her dear friend Russia flashing their nuclear weapons. How many Israelites will die then? What will happen to our nation? We will be extinguished from the face of the earth. And I don't know if God will step in," he said honestly. "What if He doesn't?"

"So, we accept the peace treaty or get slaughtered." The prime minister looked to his friend, who sadly nodded his head in agreement. He thought of God and the ancient Israelites again. Would God intervene? In truth, he was not so sure God would. Israel had turned her back on Him long ago. Why would He bother even if He was so inclined?

"This is the only recourse we have. The treaty. But I don't trust this Marcus Junius," Levi admitted.

"Nor do I or many of the Security Council," confessed the prime minister. "But we have no choice but to depend on the Federation. The Americans cannot help us. With their president assassinated, the country in confusion, and their military debilitated, they have made it clear: they cannot send troops or air support. If signing a treaty with the Federation is our only option, then sign we will. We must protect our people."

"I don't see any alternative." Levi nodded.

"I hope my granddaughter will come to know peace." The prime minister sighed, more to himself than to his friend.

Both men rose from their chairs, straightened their ties, and shook hands of agreement and resignation.

Prime Minister Ben-Zion left with his chief of staff, Levi Gur, to formally meet with Marcus Junius, the leader of the newly formed yet powerful Federation, to sign the peace treaty.

The prime minister entered the secure chambers of his offices and shook hands with Marcus Junius, who was introduced by his advisor and chief of staff, Roberto Pertucci, as Super Dux of the Federation. The rest of his senior advisors were presented and introductions were made with Israel's Security Cabinet and other attendees. The tension on the Israeli side was thick. While many of the leaders were hugely relieved the country would be protected from her adversaries, they were extremely distrustful, but there was no other option. Israel was far too small to protect herself indefinitely under a diverse Arab attack.

Reluctantly, Prime Minister Moshe Ben-Zion signed his name alongside that of the Super Dux. The prime minister would later question Levi about the significance of Marcus' new title.

Marcus stepped forward to address the attendees. "It is agreed that, for the next seven years, Israel will be guaranteed peace and security from those wishing to do her harm."

A light applause was heard through the room. It was known that the Israeli people themselves were not totally confident in the agreement, but they were willing, along with their leaders, to take the chance.

"We have over forty nations pledging support to Israel," Marcus went on. "While there are nations who did not support the treaty, notably Russia and Iran, Libya, Afghanistan, and Sudan, the treaty is strong enough to satisfy security."

For a while, thought the prime minister. The Israelis had spent billions on defense. The people longed for secure peace and the ability to tend to their lives. It was time to put money and effort back into their economy and well-being and look to the prosperous future of Israel. If it meant a treaty, then the country would have to depend on it.

The overall of the treaty had concessions: Israel was to pay trade tariffs to the Federation on exports, a hefty percent of Israel's energy production was also designated, and any Israeli military action must be aligned with the Federation's own security defense forces, known as FSDF, which Marcus Junius recently created from all the EU and NATO nations.

After photos of the formal signing, press conferences, and a banquet hosted by Israel, Marcus, now referred to as Super Dux, and his entourage left for Rome. Back in the prime minister's office, he and Chief of Staff Levi Gur were following up on a number of action items to present to the cabinet when the prime minister asked, "What is the meaning of Marcus' title, Super Dux?"

"*Super Dux* from the Latin means 'over' and 'chief,'" answered Levi. "Apparently he wants the title to identify his position in the Federation as supreme, perhaps in a subtle way."

"It's hardly subtle, if that's what it means," the prime minister responded. "He is head over a multinational organization that includes a combined military force under one man, which is him. Granted, that is where our comfort lies—we will be protected with a collective military force looking out for our interests."

"Which is really their interests, when you take into consideration the percent they are extracting from our exports and the share of the gas off our coast and the projected four hundred billion barrels of oil trapped in the rocks," Levi complained.

"The Federation's financial and military capacity is expanding exponentially with the addition of new member nations and now with the treaty. Revenue from our country will drop into the Federation's funding bucket and will help bolster the economic, social, and military goals of Marcus' groundwork for a dominant and prevailing Federation," the prime minister explained. "I know what's going on, Marcus. Our new Super Dux is positioning the Federation to become a meddlesome and domineering superpower."

Both men were well aware of the trade-offs. The Federation, of which Israel was not a part, but was now protected by, was adamant about an interest in Israel's gas and oil reserves. The gas was offshore, but the oil exploration and extraction was close to the West Bank. The Federation would protect their interests wholeheartedly from the Palestinians, which on the one hand was good for Israel, but on the other, Israel would have to pay the price for its protection.

"And consider our exports," Levi pointed out. "Our diamond industry holds stable even in these troubled times, along with our high-technology products. We have some of the brightest and entrepreneurial people in the world that weren't taken in the Vaporization, unlike the US."

"Yes, and we still have a host of products that will rally now that we are in a secure state with the backing of the Federation. Our chemical, pharmaceutical, and biomedical products will progressively regain momentum, along with our transport equipment."

"So, Prime Minister . . . " Levi smiled. "It's the price of peace. Tariffs and percents."

A week later, while the security cabinet was working on their last session of military budget cuts, a side conversation was ongoing during a break while the ministers were drinking coffee and tea.

"Have you been following those two men in Jerusalem who are preaching the 'end is near' and speaking to everyone within earshot to repent?' asked one of the ministers.

Another laughed. "They are actually wearing sackcloth!"

Minister of Internal Security Yossi Schnell responded in seriousness, "We've been following them very closely, and they pose a real problem. They're being called God's prophets Moses and Elijah by some, and Enoch and Elijah, by others. The 'two witnesses' by others. But the majority of people call them crazy."

"We don't need our own brand of religious extremism! Where are these people coming up with this misinformation?" demanded the minister of defense as he poured himself another cup of coffee. "The people who believe they are prophets cite 'two lamp stands and two olive branches' from the book of Revelation in the Christian Bible and 'two olive branches and two gold pipes' found in our Nevi'im: Zechariah 4 in the Minor Prophets. It's also in the Christian Old Testament, which is, for all practical purposes, the same as ours."

Prime Minister Ben-Zion and his Chief of Staff Levi Gur wandered over to listen to the conversation. Both men had talked about the two so-called witnesses earlier that day—two men who had been in the news for weeks regarding the unusual clothing they wore and their unrelenting message: "Turn from your sins, and turn to the one true God through Jesus Christ His Son!"

During that time, they were regarded as harmless, but increasingly annoying. People jeered and cursed at them. Newspapers wrote unflattering opinion editorials, and political cartoonists had a field day. The internet was alive with negative, nasty comments and action-filled videos. However, just this morning their behavior escalated beyond words due to the rougher crowds who were tired of listening to them. Three men, at the encouragement of others, hurled rocks at them.

The prime minister turned to the internal security minister, his head cocked to the side and his eyebrows raised. "They may be crazy and annoying, but we were informed earlier that they were attacked by some people in the crowd who were throwing stones at them. They responded with fireballs, burning the attackers alive."

Cutting into the conversation, the minister of defense barked, "They threw fire bombs? Where were the police? Why have these two men not been stopped and arrested?"

Yossi, internal security minister, had hoped that the conversation wouldn't turn to the "witnesses" at this particular staff meeting.

Internal security was not prepared to discuss the recent turn of events; they were still investigating these bizarre and unexplainable events, but he now was forced to say something. He had planned to brief the prime minister later in the day when he had more information. "Gentlemen," Yossi said calmly, "what we know and are currently investigating is that when the local police tried to apprehend the two men, fire shot out from what looked like their mouths."

The men in the room stopped their idle chatter and came closer to listen. The prime minister and his chief listened expectantly.

"What?" asked the prime minister.

"While the authorities thought it was some bizarre high-tech defense mechanism, it proved more than that. So far we have ascertained it was not a trick. The police did open fire on them to stop them." The security minister paused, then licked his lips. "Nothing happened. Nothing. They were hit, but the bullets were ineffective. The police charged, and again, fire shot out from the two men, who then continued to preach as if nothing happened. The crowd was delirious as police officers writhed on the ground, burning."

"Why are we just hearing of this now?" the prime minister demanded. "This is unbelievable!"

"We were going to brief you as soon as we had more information. We are scrambling for answers," Yossi said miserably.

"But what of the police? Why haven't the two men been arrested, Yossi?" the prime minister insisted.

Now everyone's attention was riveted on Internal Security Minister Yossi.

"Prime Minister, please, let's everyone sit down and I'll speak to all of you. It's good the Security Cabinet is all here." Yossi nodded, thinking he wasn't prepared for this now. However, he had no choice but to brief the men and women overseeing the country. "It's not as easy as you think," he explained once everyone was seated. "They have fire bomb artillery capabilities that emanates from their bodies and a defense shield we can't penetrate or comprehend."

"What are you talking about?" shouted the defense minister, nearly spewing out his coffee.

"That is insane!" cried the minister of justice, expressing what everyone else was thinking.

"Calm down, everyone!" the prime minister demanded. "We will discuss this civilly."

"As I have explained, we are investigating this as we speak," Yossi assured everyone. "At this time we don't understand how they are untouchable. But if we can keep the crowds composed, the 'witnesses,' as they are called, will not feel threatened and so will not strike back. We have police barriers up and crowd control in place."

"I wonder if this is a by-product of the Vaporization?" one of the cabinet members asked. "It seems very odd that these two men would have such unusual powers. Could the Vaporization have this effect on them?" She looked around the table for endorsement.

Yossi gave it some thought. "Yes, that is very possible and certainly worth considering." They had nothing else to go on.

All were quiet for the moment until the minister of defense spoke up. "Under the circumstances then, we should keep the crowds at bay so these two men aren't antagonized and cause any more deaths. Let them preach until your team can devise a way to kill them."

"Yes, that seems like the path of least resistance for now," conceded Yossi, which was what he planned all along. Without understanding the witnesses' power, they had no way to apprehend them without risking others getting killed in the process.

After they adjourned the defense budget meeting and were back in the executive offices, Levi, clearly worried, asked, "What do you think, Prime Minister?"

The prime minister sighed loudly. "I honestly don't know what to think. How can two men be physically invincible? I agree with our Minister of Defense. Let them preach. Ensure they are not foolishly attacked so they cannot respond with their own brand of weaponry. We can keep the people at a distance with barricades. The people must understand the risk they take if they attack these two men," he reiterated. "At this time, we cannot protect the aggressors, nor can we arrest the witnesses. Those who take matters into their own hands, or make sport of this, will suffer the consequences."

Levi nodded his head in agreement and added, "We can't stop the press either from covering them. Look at this incredible video posted online. This is what Yossi was referring to at our budget meeting." He pointed to one of the widescreen monitors mounted on the wall. It showed a heckler lobbing a brick at close range to a witness' head. The witness turned and looked at the man, who was immediately consumed in fire. The horrified crowd pushed back, no one making the effort to put out the fire. A second, then third man threw a rock. The same thing happened to them, causing chaos and panic. It was all captured on a shaking cell phone.

On another monitor, a newscaster was replaying the morning events, capturing the panic and horror of the crowd on the cell phone video. Later, when the TV crews arrived, close-ups were taken of the witnesses who were imploring people to turn from their evil ways and turn to the one living God. They begged the people to repent of their sins of greed, love of money, worship of material possessions, promiscuity, thievery, lies, and so on.

"This will get old, and the people will move on," the prime minister said.

"I'm not so sure," his friend said. "Watch!"

The videographer turned his camera on the crowds pushing against the barricades, cursing, heckling, and taunting the witnesses. The crowds were furious and looking for action and retaliation. Someone spotted an aggressive protestor and shouted for everyone to get ready. Most of the crowd held up their cell phones and some even had tablets to capture the attack. A man gleefully held up a bottle and waved it to the crowd as they moved away to make room for him to light it. Catching everyone's attention, he screamed obscenities, ignited the cloth at the top of the bottle with a cigarette lighter, and hurled the Molotov cocktail at the two men who refused to avoid it. But before it could hit the ground by their feet, it was intercepted by a flash of fire from one of the witnesses. The bottle exploded into thousands of flaming shards that flew mercilessly through the crowd, cutting and burning all in its path.

Horrifying screams and confusion erupted as people howled in pain. The fire from the witnesses continued to seek out the person who threw the bottle. It found its target. In seconds, the man's face and hair detonated in fire and his body was consumed in vicious flame. Like a fiery puppet, he jerked in terror, sending the bloodied crowd about in mass confusion before collapsing in a smoldering mass. The crowd screamed in horror but were helpless, terrified to go after the two witnesses.

The prime minister said, "Levi, what kind of power can these men have? Maybe the Vaporization is causing superhuman feats?"

Levi couldn't answer. He sat bewildered watching the screens.

Chaos erupted. Police arrived along with screaming ambulances. The screen showed some people being treated for their injuries while others crowed behind the police, cursing the two men. The police tried to disperse people in the crowd, who were moving back reluctantly.

As the squad trained their weapons on the men they did not fire. The camera zoomed onto the witnesses who momentarily stood quietly and then continued their pleas: "It isn't too late. Turn to the one true God. Confess your sins; believe in Jesus' work on the cross!"

The prime minister and his chief of staff sat stunned. This was as unbelievable as the shock of the Vaporization. Neither could articulate their feelings.

Finally, the prime minister spoke. "If Marcus Junius gets word of these two men, I don't know what he will do."

"What business is it of his or the Federation's?" challenged Levi. "Can he or anyone else reckon with this phenomenon?"

Prime Minister Ben-Zion could only shake his head. "Marcus would view this correctly, as a security threat and one that we can't control. The problem and therefore the solution are beyond logic as we know it. This is a religious situation that has morphed into what looks like the supernatural, or some result of the Vaporization. But I don't think it is the latter because they are asking people to stop sinning and turn to God, with belief in Jesus. If they get attacked, they perform a miracle with fire from out of nowhere."

"With the exception of the Jesus part, it sounds a lot like our Bible teachings," Levi reflected.

"Yes, but it is Christian theology built on Judaism," answered the prime minister. "If Marcus challenges us about not containing this, we can only be honest. At this time, we simply don't know how to manage these two men. It appears they only want to preach. They aren't looking for trouble. Unfortunately, the people are and so they are protecting themselves. And some are treating this as entertainment and people are getting killed."

"The press is all over this. It will go viral on the internet and get out of control if we don't somehow manage the media," Levi said urgently, turning to the prime minister.

"How are you going to control cell phones and the internet when the cat is already out of the bag? But yes, we need to work on this. Let's set up another meeting with the Security Cabinet as soon as possible."

As they pulled together their notes and briefs, the monitors continued with world news. Although the recent headline was the treaty with Israel and the Federation, the constant update was on Super Dux Marcus Junius and his successes and influence in the world, leading many to embrace a new world order overseen by the Super Dux.

"They haven't caught on to our two witnesses yet," Levi said gratefully.

"It's just a matter of time. The press will make us either a laughingstock or will notch up the terror factor. But listen to this," the prime minister said, nodding to a newscast. "I think Marcus has the press in his pocket."

The commentator spoke with pride. "Many nations agree to a single point of leadership in these uncertain times. The United States is considering joining the Federation and has the support of her people.

They call Marcus Junius the 'Cowboy on the White Horse,' riding to the rescue to save the day."

The screen switched to another commentator who interjected, "The bottom line is that the world's nations need a solid economy. It makes sense for financial systems to be centrally governed and regulated. Security, too, is paramount in these uncertain times. Therefore, it is logical that a collective military defense force centrally controlled should follow. The Federation satisfies all criteria, and Marcus Junius has proved himself indispensable as leader."

"It's not a slam dunk, as the Americans would say," the prime minister said as he prepared to leave. "Other nations, in particular those who did not support the treaty, are vehemently against one leader and one world order."

Before Levi could comment, he held up a hand and pointed. Both men looked back at the TV monitors filling the room. The press was now gleefully and importantly breaking news on the two witnesses.

CHAPTER NINE

THE FAMILY

"DAD, DAD!" SABRINA CALLED TO her father.

Jason stood in the kitchen, eating a peanut butter and jelly sandwich and watching with fascination and dread the continuing news about the two men in Israel, called the two witnesses with supernatural powers.

"Look!" Sabrina proudly held out her hand and to show off her newly inked tattoo.

Tearing away from the TV, Jason looked down at his daughter's hand in horror. "What have you done?"

It was an intricately and well-done design of three numbers intertwined. *666.* Trying to swallow the glob of paste in his mouth, he took a drink of milk and swallowed hard. Dazed, he looked into the happy eyes of his wife, Allie.

"Don't look so horrified. I have a matching one too," Allie said. "See? Isn't it cool? It hides the tiny scar where our bank chips are inserted. It looks just like a henna tattoo. So feminine and pretty. You're going to need one too—you have a deadline to get it, and the lines at the mobile clinics are long." She read the look of resistance on his face. "If you don't get one, you won't have access to our bank accounts, or to use checkbooks and credit cards, or make any money transactions. Bring your license and social security card with you. Don't worry, you can get a manly one—like block letters!" She laughed.

"Sabrina, Allie, how could you?" Jason burst out. "This means that you have taken the 'mark of the Beast,' the mark of the Antichrist!"

"Jason, for the last time, I have had enough of your demented talk! Do not talk like that about the Super Dux's directives. It's dangerous! You could be arrested as a traitor! And why would you even think to talk like that? He's taken the world out of chaos! And with the current condition of our country—an assassinated president, runaway inflation, crime beyond control, and a military that's laughable, he is our messiah! He's the one with the plan. Not your Jesus!"

"But Allie!"

She cut him off. "You've known for a long time that this was the way for money and commerce to be managed and transacted. The United States is now a part of the Federation. Do you think you're above the law? You're not! This isn't an option. Get the mark. Don't you realize the implications of not having it? If we are going to have a unified management of finances, we all have to be in the financial database and we all have to be recognizable at a glance in order for us to conduct business—or even stand in a fast-food line. Our government is in total agreement with this!"

"Well, of course they are! One third of our debt has been forgiven," he countered. "Why not use fingerprints or eye scans for the database?"

"Because, Jason, how could people tell at a glance if you are in the database or not by simply looking at fingertips or eyes? Do you think your local mom-and-pop stores can afford expensive equipment and computers to read eye or fingerprint scans? These tattoos immediately validate a person is in the system without anyone having to use special technology, other than a credit card scanner. You can't fake the tattoo either: the underlying chip is activated via the scanner. It's so simple and totally effective."

"What about people without bank accounts?" he asked.

"Everyone is required by law to have an approved account. You can always use cash too, because your chip authenticates your mark. As I said, you can't even stand in a line if you can't show your mark."

He couldn't win the argument. Heartbroken, he walked into the family room and sat down. He could hear Allie complaining as his daughter mocked him.

"Mom, he's acting like an idiot! I'm tired of listening to the same old junk. He embarrasses me in front of my friends, that's why I don't bring anyone home anymore. He's all doom and gloom and carries on like an old preacher or something. All hellfire and brimstone!"

"He's got issues, Sabrina, but don't talk about your father like that."

"Oh, jeeze, Mom. He doesn't let up. All my friends just laugh at him."

"I just wish he'd get over this newfound religion," her mother said. "It's all myth. We could be enjoying this exciting time we're in; instead he's doing his best to be negative. And I have to agree with you. I don't want to hear another word about what he thinks is going on."

Allie's cell phone rang. Sabrina left the room and Allie picked it up. "Hey, Mom. Oh, everything with Sabrina and me is wonderful, but I'm really getting tired of Jason. He's constantly trying to force his belief about the 'rapture' and the upcoming 'tribulation' on us. I am so over it! He warns if we don't turn to God, don't confess our sins (our sins—can you believe it?), and don't believe in Jesus, then we'll spend eternity in hell! I know it's crazy, but I have to live with it." She paused for a moment. Eventually she hung up and went back into the family room, where Sabrina was reading and texting on her phone.

The room was ominously quiet except for the prattling of the TV announcer hammering away at the danger the two witnesses in Jerusalem were posing to the Israeli people. A clip was run where the two men were pleading with the people to confess their sins and turn to God.

"I'm so sick of hearing about sins! What are sins?" Allie demanded, staring at the TV with her arms crossed tightly against her chest.

Jason kept silent. He was upset about what his wife had told her mother. Now he had to listen to her protests about sin. "What I think is okay, someone else thinks is not okay and vice-versa. So who can define what is sin?" Allie snapped, turning to her husband.

"God makes the definition," Jason softly replied. "And I can show you if you'll only be open to another way of looking at life and death."

His daughter looked up from her cell phone. "Sin is old-fashioned. No one ever talks about sin. When someone does something wrong, I don't think I've ever heard someone say, 'Oooh. Don't do that! It's a sin!'" she mocked, shaking her finger in admonishment. "C'mon, Dad, really?" She went back to her phone.

After Allie's blowup about sin, she and Sabrina left the room and Jason surfed the TV channels sitting in the family room. He was numb. It was evident he wasn't making headway with his family. He closed his mind to his personal problems and settled on a public broadcasting channel. As usual, the news was watered down. The main focus of most newscasts were the wonderful works of the Super Dux Marcus Junius, his new headquarters in Rome, and the seemingly benevolent control he had over the nations and peoples that joined the Federation. Israel was turning its attention from military spending to peacetime activities—investing in industry, agriculture, and technology. Rare was the mention of escalating crime and the floods of immigrants and refugees fleeing countries steeped in poverty and gang wars. Rare was the talk of escalating inflation. Even Islamic terrorism, while still rampant throughout the world, was getting little air time. All attention was on the Super Dux.

The newscaster beamed. "The majority of the nations are settling into a new normal and accepting the rule of the Federation and its leader. The Federation is likened by political commentators to the ancient Roman Empire. Sophisticated, all encompassing, and ruled with strength and order."

The video cut to a political pundit who knowingly said, "Life will go on, still challenging with social ills, but better in the long term!"

Jason wasn't buying into it, nor were some others. Underground groups monitored the political activities of the Federation and non-member nations posted reports and commentaries on certain websites. Many who had come to believe that the rapture and prophesy were true believed that Marcus Junius was the Antichrist. His commerce directive requiring all citizens to have *666* tattooed on their hand was straight out of the Christian Bible, in the book of Revelation 13:16–18. Some people went even so far as having the numbers tattooed on their foreheads.

Jason watched and listened as a commentator from Rome interviewed Marcus from his headquarters in the Vatican. "Super Dux Junius, how did you decide to come up with the numbered mark and the imbedded chip for purchasing power?"

"Eventually we will all have one currency, which we are working on now. This will be a universal process for buying and selling, regardless of size of purchase and regardless of country. This information will be sent to our vast and sophisticated data banks for analysis to determine the correct ways of overseeing and managing all our financial systems for the good of the Federation and the world. Even those who are not a part of the Federation will need the chip and number mark if they are to do business with member nations. The deadline to get the mark and chip is one week from today."

"But why the tattoo of *666*?" the newscaster asked.

"We needed a quick way for authorities and anyone who makes transactions to visibly identify those who have been vetted for financial transactions, regardless of country and size of the transaction. I chose the symbol *666* on purpose. I want to prove to the world that the Christian Bible saw the mark as demonic, but I am proving the Christians are wrong. They are steeped in fairy tales and myth. The numbered mark proves unity among the nations and is a program for all to participate in helping the economy of all countries." He paused for emphasis. "If they continue to resist the chip, they will suffer the consequences and be treated as traitors."

"That's strong language, Super Dux. Can you explain?"

Marcus Junius stared boldly into the camera. "I view not taking the number mark as treason, and we all know what treason is punishable by. It pains me, but we cannot have dissension at this juncture. Our framework and foundation for economic success are dependent on the number mark." Switching on his charm, he gently said, "This mark, which you all will proudly receive, is a mark of progress, hope, and unity!"

"Times have changed in the country. Gone are the freedoms we took for granted," Jason said aloud. "Our government has gone along with the Federation's mandates of law and order to keep the member countries secure against terrorism and extremism and to control commerce. Our country has actually welcomed the addition of mercenary security forces on our soil to check for people who don't get the Super Dux's mark. Who would have believed it?"

"Sorry to interrupt your conversation with yourself," his wife said with an edge to her voice. "I want to talk to you about what's going on. Shut off the TV."

He did and looked expectantly to her.

"I've been asked to go to Rome with Henry Sotheby. The company has been commissioned to design a piece for the Super Dux. I will be the chief designer. I'm taking Sabrina with me; it will be a wonderful experience for her. She'll get to see the Vatican and meet with Marcus Junius himself. We are both terrifically excited," she said coldly with a hint of challenge in her voice.

Jason looked at her in open surprise. He began to speak, but she cut him off.

"I don't care what you think. All I can say is that you have a week to get the chip imbedded in your hand and get the mark that proves you've done it. Pay attention, Jason. You have to have it, or you won't be able to pay bills or use credit cards. You must have the chip in order to scan and activate payment. No one can accept cash without a scan of your chip. It's that simple. If you don't get it, you're on your own. I will not risk Sabrina or me getting arrested and losing all that we worked so hard for because you're trying to make a point. A horribly dangerous point at that."

Jason didn't respond but sat quietly thinking. He knew this was coming. His church discussed it at length, what to do when the mark became mandatory. And more was going to happen as the seven years unfolded. But he didn't want to dwell on those terrors—terrors they would all experience until Jesus came to destroy Satan, the Antichrist, his false prophet, and all the evil of the world. Jason and all the new believers understood many would be persecuted, tortured, and killed, but he had comfort in his salvation. But in truth, he was terrified and overwhelmed with grief for the loss of his daughter and wife.

With tears in his eyes, he finally spoke. "You know I can't take the mark."

"Then starve because we won't be able to help you. No one who has the mark can help those that don't have it."

"Maybe they'll haul me off to a dungeon," he said under his breath.

"Dungeon? Hardly," she said sarcastically. "They've reinstated capital punishment for anyone who deviates from the policy."

The pain in his heart was real as she said, "We're leaving for Rome tomorrow and will be gone a month or more depending upon the amount of work I need to do. I didn't tell you sooner because I just don't want to argue anymore. When I come back, I'll either see you here, or I won't. You have enough food for about a week. Don't think about stockpiling, either. Buying in bulk is being reported."

"Oh, Allie," Jason whispered and covered his face with his hands.

She left the room but came back again. "Jason, I am truly bewildered at the change in you from being an aggressive, successful businessman who was willing to conquer the world at nearly any price, to giving it all up—including your family—to become a follower of Jesus and some magical kingdom. It's pathetic." She left.

"Dad." Sabrina silently crept in and snuggled beside him on the couch. "I'm really going to miss you, and I want you to know I love you. And I'm not being influenced by Mom. I just really don't believe the things you've been telling us, about Jesus, the rapture and tribulation. I'm sorry, but I just don't." She kissed him on his cheek. "Please get the mark and chip. It's no big deal. I want you to be here when we get home."

As she walked away, Jason held his head in his hands and broke down and cried. He cried for his wife, daughter, and all the millions of people being misled by one man who would experience eternity in hell, away from joy, light, love, and God.

His faith in God and God's unfolding plan had created an uncompromising position for Jason. There was nothing he could do now for his family, other than pray for them. Tragically, the imbedded chip they decided to take, along with the mark of 666 was confirmation that they were losing their lives. He, on the other hand, had become proactive in trying to save his. Twice a week for some time now, his church group, led by the former youth pastor James Carrancho, met in the sanctuary of the small church. They studied the Old and the New Testament prophecies and devised a plan of hopeful survival.

He recalled James saying to the small group at their last meeting, "We can't tell just anyone about our church's activities, but if you find anyone open to what we are studying, invite them to join us, but be careful. Pray about it. All religious groups are being closely watched because of extremism."

He never mentioned it to his family. It would only cause more problems and frankly, he wasn't sure how safe it would be to let them know of his activities; he loved them and didn't want to put them in jeopardy because of his choices. It was time to move on, as his daughter would say. They chose the path that they were willing to take, and he would follow the path he knew would ultimately lead to life. Eternal life.

The following day at work, Jason didn't even bother to clean out his desk. He left his work cell phone, laptops, and tablets on his desk. He gave the office a good look around and picked up a couple of awards he had displayed on the credenza. He had been so proud of himself and his team. Setting them down, he then gazed at the photographs on the wall picturing him with celebrities, corporate giants, and well-known sports figures. He smiled and turned to the wonderful view of the city. He always enjoyed the view. It'd had a settling effect. Now it was all meaningless. His life had changed the moment Lilly, his colleague from marketing, was caught up in the rapture. If only he had been prepared. If only he had taken the time to study the Bible and understand, but that was water under the bridge. His relied on the comfort of a quote he memorized from the book of Romans 8:28: *And we know that in all things God works for the good of those who love him, who have been called according to his purpose.*

There was also no reason in saying good-bye to anyone; his colleagues were certain to know pain and fear beyond their wildest imaginations. Total calamity. He was well aware that he too, would be entering a time of severe testing. He might not even live through it, but, he hoped, and God willing, he would be there for the end, when Jesus would return with a vengeance and reclaim the earth from the Antichrist, his false prophet, and Satan himself.

Leaving work for the last time, he felt no sorrow but a hollowness. This was the end of life as he knew it and memories held no sway. It was all over, meaningless. Entering the little church, he joined the group of new Christians working feverously to put together survival packs.

"We've got only a week to buy any supplies we don't already have and we must be very careful as to what we purchase. The Department of Homeland Security has stipulated that any unusual purchases be reported to curb anyone who resists getting the mark," Jason explained.

"Yeah, we don't want to raise a red flag to anyone," James agreed as he rolled a sleeping bag and tied it. "It was good that we were able to quietly collect stores and equipment if only for a short time."

"No kidding. We knew this number mark thing was coming but not this quickly. I'm sure the authorities did it on purpose so people who didn't want the mark wouldn't hoard," Mary, the older woman, said.

"Okay, there are ten of us," James said. "The others have chosen different paths of escape. We need to get out of the city and make it to the mountains. That's going to be a two-day drive. We don't want to be on the road after the ten o'clock curfew. Jason's wife's grandmother was taken in the rapture. Jason and I think we should try and make it to her place, where there's a small farmhouse in the woods, a pond stocked with fish, a creek, and a well."

"Maybe the chickens are still there," Jason said hopefully. "She had a root cellar where she put up vegetables and fruits. We've got seed packets too." He opened a small box that held a variety of seeds.

"Homeland Security and other police groups are going to soon have checkpoints. If we don't get to the farm in the next five days and are caught without the mark, we'll be tried as traitors and killed," James said.

"Beheaded, I heard today," Mary said. "The Super Dux is taking no chances on anyone going against his authority."

"We know how the story goes and how it ends. But if we can make it to the mountains, we might survive until Jesus comes back for us," Mary's husband said.

They continued packing and planning, and maps were given to all. Four cars would be taken, and Jason and James would share James' Jeep. Two of the cars would be ditched at various spots along the way, and the plan was to take only two vehicles onto the farm property. The time for departure for James and Jason would be the next day at dawn. The others would leave at staggered times so as not to have a convoy of sorts on the highway.

Jason turned to James. "You sure you don't want to take my BMW?" he teased.

James smiled. "My Jeep has four-wheel drive. We might need it."

Jason went home to an empty house. It was tragic that all he had created with his wife and daughter had been futile. He wandered through the house and spent awhile in his daughter's bedroom. He looked in her closet. Clothes, shoes, purses, coats, scarves. She could open a boutique! Though it occurred to him, he was largely to blame. *That is what I taught her: material possessions, beauty, money, classy cars are all that are important.* He looked at the pile of clothes on the floor. Her $200 jeans were tossed in a pile of dirty clothes.

In his own bedroom, his wife's closet was as full as Sabrina's, bursting with gorgeous, expensive clothes and accessories. Sadly, neither she nor his daughter would get to enjoy them in the few years they had left.

He carefully packed what he thought he needed in a duffel bag. How could he gauge it? They couldn't take much; they had to travel lightly and not cause suspicion in case they were stopped. Each were bringing clothes, food, and supplies and counting on his wife's grandmother's house to be intact.

The next morning Jason collected his last newspaper from the driveway, waiting to be picked up by James. Once in the car, they called the others and said their good-byes and prayed for travelling mercies to meet up together at the farm house. They believed that cell phones were okay for now and not overly concerned they would be monitored via GPS. In time, they conceded to ditch them, knowing they would eventually be unable to keep them charged.

Traffic was light, and Jason and James drove in silence for hours, thinking of lives lost and few gained. Many of the roads were lightly traveled and both watched in consternation as the police and other security personnel prepared checkpoints for the following week when the mark would be mandatory.

Casually he opened the newspaper. "James, this article is actually reporting that the two witnesses in Israel are telling people to 'repent.' Amazing. When was the last time you heard anyone using the term *repent*"?

"They printed that, huh? I wonder if anyone knows what 're-pent' means? Those two men are straight out of biblical end-times prophecy and is anyone taking them seriously? What else does it say?" James asked, surprised.

"There's not much more than a couple of paragraphs and the writer says that they are, for lack of a better description, 'demented.'

Apparently they're throwing fireballs at the people that are harassing them. There's not much more," Jason answered, skimming the article.

"It's all moving ahead according to prophesy; they appear during the tribulation, telling people to repent and turn to God. According to some theologians, about three and half years into the tribulation, they are killed, but brought back to life," James added.

Jason folded the paper and put it away. Three and a half years wasn't that far away.

The next several miles Jason and James discussed the article until Jason noticed something odd. He commented to James, "There's not any traffic going in the other direction. There must have been an accident."

"Yeah, you're right." After a few miles he asked, "Do you smell smoke?"

"Yes, I do. And it's getting stronger. There must be a forest fire or something."

"Are those hail stones coming at us?"

Baseball-sized hail began raining down, cracking the windshield and putting deep dents in the hood of the car. "What the heck is happening?" asked a frightened James.

"Oh, no! Look!"

As they crested the hill they saw a vast plain as far as eyes could see covered in flames, with fiery tornados, smoke, and disabled cars. "We've got to turn around, quick! The flames are running along the road," Jason screamed.

James tried to turn around, but the cars behind him stopped him dead.

"We've got to get out of here, or we'll be burned alive!" Jason coughed. Ahead of him the swirls of fire were engulfing cars and screaming drivers. Black smoke of burning rubber, timber, and charred bodies was descending and rolling toward them in a deadly cloud.

Panic set in as the people in the cars behind them realized they were trapped. People jumped from their vehicles and ran on foot in the opposite direction of the oncoming firestorm, only to be bludgeoned to death with the hail stones.

Jason threw his SUV into four-wheel drive, turned hard to the left, and drove down the muddy median strip onto the opposite side of the road. Others were trying to do the same, but those in smaller cars sunk in the mud, blocking others in their attempt. Hail pummeled the cars.

The fire was approaching like a wave, and those on foot didn't have a chance. Hail, smoke, and heat got to them before the fire. Cars exploded, bodies flew apart, and shrapnel filled the black, dense clouds swirling crazily around the roadway. Blood was caught in the haze of the smoke, covering everything.

James flicked his eyes from the rearview mirror to the road every few seconds. Jason craned his body to watch their back.

"What'll we do?" Jason cried in terror.

"Look at the map, see what the area looks like. We've got to escape from it!"

Jason flicked on his phone. He scanned the map. The driving app showed a roadblock ahead. "It can't be. They can't have a roadblock set up now!"

James shrieked, "Are they crazy? We'll be fried!"

"Wait, there's an exit three miles before the roadblock. Let's take it," Jason yelled.

CHAPTER TEN

THE UNITED STATES

DANNY POWELL, CHIEF OF STAFF to former Vice President Sarratt, the newly appointed president, reviewed the vote to join the Federation. "It's the only way out of the hole we've admittedly dug for ourselves."

"Well," drawled President Sarratt, "it's not entirely the government's fault because no one in the administration could have foreseen the calamity the Vaporization would bring about."

"But," Danny pointed out, "the United States poorly positioned itself to begin with by escalating its debt on a yearly basis. We've been in a fragile economic position for some time. To make matters worse, not too long ago the country made the disastrous decision to pass the immigration reform bill. That allowed thousands of children from Central America with a parent in the United States to gain citizenship—not to mention allowing tens of thousands of unaccompanied minors to stay in the country. And to add insult to injury, the adults who were in the country illegally for over five years were given deals allowing them to stay! The cost of legalizing all these undocumented immigrants cost the government 5.3 trillion dollars! Trillion!"

"Ironically many were vaporized. Nonetheless, the United States is grappling with an accelerating debt, ongoing illegal immigration, a reduced military, diminishing tax dollars, terror attacks, and crime.

What choice do we have?" complained the president, referring to the agreement made by the House and Senate to join the Federation. An agreement of which he lobbied diligently for. It was the only way to bail out the United States.

"Because of the consequences of the Vaporization, we are crippled and must rely on others to assist us," the secretary of state, Joan Willis, agreed. "Our treasury is diminished, our military is weakened, and among many other situations that you all know and can attest to, we can barely run our federal and state governments. We cannot go on thinking things will get better. They won't."

Danny continued, "I'm preaching to the choir, but the obstacles we're facing without solutions are daunting. Citizens are killing one another over color of skin, language, televisions, and cars. It's as if the dark side has taken over personalities and the response to the smallest infraction is violence. It's nearly impossible to control. Jails and prisons are full; in fact, prisoners are being released because of shortages in staff and food."

"Disease is now sweeping across the country," President Sarratt added, gesturing to a stack of reports on his desk. "A huge concern reported by the secretary of Health and Human Services addresses the outbreak of measles, whooping cough, and scarlet fever that previously we never had to worry about. It's spreading like wildfire. Health care workers are few; some hospitals and clinics have simply closed. We don't know how long vaccine supplies will last or how we can replenish them. And we can't agree on how to control the spread of disease. Quarantine is the only answer, but again, because of lack of staff, we can't enforce it."

"Thousands of people are dying. So many, that bodies are being burned in commercial furnaces and the ashes buried in common graves," Danny observed.

"'There is no room at the inn,' I heard one commentator sarcastically observe. The newscaster was covering the Speaker's remarks on the problem of disposing of so many bodies at one time," the secretary of state said in revulsion.

As President Sarratt listened to the secretary's and Danny's reasons for the weakened and ineffectual governing, he was relieved that the parties in both the House and the Senate realized that in order to keep the country running, the country needed to be a part of the Federation. While they were looking for resources such as staff and money to help keep the country operating, he personally wanted more. He understood the Super Dux's vision and wanted to be a part of it. While others hoped to hold onto the old way of running things, it was clear that a new approach was needed to keep the country together. The country was too broken and ungainly for what was implemented in the past to enforce rules and regulations. In the president's mind, the Constitution was obsolete and the House and the Senate were ineffectual. The Supreme Court could not impose any decisions.

Later, in a private meeting after the vote to join the Federation, one congressman from Colorado said to a representative from California, "It's unbelievable this could happen in the United States. That we would have to turn to others to help our country is unthinkable." He shook his head morosely. He was not alone in his thoughts.

President Sarratt contacted Marcus when the vote was made official. "Super Dux, I can personally confirm that the United States will join the Federation. The country understands that you are in charge of the Federation, but they have prepared a draft document of how the United States and the Federation can work together without the US losing the ability of governing her people."

"I'm listening," Marcus said encouragingly.

President Sarratt explained, "As providence would have it, our House and Senate are smaller in members due to the Vaporization and an unprecedented number of suicides. Sickness, too, is continuing to spread across our country, killing record numbers of people including our leaders."

"I know," Marcus sadly agreed.

"Representatives, congressmen, and their staff have been greatly affected. Simply put, I believe the two legislative branches are unable to satisfactorily perform their duties, although they won't admit this, but they have come to grips that our country is in dire need of help. They are looking for resources, professional people, and money. However, I want to take this a step further. While the House and Senate are looking for Federation resources, I envision a more encompassing relationship. One where we can we fuse the governing responsibilities of our country with the Federation."

Because Marcus had anticipated the call, he already had a strategy in place for absorbing the United States. The two men spoke for two hours hammering out a well-constructed plan.

Later, President Sarratt met with his chief of staff, Danny Powell, to prep him for the upcoming plan he and the Super Dux had agreed upon. "Tragically, Danny, the United States isn't alone in failing to control their calamities. Other nations, too, are worrying about inflation, disease, unprecedented natural disasters, and civil wars."

"Yes," his chief of staff answered. "I've been studying the reports. Many are joining the Federation, citing strength in numbers, but after a period of time some nations were questioning the benefits too." He held up a synopsis of dissatisfaction among Federation members. "While press and media outlets are touting harmony, security, and economic growth per Federation propaganda, there are ripples of trepidation among many members."

"Danny, I understand. I think we will both be on the same page as I explain this to you. The Super Dux has wonderful plans and vision, so as more nations join the Federation and give up much of their own governing powers to create a unified organization, control in decision-making must happen. The Super Dux is persuasive. He has positioned himself as autocrat over the Federation."

"And steadily proving to be an elitist." Danny smiled. "He's enforced severe limits on freedom of expression and created a single party representing member nations where he alone makes final decisions." He pointed at a document backing up the information.

"This is true, Danny," the president said a little condescendingly. "To enforce his rule, he built a military-centered political system that forces the citizens, municipalities, and states to submit to his dictatorship."

Equally disturbing, those without the mark of *666* were being beheaded publicly. The executions were treated as sport and covered by TV networks throughout the world. Most of those beheaded called themselves Christians and would not accept the "mark of the Beast" as they called it. They infuriated the Super Dux, who refused to call them Christians. He didn't want anyone to acknowledge the existence of Christianity. He was now on a very public mission to wipe them out and renamed them "traitors." He hoped the beheadings would send a frightening message to anyone who refused his mark.

"I want to let you in on the plan. This is confidential between you and me," President Sarratt said. "I'm sure you will be excited to be a part of this."

Danny listened carefully and with conflicting emotion.

Later, President Sarratt laid out the Federation's plan to his next line of advisors and aides. "The Federation has accepted our request to join. We've been directed by the Super Dux to disband the House and Senate. Because we have joined the Federation, we won't make laws here anymore. We will implement the laws created by the Federation," the president said factually. He was pleased that the Super Dux agreed with him in dissolving the House and Senate. The two legislative branches were a quarrelsome bunch that could never agree on anything. They wasted valuable time and astronomical amounts of taxpayer's money that supported them, their staff, their overhead, and their wildly expensive projects. Without the expense of maintaining the House and Senate and so many of their frivolous bills, taxpayer money, already severely reduced, would be diverted to the Federation, who would manage the US government more efficiently using a vastly smaller staff.

"What about the cabinet?" asked one of the privileged aides.

"We're rearranging the cabinet too. We still have to have overseers for each governmental segment, but we have been mandated by the Super Dux to get rid of old wood. We want a fresh group of people who will enthusiastically support the Federation and all the Super Dux's directives." He nodded to Danny to hand out confidential copies listing the new heads of the cabinet. "I handpicked these men and women so we can count on their performance and loyalty."

Giving them another document, he said, "Here's the Super Dux's outline of governmental structure. I will still head the cabinet. No secretary of state. If needed, I will take over that role, but the Federation's staff oversees those responsibilities. Our defense department will be combined with the Federation's Ministry of Defense. The departments of Justice, Treasury, Commerce, Energy, Homeland Security, Education, and Labor will fall under the similar ministries in the Federation. However, we will have direct control over Interior, Agriculture, Health and Human Services, Transportation, Housing and Urban Development Ministries."

"Hmm. The Federation takes the lion's share of powers, eh?" Susan, an aide, angrily retorted as she read over the new structure.

The president looked witheringly at the woman. "The Federation, in case you haven't observed, has saved the United States from implosion. Keep your remarks to yourself."

The aide ducked her head and continued to study the documents.

"Next, I want to address the problem of disease. We are experiencing the rapid spread of measles and chicken pox. I would like to say that this is unacceptable, but we are short on vaccines, so we are going to quarantine all those with symptoms and diseases. The Federation will send us manpower for enforcement. Here is the list of dormitories on the various college campuses we are taking over."

"What about the colleges? They need their dorms to stay open," asked a surprised advisor.

"We're taking over those college campuses that are strategically located in certain disease hotspots in an attempt to isolate the spread." Danny handed out another sheaf of papers. "You'll find all of these documents on our secure intranet."

To underscore the priority of controlling disease, the president explained, "Our country is not the only one experiencing resurgence of diseases. Ebola is galloping through Africa again, Cuba has a unique strain of HIV that is quickly becoming full blown, and

Europe is reporting cases of tuberculosis and dysentery. Each nation of the Federation is required to take strong control to contain and manage the health problems. We must do the same on our side of the pond, even if it means mass quarantines. It will also mean mass deaths. We don't have staff or supply to manage these sicknesses, and the Federation is sending limited personnel to help us, so there will be many deaths. We'll have to dispose of the bodies, so at each site we'll need to construct crematoriums." The president nodded to Susan. "Schedule a meeting with Health and Human Services and the Federation's health minister. I'll be in on that meeting too."

"We have the new structure of government. How are we going to implement all of this?" asked a concerned aide, who was joined by another.

"Revamping the government's organization would prove impossible!"

"As we speak, the Federation forces have already secured the cabinet," the president calmly explained. "The secretary of defense, the secretary of homeland security, and other pertinent personnel in the hierarchy are currently agreeable to the changes."

"In other words, it's a coup, of sorts," Danny clarified, slightly smiling. "And a done deal."

The excitement and consternation of the peaceful coup was soon upstaged when an urgent message surfaced on the tablets of several staffers. "Mr. President," Susan shouted, "it looks like an unusual natural event is unfolding across the United States. Huge fiery tornadoes are engulfing natural areas, burning up trees and grass. Hail? Oh, wow, hail is falling in record sizes!"

"Turn on the monitors," the president instructed.

Seven monitors displayed seven distinct regions: Africa, Antarctic, Asia, Australia/Oceana, Europe, North America, and South America.

An eighth monitor displayed only the US. All eyes were riveted on the country as the aide switched to the app that isolated natural disasters such as forest fires, floods, earthquakes, tornadoes, cyclones, volcanoes, tidal waves, and other natural phenomenon.

"Turn on the fire app," an advisor said to an aide.

She clicked it, and to their utter disbelief, firestorms were raging across the screen.

The aide quickly tapped into her tablet, read the stats, then cried, "Mr. President, this is unspeakable! The percent of damage is happening all at once! It looks like nearly a third—Mr. President, a *third*—of the forested areas of the world is on fire and being pounded by hail." All seven monitors came alive with firestorms. Fine-tuning the data, she said, "It's occurring mostly in large vegetative areas. Urban areas aren't being affected. This is astounding. It would be catastrophic if this was happening in cities!"

"There'll be plenty dead regardless," a technician grimly observed while scrolling quickly through the stats.

The president got up to leave, anticipating the volley of phone calls and urgent messages that would inundate his staff. "Let's go. Set up a conference call now with the Super Dux."

An aide looked up from his tablet and said in astonishment, "It's already scheduled. The Federation has it at one o'clock."

"Greetings, member nations," a somber Marcus Junius intoned via the secured web meeting. "We've also invited nonmember nations who are dealing with these firestorms. To save time, rather than giving individual briefings—it's still early into the event—I'm directing each country to send an update on the hour on the status of these storms in your countries to our emergency management chair via the secured link on your screens and email. We will compile the information and update all member and nonmember nations on the status of worldwide destruction. We ask that you chart the information in the following format that will be sent to your emergency response secretaries. One: Provide the longitude and latitude of the areas that are being burned and damaged by hail. Two: Approximated total square kilometers. Three: Approximate dead. Four: Approximate value of damages. Five: A synopsis of how you are responding."

Danny turned to President Sarratt and whispered, "And what are they going to do about it? This is massive in scope. It's affecting the entire planet."

"It'll give them an idea of the magnitude of the agriculture and population losses. In an encompassing situation like this, only when the dust settles, so to speak, can the Federation determine who needs the most help for recovery," the president rejoined.

More like assessing losses of crops and timber, Danny thought.

While the president was on the conference call, staff tracked the progress of the firestorms across the world on a similar bank of monitors in the White House Situation Room. It was frighteningly clear that there was no controlling the ravishing fires or the freak hailstorm. It was an impossible task. The leaders might be able to update each other on the status of the devastation and loss of life, but there was nothing they could do against the power and heat of these storms. It was a situation one could only watch and pray, if one believed in prayer. Very few did.

"If anyone believes in a god, then their god should be cursed!" grumbled a technician as he tracked the progress of the storms.

A commotion rose from the analysts tracking the storms. Warnings were now coming from NASA that a huge mass was hurtling toward earth at phenomenal speeds.

"Why haven't they been tracking this? Why are we just finding out about this now?" they shouted in sheer distress. "What has NASA's Meteoroid Environmental Office been doing? Don't they have a smart cameras network that tracks and triangulates these threats close to earth?"

"What about the European Space Agency?" someone demanded, frantically putting a fix on the projected point of impact. "They have a radar system in France, Spain, and Switzerland capable of tracking asteroids and meteors!"

"Even if it appeared on their radars, it's traveling too fast to warn anyone. It looks like a mass the size of a mountain, or planetoid."

All eyes trained on an enormous monitor showing the world as a whole. They howled in disbelief as the colossal mass slammed into the Atlantic Ocean. Like a nuclear explosion it erupted in the sea just outside the Strait of Gibraltar.

"Oh . . . my . . ." breathed a tech. "The waves are titanic! They're rolling through and over the Strait!"

They could see, from satellite images, the waves slamming the coasts of Portugal, the southern portion of Spain, and the coast of Morocco. They were pounding relentlessly all coastal cities bordering the Mediterranean Sea.

"We're getting reports that the force of the tsunamis can't accurately be tracked, but they must be beyond a Force 9. Look." Another tech zoomed in on a river that emptied into the Mediterranean. It was overwhelmed by the extraordinary force and height of water. And it wasn't just one massive wave. The resulting force of the meteor sent a series of immense waves building in all directions, affecting all five oceans because of the trigger effect of underwater earthquakes. The immensity of the power and swiftness of the vast walls of water inflicted incalculable destruction to life in the water, coastlines, and rivers.

"This is a force nothing like any geologist or seismologist has ever recorded!" cried another tech in horrified awe.

The Federation meeting on the firestorms was interrupted with the news of the meteor hit, resulting in underwater earthquakes and tsunamis in all five oceans.

"What happened? What caused this? If it was a meteor, shouldn't we have known, been tracking it and been prepared? Why did this happen?" asked a stunned commissioner from Spain.

"The loss of life will be staggering," someone uttered.

"Ladies and Gentlemen, we are ending this call due to another recent disaster that must be evaluated," a frazzled administrator said. "Please update the Federation emergency response chair on the hour regarding the status of your countries' damage and loss of life."

All audio and visual went dead.

No one slept that night as analysts and scientists around the world evaluated the damage. The following day in the Situation Room, President Sarratt asked for updates.

"It's beyond comprehension," his chief of staff gravely said. "The impact triggered underwater earthquakes in the other oceans as well. We'll be assessing the damages for weeks, but we've had massive loss of life, and the sea kill is staggering. We're seeing dead animals miles inland where the coastlines were hardest hit. Ships in the Mediterranean, those working the northern west coast of Africa,

Portugal, Spain, and some in the Atlantic sunk. The Suez Canal Authority, what's left of it, reports mass destruction."

"Mr. President?" a staffer interrupted, numbed by the onslaught of what appeared to her to be supernatural tragedies. "There's been a horrific earthquake in California. Seismologists believe it's a result of the meteor."

Looking at the screens, the group paled.

"It's finally 'the Big One,'" the president whispered. "It's off the Richter scale." High definition satellite images showed structures of all sizes collapsing, highways buckling, and deep ravines opening and swallowing buildings, power lines, buses, trains, cars, and people. The multiscreen monitors flashed crumbling, exploding images in three-second intervals. Water pipes burst, propane, fuel, and gas tanks exploded. Cars toppled off of bridges, sending drivers and passengers to imminent death. The quake lasted four minutes. How many disasters could continue to rock the world at such magnitudes?

"There's no way for first responders to get in there," a frightened aide moaned, scanning the destruction. Fires raged out of control. Broken pipes gushed water hundreds of feet in the air. "Eighty-five percent of the water comes from outside the region in through aqueducts across the Andreas Fault."

"No power, no water, no way to get to victims." Another staffer choked. The dazed staff all turned to their leader.

The president pulled himself together. "Calm down! These are unusually trying times, but we will get through this. We'll get help. We're valued and important members of the Federation and together we'll rebuild and achieve the greatness of this nation once again. Super Dux Marcus Junius is a miracle worker—you have seen for yourself his great accomplishments. He will rise to the challenge. We will recover, we will rebuild, and we will regain our strength."

There was spontaneous applause. All were grasping for hope.

Then his aide Susan spoke up. "Maybe these supernatural events are warnings. Maybe we should turn to God and—"

"Susan, that's enough!" the president said sharply, holding up his hand to stop her from saying anything more. "You think God or a god would do this? Why? For what reason? You, ma'am, better rethink your allegiance. There is no room for religious extremism. The Super Dux has branded all religious fanatics, particularly those believing in the rapture and tribulation, traitors and you know what the penalty is."

"I said God, not Jesus," Susan said, desperately trying to defend herself.

"What's the difference?" the president firmly asked, not expecting an answer. "We can't have this discussion. Remove her!"

Security moved forward. Horrified, the staff, aides, and administrators watched as Susan's hands were pulled behind her back and handcuffed. She was roughly pulled from the room by the ever-present guards.

"Ladies and gentlemen, continue to monitor and access the situation. I want a detailed briefing in an hour." The president motioned to his chief of staff and closest advisors to follow him to the Oval Office. Once outside the Situation Room, he instructed Danny to set up a call with the Super Dux as soon as possible, and to an aide he said, "Arrange Susan's disappearance. We cannot have dissension in these times of chaos. Don't alert the press. They already have enough to cover."

CHAPTER ELEVEN

THE FEDERATION

"IT'S UNSETTLING TO LOSE SO many important businesses, people, and ports in California," Roberto grumbled to Marcus, who was clearly angry at the constant bombardment of disaster.

"With the membership of the United States I was depending upon trade tariffs to pad the Federation's treasury from their exports and imports. Particularly from a state so well-known for its consumerism. After the tremendous fires gobbled up crops and hail killed livestock, I didn't expect tsunamis and earthquakes to sop up what was left," Marcus said coldly.

"If there is any good news," Roberto offered, "the Vaporization didn't take many wealthy business people throughout the United States.. At least New York and other major cities are affluent hubs and still useful to us. Damages from the tsunamis were bad, but not totally destructive. The ports are recovering enough to get ships in and out."

"Okay. California's been dealt a crippling blow, but I'm not planning on extending any help to the state through the Federation. California is no longer of value. Let it sink into the Pacific. As far as I'm concerned, it's a write-off."

Nevertheless, the damage around the world was astounding. The firestorms and their destruction of vegetation were mind-boggling; nearly a third of forests and grassy plains were burned up. And the mountain-sized meteor that crashed in the ocean proved devastating. So much sea life was killed that the waters were bloodied and littered with carcasses. Human bodies were strewn like discarded dolls across the land and whole seacoast towns disappeared. Many ports, harbors, and anchorages, particularly on the southern European, North African, and Mediterranean coasts were wiped out.

"Roberto, I'm leaving the clean-up, rescues, and aid to the individual countries. I'm not spending Federation funds on response or recovery. Reason is, we have to deal with the reduction in shipping which means a reduction in revenue generation. We expected revenue from the US and that, too, is going to be marginalized."

"Marcus, you know there is a growing unrest among some of our member nations," Roberto said cautiously.

"I'm well aware. Some of it is due to my authority, but these ongoing catastrophic events are trying everyone's endurance. I have to keep an iron grip on the Federation and its citizens. Maintaining power and containing unrest is my focus." He had more to conquer in order to form a new world order, and he would succeed, but he needed to hold onto power and acquire money.

In the meanwhile, he had a meeting set up at the request of the powerful cardinal of the Vatican. He was one of the supportive clergy who welcomed and negotiated the Federation's move into the departed pope's offices.

"Cardinal Giovanni, welcome. Please, sit." Marcus directed him to the seating area as his servants poured coffee and set up little cakes and fresh fruit for the two men.

The room was opulent, drastically changed from the humble furnishings of the recently "vaporized" pope. Heavy antique brocade drapes framed the large window looking over St. Peter's Square, and invaluable works of art by the Italian masters hung on the walls. Priceless antique rugs and chairs complimented one another in rich red, gold, purple, and blue. The seating area was comfortable and informal. Rich Italian leather couches and chairs were situated around an ebony-and-marble coffee table. Warm sunlight streamed into the vast office.

"Super Dux, I thank you for seeing me," the cardinal began. "I have an appealing idea I would like to share with you. I would like to speak confidentially, if you please." The cardinal looked to Marcus' chief of staff, Roberto Pertucci.

"Certainly, Cardinal Giovanni." Roberto silently left the room.

"Super Dux—"

"Please, call me Marcus." The Super Dux smiled. He had a certain feeling for what this was about. He had been playing a revelation in his mind, and perhaps this was the pivotal point. Earlier, he had Roberto do a covert investigation of the cardinal, who had offices in the other side of the building. Phone taps, electronic surveillance, and computer files showed the cardinal was not a man of the cloth. He was ambitious and incredibly clever. Roberto discovered the cardinal had a plan to increase his own power and visibility while at the same time enhancing the Super Dux's powers. A win-win situation.

"Marcus, the world was in shambles, but thanks to your immense talent and vision, you are quite successfully making a silk purse out of a sow's ear contrary to what one would believe possible." The cardinal paused for a sip of his coffee. "And then, as you were making such wonderful progress, recent horrendous natural events have been an economic and social blow to the Federation's growth."

Marcus stared at him in thought. "Yes," Marcus acquiesced. He had no intention of elaborating about any concerns regarding the Federation and refused to be on the defense. Switching the subject, he said, "It was heartbreaking to lose Venice. Gone. All those beautiful old buildings, and to lose St. Mark's Basilica! It was devastating. But, we must move forward, wouldn't you agree?"

The cardinal shifted in his chair. "Losing St. Mark's was distressing," he said absently, but he, too, wasn't going to pine about what was irretrievably lost. He had other plans. "This is why I am here. I'll come directly to the point. I have visions. I see you not only as a political world leader but so much more. I see a supernatural greatness."

The cardinal paused to let it sink in, but Marcus was already ahead of him. It was all part of a plan that was revealed to him in his own visions. "I agree with you. I need power beyond politics. You've heard of the two witnesses in Israel who are asking the people to turn to God before it's too late, before God's final judgment? Well, I defy their God. It's the Christian's continuation of their idiotic myth. To prove this to the world, to the Christians, and to show my supremacy, I must destroy these two men, but in order to do that supernatural power is required."

"Your assessment is correct," the cardinal agreed. "These men have powers beyond flesh. At the moment, no one can stop them. The Jews are just trying to control the situation rather than resolve it."

"Because they can't," Marcus answered harshly, "and I will. We both agree, there is a powerful spirit that can be channeled into humans of his choice. I want to move into the realm of total rule using that power, and you will help me."

"I can, Marcus. I have known for some time that in truth, I am not a follower of the Christian's God. I look to the same power that you look to. The one who has defied the Christian God." He smiled. "I have communicated with this being and using his authority, you and I will control the world."

"Not equally, Cardinal Giovanni. I, too, have been dancing with the devil; I have been given visions beyond human imagination. To be clear, you will work for me, but you will enjoy your position, and we will depend upon each other. A team so to speak. I'll be the captain. And as you have said, we will have extraordinary command." A question popped into his mind. "By the way, whatever happened to those two priests that were going to assassinate the pope? One of our spies informed us of the plot when we were still the European Union."

"Yes, yes. The CIA informed us of the plan approximately the same time President Foster of the United States was to be briefed. We took matters into our own hands and killed them. We didn't need the United States to protect us," the cardinal responded in pride. "Also, those who are still at the Vatican are taking orders from me. Any clergy who was not vaporized, and subsequently turned to God, left to preach to anyone who would hear them. Obviously, they have not taken the mark."

"Really? I want you to work with my undercover task force to hunt them down. They are traitors and must be killed. Can you do that?" Marcus asked arrogantly.

"I'm sure," the clergy man said with a slight hesitation.

"You have the power to succeed, Cardinal Giovanni. Do it."

A servant discreetly knocked and came in with fresh coffee. Both men waited until the young man left before Marcus continued. "There is more I want to say to you. I have a critical goal that will place me in a position of getting closer to world domination. You know the Federation made a seven-year treaty with Israel. It was for her security and protection. I am going to break the treaty with Israel and crush her. She thinks she is safe, but she is ripe for the harvest because she has foolishly diverted her energy and resources from building up her military to rebuilding her economy. Her military is in a stagnant position, but her economy is flowing. I want to show the world that I have the power to utterly consume. Overtaking Israel will be that confirmation and the coins from her purse will be added to our treasury."

"This plan is an excellent step in showing the world your strength. The people must view you as unstoppable." The cardinal nibbled a cookie, then said pensively, "By conquering Israel, they will at first be stunned, some will be angry, but the end result will be that they see you as a superhero. The world must fear and be in awe of you. Who, since Israel became a nation, has been able to dominate her?" He shook his head, reached for another cookie, and chuckled. "You will transcend power and otherworldliness becoming a god in their eyes. And I will be the prophet who will underscore your supremacy by displaying supernatural wonders and signs," Cardinal Giovanni vowed.

"And you no longer will be called a cardinal. You will be called, "Prophet!" Marcus declared. At the close of their meeting, the cardinal beamed as he left the Super Dux's office. It was all falling into place; the supernatural was remarkable.

After Cardinal Giovanni, now called the Prophet, left Marcus' suite, he called in Roberto, as well as his Minister of Defense and his Minister of Federation Security to structure the attack on Israel. He wanted it to happen soon; the country was to be taken by surprise. However, he wanted the effort to be perfectly executed—not rushed. He gave authority to his ministers to use any means necessary to conquer quickly. He laid all of the resources of the Federation at their disposal. He wanted the Israeli people destroyed and he wanted their land and spoils.

There was no question in the ministers' minds that the Super Dux was working toward limitless power. The men readily agreed. It was an exciting time. Power, glory, war, spoil, kingdoms, and peoples were to be ruled under the Super Dux and they would be an important part of an empire that would surpass all previous empires! In solidarity, they gathered their notes each planning their strategies to wipe out Israel.

Before Marcus moved on to his next meeting with his member nation commissioners, he was scheduled to attend a luncheon with Henry Sotheby of the jewelry empire and his renowned designer, Allie, and her young daughter. Also attending were three wealthy patrons of the Federation. He welcomed the mental diversion. He wanted a signet ring and perhaps that would clear his head for the next meeting.

He saw that Allie was a stunning woman and her daughter was equally appealing. He was pleased to see that when they both extended their hands, each had *666* tattooed in exquisite calligraphy. "Your marks are stunning, ladies," he said. "May I call you Allie and Sabrina?"

"Oh, please do, Super Dux. We are thrilled to meet you." Allie shifted nervously in her seat while Sabrina gawked at the stunning ornate decorations, statues, and paintings adorning the opulent suite.

"And where is your husband?" Marcus asked conversationally as they took their seats at the table, beautifully appointed with crystal, linen, silver, and fine china. Allie was on his right and Henry Sotheby on his left. Sabrina was beside her mother and the others were seated around the oval table. The centerpiece was a simple display of white orchids and red roses.

"He was unable to make it to Rome, Super Dux. He extends his apologies," Allie said nervously. She didn't want to elaborate any further. Anyone in his right mind would have jumped at the chance to go to Rome and meet Super Dux Marcus Junius and she didn't want to have to make up excuses for a husband who clearly held traitorous thoughts. His behavior frightened her and if he didn't get the mark, didn't get off religion, she didn't know how his behavior could affect her and her daughter's well-being. She didn't want to think about him. She didn't want anything to ruin her luncheon with the most powerful person on the planet. So she deftly changed the subject.

"I understand that you would like me to design a ring for you?"

"Yes, Allie. I would like a gold signet ring, embossed with 'Super Dux of the Federation.' I'm not sure about the stones. I'll leave that up to you to decide. It is to be large, readily visible. And I'm going to use it as a seal. I don't know if it should have a main stone carved with the seal, or stones around the signet. I'll let you sketch up some designs so I can choose."

The luncheon proved light and fun, and Marcus was able to glean huge donations from the three patrons in exchange for promised real estate. Henry Sotheby was a typical snob, but the mother and daughter were interesting. Both were lovely, somewhat reticent, and a trifle nervous, but he expected that in his presence. After all, he was the most powerful man on earth and soon to be the most feared and revered. He briefly wondered why her husband didn't attend. The man missed a chance of a lifetime.

After his gracious exit from his luncheon guests, he called Chief of Staff Roberto. "I just had lunch with the people from Henry Sotheby's Jewelry. A Ms. Allie is going to design my signet ring to be used as a seal. I also want a crown—something reminiscent of Julius Caesar. I didn't want to mention it in front of the other guests. Ms. Allie and her daughter have a guest suite here in the Vatican as does Henry Sotheby. Track them down and find out their start schedule."

"Cost?" asked Roberto.

"Oh, something in the two-million-dollar range. I don't want to get too flashy, but I want to make a point when the time comes."

"I understand, Marcus." Roberto seemed to be enjoying himself.

As soon as Marcus sat down with his commissioners, word came that yet another flaming meteor, the size of a small planet, had exploded into billions of shards and particles as it entered the earth's atmosphere.

"Hurricane force winds are sending the flaming wreckage across all continents. Some pieces are large but innumerable particles are collecting together like dust clouds. Particles are falling on people, animals, land, sea, and fresh water sources around the world," briefed a frightened staffer. The impact of the dust alone would be devastating. The larger fragments were fireballs hurtling through the air crashing on people, buildings, and infrastructure.

"Monitor the results and report back to Roberto on the hour on casualties and damage," Marcus instructed. The staffer nodded and left the room, as Marcus broke up the meeting. The exhausted and stressed-out commissioners hurried out or, for those not present, disconnected their call to attend to their own countries. The calamities seemingly occurring one after another were wearing down an already damaged and drained populace. Since the Vaporization, each season brought fresh trouble. "Is this the new normal?" they asked one another. "One stultifying event after another?"

Hours later, reports came in that the particles landing in fresh water turned it toxic. Huge reservoirs, rivers, and standing waters were contaminated. Authorities had no way of cleansing the vast amount of water. Millions of people would be dying from drinking water unless a way was found to sanitize it. It was unthinkable that yet another supernatural disaster had happened.

Months later, Marcus looked out of his office at St. Peter's Square. Dark clouds of dust still swirled around the patios, falling on hurrying pedestrians trying to seek shelter. It was a bizarre sight. It looked like thick gray fog. He pulled the drapes and flicked on the lights. Was there more to come?

"Or warnings?" He lifted his fist and said aloud to no one in the room. "Warnings mean nothing to me! And I will still proceed to attack your beloved people, the Jews," he shouted loudly, looking up to the ceiling.

"Did you need me, Super Dux?" Roberto entered the office with bottled water.

"No. I was just venting out loud. With all this pollution in the air from the meteor, the day is like night out there in the square. I'm getting sick of these catastrophes! One after another!"

Roberto fully agreed with hidden fear. "Because of the density of the dust, daytime is shortened by nearly a third."

The Super Dux took a long drink of his water. "It's a strange and an uncomfortable environment," he conceded. "People who escaped the fires, the tsunamis, the earthquakes, terrorism, disease, and poisoned water are discovering it's more difficult to cope in the constant gloom."

"The suicide rate has mushroomed. Sickness of all sorts is manifesting itself. Skin conditions have worsened. Eyesight has weakened. Overall health has so affected people that many are inert giving into deep depression." Roberto said with worry. He thought of all the people he had to deal with on a daily basis. No one was well. It was truly frightening.

"I know what's going on, Roberto. I know! Fresh food supplies dwindled. Gone are the fruits, vegetables, and herbs that could be found in farmers' markets around the world. Even supplies of fresh meat are limited due to the decimation of herds due to lack of grass and clean water. Famine, never experienced in the Federation, is now a part of the mounting horrors we're all facing, including the United States! I don't want to hear about it anymore. We have a world to run!"

Roberto picked up his papers and handed them to the Super Dux to review while thinking of the unusual levels of pollution and meteor dust in the air along with smoke of ongoing fires consuming structures and flammable materials. It was overwhelming. No wonder the days were dark and nights almost black. The sun, moon, and stars barely penetrated the earth's filthy atmosphere.

As the Super Dux scanned the strategy for the attack on Israel which was held up because of the current crisis of thick dust and polluted drinking water, Roberto pulled aside the drapes to look out the window onto St. Peter's Square. Birds were no longer flying, feeding, or perching. Squirrels, once abundant in so many urban areas, were rarely seen and pigeons that were always abundant scavenging the worn grass or cracked pavements were gone.

Marcus turned to Roberto and said, "Close the curtains. I don't want to be reminded of the pollution. What more have you heard about the two 'witnesses'? Has the Israeli Prime Minister killed them yet?"

Roberto dropped his hands from the curtains. "No. They're impossible to destroy. They're still ranting and raving about the coming wrath of God and begging the people to turn from their idols of money and material possessions and from their sins. Of course, the crowds laugh at them. Who believes in sin? I mean, what is sin?"

"Sin, is subjective, Roberto. That's another argument I have with these religious fanatics. They think their God has the right to define 'sin.'"

Roberto continued, "As I said, these two men can't be destroyed. Bullets, grenades, mini-rockets—nothing gets near them. When attacked, they hurl fire at their opponents. The Israeli government has been trying to keep the people away, but the crowds won't listen. This is great sport to them, and they continue to harass the men. They've threatened to 'shut up the sky' from rain and it appears they have done so. Israel is experiencing a severe drought," Robert said in worry. "They also have the ability to strike the earth with disease, and turn water into blood." He shook his head. It was scary.

"Has that happened?" This intrigued Marcus and he put down the papers in his hand, focusing on Roberto. "These men have their own mystical arsenal?"

"According to the Israeli internal security minister, it has happened and they have some supernatural powers. People, who have cursed them in the worst possible ways, have gone home to find blood coming from their faucets, or wake up with some unknown disease."

"Who are they? Where did they come from?" The Super Dux planned on killing them, but he needed better intelligence than what he was hearing in the media.

"I don't know who they are or where they are from, but there is no doubt they have supernatural power. People, who still can afford to fly, are coming to Israel on tours to see these two men, now known internationally as 'two witnesses.' Tour guides hire professional tormentors to attack them. A large reward is given to anyone who can hit them with rocks, guns, or whatever, and not get burned up in the process," Roberto explained.

"And?" asked Marcus.

"And so far, no one has been able to strike them. Conversely, all who have attempted have been struck dead by either one or the other of the witnesses. It's been a boon to the Israeli tourist industry. It's ironic. These two men are viewed as deadly entertainers who are deeply hated, but the crowds can't stay away from their miracles." Roberto couldn't help but think that they were messengers from God.

Who else could give them that kind of power and why would they preach repentance of sin and turning to God if they weren't of God?

As if Marcus could read Roberto's thoughts, he stared at him until Roberto uneasily turned away. "You're not getting weak on me are you Roberto? I count on your guidance and support. If you're wondering if there is a God, I will let you in on a secret, but it is not to be disclosed to the world until I am ready. I was going to wait, but I think you need some reassurance."

Concerned, Roberto listened.

"I have the power of God if you want to surmise there is a God, which there is but He is not omnipotent as the Bible or Torah would have you believe. I, Roberto, yes, I am more powerful than the God of the Jews and the Christians. And soon I will show you and the world this amazing power."

Roberto was stunned at the announcement. He didn't disbelieve, but he asked Marcus, "How? How did you get sovereignty above God? How will you prove it?"

Before Marcus could elaborate, his minister of defense barged in his office. "We've been preempted! Russia and Iran are invading Israel."

"They can't possibly do this!" shouted Marcus, jumping up. "Get our supreme commanders, our senior staff, into our Command and Control center." Turning to an ashen-faced Roberto, he said, "I want my Prophet, Cardinal Giovanni, there too. Get going!"

Inside the Command and Control center, Roberto looked aghast as the monitors of the tracking systems showed forces assembling and moving like a slow storm cloud, covering the land toward Israel.

"They're coming to the mountains of Israel. Lebanon and Syria must be with them. Maybe Jordan too," said the minister of defense.

"A coalition of nations led by Russia and Iran," stated the Super Dux coldly. "A Russian-Islamic invasion. How appropriate. And Israel thought she was safe from her Islamic neighbors and that we, the Federation were going to protect her!" He turned threateningly to his security and intelligence chief. "And we, her supposed protector, had no knowledge of this effort building? How could this be?" He was enraged. Russia and Iran had one-upped him and beat him to it! He turned to his defense minister. "What of Russia? Has she been a sleeping bear we didn't know would wake up? Were we, in fact, the ones lulled into sleep, thinking she was of no importance?"

"Super Dux, Russia and Iran signed a cooperative agreement to back each other militarily, but that was a long time ago. It's been well documented that Russia has developed relations with Muslim and Arab nations for years." The defense minister was sweating profusely. He had failed his watch. "But it's all about the oil. Russia needs the energy."

"We have been watching Russia." The intelligence minister joined in defending himself and the minister of defense. "But her main activity has been restoring the nations she lost when she was the Soviet Union. She has been succeeding without aggression. We didn't feel she was a threat. The nations returning to the Soviet Block are weak, pathetic. They are cubs returning to their mother."

"Afghanistan is hardly weak nor are the other 'Stans,'" Marcus shot back. "They are brutal and ruthless in their fighting and Islamic ideologies. How could we miss the coordination of such a massive war effort right under our noses?" Seething, he walked to his chair and sat down. Looking at his gathered people, he ominously said, "Russia and Iran have nuclear weapons. Russia and her 'cubs' offer masses of soldiers to the effort, and the Iranians have a hatred so deep for Jews they would revel in wiping them off the map. We already know this. But the question remains, how did this effort go unnoticed?"

The room was quiet without answers. Cowed, they watched the red dots on the surveillance monitor slowly move across the territories of Syria and Lebanon, to the mountains of Israel and the Golan Heights and northern Jordan. "We all know what they want. First to slaughter the Jews, then to occupy the land, and then to take over the spoils of war . . . including the hundred billion barrels of oil in the ground in the Schfela region of northern Negev," Marcus said through clenched teeth. "It is not humanly possible for the Israelis to avoid complete destruction. They are overwhelmingly outnumbered. And we can't assemble our armies in time," he concluded. "We can only wait and see the outcome. This is not over yet. Have our troops on high alert."

"They already are, Super Dux," a distressed minister of defense answered.

CHAPTER TWELVE

ISRAEL

"THIS WAS NEVER ANTICIPATED, PRIME Minister," the Israeli minister of defense uttered miserably. "In signing the treaty, we were promised to be protected and we believed. The Federation Security Defense Force said they never anticipated this either, and at this juncture there is nothing they can do!"

"Or want to do, Minister. They lied. I never trusted them, but I had hoped we could turn Israel from building defenses against war to building our prosperity," the prime minister responded. *What fools we were to trust them.* He watched troops amassing along Israel's borders. The Iron Dome would not help in this case. This was an infantry assault, and perhaps that was the reason Russia, Iran, and their coalition sought to attack by land.

For a fleeting moment he recalled the conversation he'd had with Levi on trusting God, or other nations, for defense. *Looks like we Jews did it again.* He sighed. *We turned from God and put our hope in other nations to protect us, only to have our benefactors desert us at the critical hour.*

At the same time, Levi recalled the prophet Ezekiel's words in chapter 38 about Israel living in safety. Immediately he did an internet search and found: *"In that day, when my people Israel are living in safety, will you not take notice of it?"* Israel did dwell in safety after signing the treaty but only for very short time. As he read further, he realized he should have paid attention to verse 14 in the same chapter when Ezekiel prophesied, *"In days to come, Gog, I will bring you against my land."* God was referring to an invasion against the land and people of Israel.

Bits and pieces of Ezekiel's prophesy began surfacing in Levi's mind as he surfed the book. Ignoring the confusion and desperation around him, his heart quickened as he read. There was more to the prophesies, much more.

The minister of defense dispelled any thought of hope to the assembled Security Council and other high officials as he got off the phone. "We're scrambling to put our troops in place. We're constrained on rocket power because the enemy is now spilling into our territory from the mountains and we can't afford collateral damage of our own people. We can only use standard ground weaponry."

He turned to the prime minister, knowing that it probably didn't matter. The Israeli people would be slaughtered anyway. "We're grossly outnumbered. There must be several hundred thousand troops assembled. We'll put up a fight, but I'm afraid this is one war we can't win. I fear this is the end of our people and country." He took a breath to steady himself. "After all these thousands of years, we'll now face our extinction. Look, the enemy forces are descending like a cloud."

All eyes were on the many screens projecting different angles of the onslaught. A few of the men and women in the room were crying. This was the end of Israel.

Prime Minister Ben-Zion thought of his granddaughter Sarah alone with her nanny. He should be there with her. How to choose?

Staying at his post, commanding, or being with what was left of his family?

Levi, excited, broke the spell of fear and utter hopelessness. "Listen, people, please listen. Prime Minister," he said, grabbing his arm, "there is hope! Yes, they will invade us with a vengeance as written in the book of Ezekiel. See here in chapter 38, verse 9? *'You and all your troops and the many nations with you will go up, advancing like a storm; you will be like a cloud covering the land.'* This is the invasion covering our land!" Levi said excitedly to the horror of those listening. "But then in chapter 38, verses 18 and 19, Ezekiel writes, *'This is what will happen in that day: When Gog attacks the land of Israel, my hot anger will be aroused, declares the Sovereign Lord. In my zeal and fiery wrath, I declare that at that time there shall be a great earthquake in the land of Israel.'*" Levi was beside himself with excitement. "Friends, God will intervene!"

"Who is Gog?" someone asked in confusion, tearing their eyes away from the repulsion on the monitors.

"Gog is the prince of Magog, which is Russia!" Levi explained. "This is what God is going to do." With a shaking finger, he read verses 19 through 23:

> "In my zeal and fiery wrath I declare that at that time there shall be a great earthquake in the land of Israel. The fish in the sea, the birds in the sky, the beasts of the field, every creature that moves along the ground, and all the people on the face of the earth will tremble at my presence. The mountains will be overturned, the cliffs will crumble and every wall will fall to the ground. I will summon a sword against Gog on all my mountains, declares the Sovereign Lord. Every man's sword will be against his brother. I will execute judgment on him with plague and bloodshed; I will pour down torrents of rain, hailstones

and burning sulfur on him and on his troops and on the many nations with him. And so I will show my greatness and my holiness, and I will make myself known in the sight of many nations. Then they will know that I am the Lord."

No sooner had Levi finished reading the passage when the lights blinked in the command center bunker, the floor shuddered, and metal upon metal screeched.

"Oh!"

A shocked exclamation erupted from everyone, followed by stunned silence, as the satellite and drone images on the monitors showed a massive earthquake hitting the battleground. Immense swaths of land heaved up in great waves, broke apart, and caved in upon themselves, burying alive screaming foot soldiers. In other places, the earth cracked apart like a fragile shell exposing deep, ragged ravines.

Innumerable troops and tanks tumbled into the countless yawning mouths of the earth. Whole sides of mountains and hills collapsed, sending columns of men tumbling to their deaths. Giant boulders flew through the air at great heights, crashing mercilessly against armored vehicles and men with such violence and swiftness the armies were rendered helpless. There was no way to protect themselves. The onslaught raised huge clouds of thick toxic dust as grenades, rockets, and tanks exploded. Panic and confusion fell on the enemy, and, in their dread, they shot blindly at any supposed threat, killing their own troops.

Those watching from the command center were rendered speechless as the technicians zoomed in close to those wounded and dying. "Look! Look at the skin on those men!" a horrified tech cried.

A man, whose uniform was in tatters, was writhing in pain. Along his face, arms, and legs were gruesome and loathsome boils mixed with blood and pus. Many in the command center put hands over their mouths in shock. It was a grisly sight as more soldiers fell to the ground exhibiting the same contagion.

"What is that?" asked the prime minister. "Were they carrying some kind of chemical weapon and they've contaminated themselves?"

Levi repeated, *"I will execute judgment on him with plague and bloodshed."*

Suddenly, a torrential rainstorm swept across the battlefield with hurricane force winds. Giant hailstones pummeled the remaining troops. As explosions raged, fiery rocks flew through the air, igniting those still alive. Bodies, metal, and rock swirled in the force of the winds while fires continued to race through the downpour.

Levi whispered as he pointed the passage out of Ezekiel 38:22-23 to the prime minister. *"I will pour down torrents of rain, hailstones and burning sulfur on him and on his troops and on the many nations with him. And so I will show my greatness and my holiness, and I will make myself known in the sight of many nations. Then they will know that I am the Lord."*

The prime minister stiffened as he read from Levi's outstretched tablet. The room erupted into cheers and more tears. As staggering as the spectacle was, the enemy was overcome! The room quieted down in stunned realization that Israel was safe again.

"Was it of God?" someone asked.

Arguments broke out. Some thought yes, some thought it was a coincidence of extreme natural events. There was no time to listen to opinion. It was time to move to the battlefield, which was hours away from the Command and Control center.

The motorcade carrying the prime minister and his staff made its way to the perimeter of invasion and attack. Standing on a small rise, overlooking the battleground, they were stricken by the vast amount of bodies. Hundreds of thousands! Too many to count. Also incalculable were the burning broken weapons and the twisted, smoking, metal hulks that were once armored vehicles. The sky was blackened with oily smoke, dust, and carrion birds.

"I remember when only forty pair of Griffon vultures lived in Israel. The Egyptian vulture was diminished by seventy percent and the bearded and the cinereous vultures disappeared more than two decades ago," the minister of defense said in wonder. His unlikely hobby was bird-watching. "Now look."

Flanked by high ranking officers, staff, and the Israeli Network, Prime Minister Ben-Zion gazed stoically at the scene spread before them. Thousands of birds were hopping body to body, yanking, pulling, and tearing pieces of flesh to eat. Their bare necks were covered in grisly blackened and pink flesh and their feathers were matted with smeared blood. There was no squabbling, because there was plenty for all to eat.

The stench was building, and the prime minister and his entourage backed away. Directing his comments to the minister of defense, he ordered, "I want these bodies buried, and the weapons and vehicles reduced to ash. Bury it all here in the valley."

"It could take years to accomplish all this," the minister responded, thinking of the greatly reduced number of soldiers who would be doing the work. "But we will do this, Prime Minister Ben-Zion. Whether it is seven months or seven years."

The following day, when the officials gathered back at the government executive offices to coordinate next steps in response, recovery, and communications, the prime minister left a meeting to take an important call. Hanging up, he motioned Levi to gather only senior staff to his conference room.

He stood while others sat down and began, "The Federation was shocked at the outcome of events in the attack from Russia, Iran, and their coalition. The Super Dux was adamant that he had no forewarning of such an assault. He underscored that there was no time for the Federation to muster their troops to help. It happened far too quickly. And just as we had no intelligence on such an attack, neither did the Federation. He asked for the details, and when I told him it would take us literally years to bury the dead and destroy the weapons that were of no value, he couldn't believe it. I told him to look at his spy satellite aerial shots. He could see for himself."

"What are your thoughts regarding all of this?" the minister of defense asked.

"I initially thought they were lying when the Federation Security Defense Force first contacted you. After speaking with the Super Dux, I believe he and the Federation did not know of the attack. There was nothing they could do," Prime Minister Ben-Zion said simply. "Just like us."

Outside his office, the prime minister took his chief of staff aside. "Levi, this victory was of God. Do you agree?"

Levi, still in a state of shock, answered, "Yes, Moshe. It had to have been of God. How can it be explained otherwise? It follows Scripture too closely. Some of us are just too blind to see!"

As discussions and arguments ensued throughout the government and media, the prime minister, his chief of staff, and only a few others believed the battle was the work of God. Nonbelievers considered it a coincidence that just happened to coincide with Scripture.

They argued that these were unusual natural events as a result of the turbulence in the atmosphere that started with the Vaporization and continued with fires of unknown origin and meteors crashing into the sea and land. It was not of God. It was of nature, the universe at its worst. The oozing boils that they saw on the soldiers were a result of contamination from their own chemical weapons and not a plague.

"I am still amazed that so many of our people do not see this as God's victory," the prime minister said as he reviewed comments and op-eds in print and online media.

"Moshe, you and I have been friends for years," Levi said. "We both have intensely studied the Scriptures and have enjoyed our discussions. While we may have argued it as history, or tradition, I think we'll both agree, there has always been a seed in our hearts that it is truth."

"Yes, Levi, I agree. Sometimes it's easier to get caught up in contemporary opinion and commentary than validating ancient knowledge, but I have always believed in the one God. And now I am convinced. God's words spoken through the prophets are true. That battle that we just witnessed"—he paused in his own revelation of understanding—"was the battle to literally end all battles for the Jews. It was impossible for us to defend ourselves against the hordes and masses of enemy troops and weaponry. Absolutely impossible. Yet, according to Scripture, God with His mighty hand, using weapons from His own created arsenal, destroyed hundreds of thousands, along with their highly sophisticated weaponry."

"We need to understand Jesus' role in all this," Levi said.

"Yes, my quest now is to understand more of this man," the prime minister said. "Suppose it is all true. I admit I have recently spent time in the Christian New Testament, reading some of Jesus' words throughout the Gospels. And I'm studying some of the apostle Paul's explanations of the so-called rapture—although he doesn't call it that—and I'm studying the book of Revelation, which is difficult. I'm inclined to believe that Jesus is the Messiah and that He is coming back."

"I, too, have been following the same path as you, Moshe. What eluded us was Ezekiel's prophesies. We also misunderstood the book of Daniel. The seven-year tribulation is mapped out. We can see what has been going on in the world! The catastrophic disasters! And as I studied our own book there are other clues we can recognize today as being fulfilled or soon to be fulfilled: the short-lived peace of Israel, the attack of Gog and Magog, and the prince to come who is a fierce king and a despicable man. All these descriptions are found in the book of Daniel. I think we both know who this man is."

"The Super Dux, Marcus Junius," the prime minister simply responded. "In the book of Revelation, he is called the Beast, and he requires all to take his mark, *666*."

"My friend, Moshe, we are in for a frightening time. And now I know that we can't depend on any countries to help us. We are going to experience terror beyond any terror we have encountered, but if prophesy is true, we must be steadfast, learn more about Jesus, and wait for Him to rescue us," Levi concluded.

"Yes, but how do we influence our fellow Jews not to take the mark, and to decide for themselves, in their own hearts, to study prophecy and look to Jesus, the Christ? For we can't convince or force anyone." The prime minister was quiet for several moments, thinking, then spoke up. "Let's call a meeting in the next several days. I think I have a way of opening the dialogue."

The following month, when all the officials and staff were seated, the prime minister opened the meeting. "Ladies and gentlemen, I would like to propose a significant and prestigious project to consider for our recent, incredible victory." He paused for effect, then stated, "We rebuild the temple!"

From around the room came gasps of astonishment. Surprised glances were exchanged, and comments made. "The temple? Why the Temple Mount had been occupied by the Muslims since 1187, when they took it over from the Crusaders," someone from the back of the room said.

Another added, "It is time for us to take back what is rightfully ours. King Solomon built the first temple in 1000 BC. The Muslims are in no position to hold onto what justly belongs to the Jews. Since the attack, the Palestinians are in disarray; they're gravely weakened. While the Palestinians will be infuriated, there will be little they can do. The Muslims are no longer the power they once were. It is time to take back what is rightfully ours."

The room erupted in cheers and arguments. Some were concerned about more warfare or terrorism; others were forcefully pro-Israel. "The temple must be built!" they shouted. "We will be making a courageous statement to the world," others argued.

"For nonbelievers it will be a monument to victory. For believers of God, they will see their temple rebuilt in their lifetime," the prime minister declared. "There is much more to discuss, but I want to also bring up what some of us believe was God's intervention in saving

Israel." The prime minister held up a hand as the minister of defense began to protest.

"Let Prime Minister Ben-Zion speak," directed Levi.

The prime minister laid it out in simple format, what he and his chief of staff believed to be true concerning prophesy in Scripture and what had and was being played out now in the world: from the rapture explained by the politicians and media as the Vaporization, to the cataclysmic events that were occurring worldwide that were paralleling Scripture regarding the times of tribulation.

The senior staff and the cabinet were at odds with the arguments and examples of prophetic Scripture that described the events. Many outright and angrily rejected the possibility, and few others considered that maybe God might have a hand in all this.

To emphasize the current evidence, the prime minister asked the minister of defense, "How can you not agree about the two witnesses found in the Christian book of Revelation? They are standing in Jerusalem as we speak!"

The minister of defense bristled. "Those two men mimicked what was written in that book."

"How do you explain the fact that nothing harms them?" an equally angry Levi heatedly asked.

"I don't know. But they are not from God! Maybe from Satan!" the minister of defense retorted.

That brought a strained laugh to the meeting. The prime minister was astounded. "That is blasphemous, sir! They're telling people to stop sinning and turn their allegiance from Satan to God, through Jesus!"

"*Jesus?* We are Jews, man! We don't believe in Jesus, other than He was an ancient prophet. That's it! Not a messiah, savior, or son of God! He was a mere man."

"What about the protection our troops had against the Russian and Iranian coalition?" the prime minister asked. "You heard the chief of staff read from the book of Ezekiel. You saw what God sent to decimate hundreds of thousands of men and weaponry!"

The minister of defense held his hands up. "Prime Minister, with all due respect, we could argue this all day long. You are not going to convince me or others here that this is God's plan. Many of us don't believe in God, or if we do, we believe in an abstract way, that if there is a God, He is not directly interacting with our country. We must depend on ourselves and our leaders." He stared hard at the prime minister. "We will vote on the issue at hand. Rebuilding the temple. The temple has true historic significance. It would give the people a reason to rejoice. Our enemies have been destroyed."

The look the minister shot his leader was not lost on either the man elected as prime minister or his chief of staff. A seed was being sown by the minister of defense as to the capability and allegiance of both men.

"Levi," the prime minister said on the way back to his executive offices, "the majority didn't believe that God had any influence on the attack or anything else that has been going on in this world."

"I know. The Federation has lulled our minister of defense into a false sense of security. Will they protect us if we are attacked again? We don't have the arms and men to effectively defend ourselves; we lost so much of what little we had in the battle. The only effective defense is our Iron Dome, but if it turns into a ground fight, there's no contest. We'll be woefully outnumbered."

Levi directed his friend into a quiet corner of his office. "Please, sit down. I have more information. As you know, many Israelis have not taken the mark 666 because our country is not in the Federation and, so far, the citizens can buy and sell in our own country. However, for anyone traveling outside of Israel or trading outside the country, the mark is required. Of course, some took it because they believe in a unified world economy and look forward to when Israel will join the Federation. It will be only a matter of time before our people will be forced to take the mark."

"We must keep our own records, independent of the Federation of who takes the mark," the prime minster instructed.

Levi nodded. "We're now being told by internal security that thousands of men are spreading through the country preaching about salvation in Jesus. We've also heard that many more thousands are going out from the country as well, preaching the same thing. Obviously they do not have the mark and are preaching against it."

"Remarkable," Moshe answered. What was happening? Was the Spirit of the Lord moving among some of the Jewish people and opening their eyes?

"They sound a lot like the two witnesses. They preach turning from sin, and are emphasizing that these are the 'end times' of the world. They warn of the upcoming judgment. Some people listen to them and believe even at great risk to their lives. Yet others ridiculed them and compare them to the insane two witnesses," Levi explained.

"Have they been attacked?"

"Yes, but like the two witnesses, they're supernaturally protected and haven't been harmed."

Moshe stood up. "How many evangelists are you talking about, Levi?"

"We haven't an exact number. But a lot. In the book of Revelation it says: *144,000 from all the tribes of Israel*. Moshe, it's all coming to fruition. All the prophesies. I'm betting 144,000 Jews are out there preaching."

"We must stand strong too, and, if we can, influence those who're willing to hear, regardless of our own senior staff. It's not going to be easy and it might cost us our positions and lives." The tired prime minister rubbed his eyes.

"Yes, Moshe, and remember in the book of Matthew it says, something like, '*What good will it be for someone to gain the whole world, yet lose their soul?*'"

He stopped talking to think of how to present this next bit of information to his leader. He was hoping for a more opportune time, but now was as good as any other and he had to get it out. "Also, Moshe, I have heard talk. They're planning on impeaching us. The minister of defense will probably take your place until they can set up new elections."

Prime Minister Ben-Zion was not surprised. "None of this might matter anyway. We have been witnessing extraordinarily supernatural disasters and wars, seemingly one after another. Truly, these are God's judgments on us."

CHAPTER THIRTEEN

THE FAMILY

AS JAMES AND JASON SAT in an abandoned house for shelter, Jason recalled the day they escaped from the highway that was leading into the fiery wind storms. It seemed so long ago when they were making their way to Allie's grandmother's vacant farm house. He remembered vividly that the road behind them was strewn with stalled and damaged cars and, for those who tried to escape the fire and hail, their broken bodies littered the road and shoulder. James drove as fast as he dared through the dense smoke along the narrow country highway they found at the next exit. Miraculously, they escaped the intense heat and, with the exception of cracked and broken windows damaged by the pounding hail, they were able to get far away from the pandemonium of panic and consuming flames.

The road meandered around hillsides where the fire on the side of the ridge had burned itself out. Hail had stopped falling and, from what they could see in the reduced light, only charred trees, blackened soil where grass and brush once were, and great puddles of melting ice remained. It was bizarre.

James broke into his friend's reverie and said, "I still think of our friends from the church group. We were all to meet at the farmhouse and I wonder if they ever made it through the firestorms."

"We left at staggered times on purpose, not to raise any concerns, but do you think anyone was really watching us? Maybe we should have left at the same time, taking our chances of getting caught leaving the city," Jason said, looking at his friend with sadness.

"I don't know. I was told that churches were being watched and after I was visited at our own church by the security police and questioned, I understood how seriously they were taking any kind of dissent," James added. "What's done is done. We can't change it."

"If we were traveling even a few minutes earlier that day, we'd be caught in the fire and be dead," Jason said in awe.

"And we were spared, I believe for a reason," James said quietly.

Away from the firestorms, Jason and James had eventually made it to the farmhouse praying that this could be their long-term shelter, but when they arrived, their hopes were dashed as they cautiously approached the building surveying the yard. They had counted so much on this shelter. The once cozy little house was in shambles. One complete side had been gutted by fire. Broken pieces of furniture, hurled through busted windows, lay in pieces on the veranda. Inside it had been vandalized and looted. The number *666* was spray-painted on the walls. The food cellar was empty, the pantry bare, and the chickens gone.

They camped in the living room that evening after walking the grounds and searching the barn for anything they might be able to use, which was nothing. Anything of value was taken or destroyed. Later, in the house, Jason found old photos in one of the bedrooms. He sat heavily on a single chair and looked through the thin stack. One was a picture of his wife and daughter holding a fat hen.

"See, I still have the picture I found in the farmhouse." He dug into his pocket and pulled out a worn photograph and held it up for his friend to see. "It was years ago when we thought we were happy and safe, but we were really lost." He bit his lip and softly cried. Wiping his eyes, he put the photo back in his shirt pocket. This was all that would be left of his family; gone was their early love, their hopes and dreams. All changed in a moment.

"Let's get some sleep, my friend. The past is past. No use going over history." James closed his eyes. It would be another long night.

As they burrowed each in their sleeping bags, they waited for dawn to commence their trip as far south as they could get. It was the only area for survival against the unnaturally harsh winters. Fitfully, same as every night, they slept.

The next morning, having long abandoned the Jeep, they went on foot following country roads that were little traveled. If they heard a car coming, they ducked into the woods. Without the mark they were in danger of being arrested as traitors and so were ever alert to strangers. Trudging for hours, Jason spied a small country store at the fork in the road.

"Let's take a chance and see if we can get more supplies." Jason pointed to a dilapidated building with two gas pumps barely visible in the fog of smoke and ash.

"You want to take the risk?" James asked. "I'm not so sure that's a good idea."

"Look, I'll tape up my hand up like I hurt it. If they give me a hard time about having the mark covered over, I'll leave. You wait outside and be prepared to run."

Jason went into the near-empty store and threw a fifty-dollar bill on the counter and told the clerk who was bending over a cooler that he would like a few groceries. "I left a fifty here," he called and hurried through the store.

"Sure," she called back.

His heart was pounding, but he was hungry. There was little merchandise in the store. A couple of boxes of cereal, some crackers, two cans of tuna fish, and jelly. Jason scooped them up in his arms and quickly went to the front of the store. He planned to exit, leaving the fifty-dollar bill to cover less than twenty-five dollars' worth of groceries, but he felt obligated to stop at the counter.

The woman now was sitting at the cash register with a bottle of water in front of her and, as Jason looked, she didn't have the mark on either her hand or forehead. They stared at one another wordlessly as Jason put his meager purchases down. He spied two gallons of water on the floor. Slowly, he stooped and grabbed the last two gallons in each hand and placed them beside his other things.

"There's not much left in the store," the young woman admitted. "You got the last of the cereal. Most people are stocking up around here; they're afraid of the fires." She looked at the two gallons of water on the counter. "If you're on foot, best be looking for a well too. Clean water is really hard to find."

Jason didn't say anything but waited for her to ring up his purchases. James entered the store, worried for his friend. The young woman looked James over then turned to Jason. James picked up the two gallons of water.

Making no move to the cash register or to the bill on the counter, she proceeded to put the groceries in two bags. "Where are you going?"

James and Jason exchanged looks. Was it safe to say anything to her? She didn't have the *666* mark. Maybe she was one of them. But maybe not.

"I see you don't have the mark," she observed, pointing at their hands. "You don't fool me with that bandage. See here? Neither do I and I don't intend to get one." She held out both hands, then brushed the hair from her forehead. Both men still kept quiet not sure what to say. Was this a trap or were they just being paranoid?

"I'm a believer!" she blurted out and started to cry.

Without hesitation, James stretched out his hand to her, his heart aching. "We are too. We're trying to escape the authorities, if they even bother to track us, but we don't know. We're trying to get south." He nodded toward Jason.

"Can I go with you?" she pleaded through her tears. "I can't stay here. My parents and the rest of my family were taken in the rapture. I came to realize that what the Bible said about the end times is true. I'm so scared and alone! Please!"

"Of course! What's your name?" both men chimed in.

"Joanna Wright."

"Let's get out of here!"

They followed her to her home so she could gather some things. It was a humble little house near a small white church. As if to explain, she said, "My dad was a preacher here in town. My whole family lived here for generations. When I graduated high school, I got a scholarship to Stanford. I never looked back. I wanted as far from here as I could go. After getting my master's degree in political science, I landed an internship at the White House and just last year ended up on the staff. My dream job!"

"So what happened? Were you there when the president was assassinated?" Jason asked.

"I left just a week before. I was on staff when the president determined that some kind of cosmic physiological interference happened causing certain people to disappear. They named it Vaporization. I told them about the rapture, and they didn't believe me. I wasn't completely sure about what happened—then. It was only later that I knew for certain that it was the rapture and, I was, as the best seller says, 'left behind.'

"When I realized the truth, I left my job and hurried home, knowing so many would be gone. The town is nearly deserted. I took over my brother's store, hoping to meet more like me, but everyone has the mark and it was getting scary not having it myself. People ask so many questions. I just said I wasn't able to get it yet. And I know I can't give any more excuses. I didn't know what I was going to do. I'd have to go into hiding. Alone. I am so afraid!"

They hid in her house and spent the evening listening to James talk about prophesy and the catastrophic events they would likely experience during the tribulation. It was frightening, but at the same time there was hope. They knew if they lived until the end that Jesus would rescue all believers. Even if they didn't make it until He returned, they were comforted knowing they would have eternal life with Him.

The next morning, they left, with backpacks filled with provisions from Joanna's house. She gathered hats, gloves, and hiking boots. Life in the world as they knew it was irreversibly over and had been for a very long time. They walked the woods alongside the roads to avoid being seen, always consulting their maps for the next town that might provide shelter and supplies. There was no wiggle room for getting lost.

As time went on, they followed a routine. First, they scouted out homes on the outskirts of towns that were vacant and scavenged for food and water. They had to be careful because others were taking advantage of empty homes too and looting them. These were violent people, carrying weapons, many high on drugs and alcohol, and enjoying the freedom of trashing and burning homes. If the threesome couldn't find any home with supplies outside of town, they made their way to more populated areas after sunset. When in dire need, they looked through the Dumpsters behind grocery stores and restaurants.

Sneaking through a darkened small town one evening, they ducked into an abandoned house looking for food. Throughout the house were stacks of newspapers.

"Thank God for hoarders," Joanne said as she bagged boxes of food that were still on the shelves. "And I don't mean that sarcastically."

While gathering up some canned goods for his pack, Jason picked up a couple of the papers and stuffed them in his knapsack. When safely back at their campsite, he opened one and was astonished to learn that a huge object, the size of a mountain, had crashed into the ocean resulting in underwater earthquakes and tsunamis worldwide, causing destruction of marine and human life.

"The 'Big One' hit California too, as a result of the meteor they think," Jason exclaimed, then read the article aloud.

"We knew it would happen sometime," Joanna said.

"Oh, man. Here's another story. Vigilante groups are prowling the streets in towns and cities. Anyone caught without the mark 666 is beheaded on the spot!" Jason said in horror. "No one is stopping them!"

He also read a series of articles about the Federation, Super Dux Marcus Junius, and all he was doing for the world. It mentioned a treaty he had signed with Israel shortly after the Vaporization to protect her against hostile nations.

"Is he the Antichrist?" Joanna asked James.

"From what Jason just read to us, I would say so. He's trying to pull the whole world under one rule. It sounds like everybody thinks he's great—so far. Even the United States has joined the Federation. And the treaty with Israel? Right out of the book of Ezekiel!"

The three talked deep into the night, discussing prophesies and what was to come. Tired, they finally turned in.

Jason shivered. It was going to get worse. He thought of his two friends, James and Joanna. What would he have done without them? He found Joanna so sweet and attractive, but he knew in his heart that there would be no move toward romance. It would be comforting to hold someone, feel human warmth, but it was time to take a different look at the life they were leading: the end of the world, as humans had once known it, was to happen shortly. It was a staggering thought, but still he wondered if James thought of Joanna romantically or if even Joanna thought of them in that way. Now looking at their sleeping forms, each in their own sleeping bag, he realized they all internally made the same choice. They were friends and equally important, a family.

They continued walking southwest bunking in abandoned houses, trailers, or outside in campsites. Through the grace of God, they managed to stay alive. One night they found an empty home that still had electricity. As they were collecting supplies from the house, Joanna turned the TV on to catch up on what was happening in the country and world.

"The Israelis are still undertaking a massive clean-up that includes bodies and weaponry in the Megiddo Valley," a reporter said. "The aftermath of the recent attack by Russia, Iran, and their collation shows the incredible extent of the carnage wrought by extreme natural weather and earthquakes."

Video footage showed small groups of civilians and soldiers burying bodies strewn across the battlefield. The camera panned across smoky burn piles of weaponry and armored vehicles being tended to by soldiers.

"What happened?" Jason asked, totally confused and riveted to the TV.

"Ezekiel prophesied that Israel would be invaded, but God would intervene and save them. It looks like that happened. God used 'extreme natural weather and earthquakes,'" James explained. "And you know what? That means that Russia, Iran and others preempted the Super Dux in attacking Israel. Remember prophesy?"

"I thought that Israel and the Super Dux signed a treaty."

"Only to be broken," Jason replied. "His plan was to break the treaty and go after Israel, but the others beat him to it."

That night they slept little, always thinking about their families, their lost friends, and the ongoing and upcoming world events. The following morning, they were mentally and physically exhausted, but after a time of prayer, they felt renewed and continued on their journey. What never left their minds was the prophesied sequence of events of God's judgments. What was to come?

They traveled on. It seemed like when they were totally out of food, they would come across an undiscovered larder in an abandoned home to meet their needs. Occasionally they felt safe enough to stay in certain areas for a period of time, but inevitably, they moved on. They avoided cities and followed the map through towns. They were astounded to encounter so many destroyed buildings and homes.

"It seems like everyone's gone crazy," Joanna lamented. "I can understand breaking into homes to see if there is food and valuables, but why so much destruction? It's like the damage is done by pure hatred."

"Yeah, the hate is palatable. Why break furniture, set fire to curtains, and rip out plumbing? It doesn't make sense," James said.

They stood in an abandoned home, looking at the destruction in the kitchen. Cabinet doors were torn off their hinges, glasses and plates were broken on the floor, and the wooden chairs broken to bits. Someone had thrown a stool through the kitchen window.

"Well, let's check for anything anyway. The vandals might have left something behind to use or eat," Jason suggested.

They found overlooked canned goods and although they were heavy to carry, it was food. Dividing up the bounty, they made their way down a wooded path when suddenly a muted explosion sounded in the distance. The three friends looked up into the sky. A breeze whispered around them carrying thick dust and debris. It swirled everywhere coating them and all that was around them.

Squinting into the sky as dust floated down like rain, James warned, "I think this is one of God's judgments that's written in the book of Revelation. If I'm right, we can't drink from any exposed water source. This acid rain will poison the water. It'll kill us. We can only drink bottled water or water from covered wells."

"We need to find a covered well then because we can't go to a store for bottled water." Already thirsty, Joanna slowly followed behind them. "Good thing I'm a country girl at heart. Maybe God left me behind so I could find water for you," she gamely teased.

A covered well she did find in the backyard of a deserted farmhouse not far from where they discovered meager food stores. At the well, they filled their jugs and canteens, as much as they could carry when they would leave the following morning. Because so many of the natural areas were burned, animal life was nonexistent. Birds, squirrels, frogs, crickets had all but disappeared.

"It's so strange to be in the country and not see or hear a living creature," Joanna said sadly. "They're all gone!"

After spending the night there, they sat on the porch of the farmhouse, mulling their next move. James pulled a tattered paper from his pocket. "I wasn't much of a theologian, but I knew enough about the rapture to know that the tribulation would soon follow. When I realized this, I went to the book of Revelation, which is really hard to understand, but I wanted to know more about the tribulation so I could be prepared. From what I've read, it looks like God has seven seals, seven trumpets, and seven bowls that are series of

His judgment through the time of tribulation. I tried to share this with my own family, but they wouldn't listen either," he said, looking pointedly at Jason.

"I copied this from www.gotquestions.org. Let me read it to you. 'The first trumpet causes hail and fire that destroys much of the plant life in the world. The second trumpet brings about what seems to be a meteor hitting the oceans and causing the death of much of the world's sea life. The third trumpet is similar to the second, except it affects the world's lakes and rivers instead of the oceans.' It appears to poison the water sources," James added. "'The fourth causes the sun and moon to be darkened and the fifth trumpet results in a plague of 'demonic locusts' that attack and torture humanity. The sixth trumpet releases a demonic army that kills a third of humanity and the seventh trumpet calls forth the seven angels with the seven bowls of God's wrath.'"

"We went through the first one, when we were trying to get to Grandma's house and came up against the firestorms. The second one, Jason read to us from an old newspaper about a meteor slamming into the ocean, killing sea and human life. It probably was instrumental in California's big earthquake because of underground tsunamis." He held up his list. "I think we just went through the third trumpet: Do not drink the water!"

"We've got to find a protected place to set up a permanent camp with a well," Joanna said, tired and weak. "I don't think we should stay here because it's close to that other house that the vandals destroyed."

"And we need to be near a food source, or have the ability to have a little plot of land to grow things," Jason said, thinking about the seeds they collected. He lost the packets of seeds he carried from his survival pack. He had put them in a small box, and when they went from one dwelling to another, he realized he had left them behind. Now, all they had so far were tomato, cucumber, and pepper seeds along with some melon seeds from garbage they discovered in the Dumpsters. Until they could grow things, which would take a few months, they were surviving on whatever food they found in deserted homes. There were no fruits or vegetables left behind. Gardens and crops were ravaged; abandoned stores were empty.

"And it doesn't matter that we have money," James added. "We can't buy anything without the mark 666. If any of those gangs come across us without the mark and we're trying to bribe anyone for food, they'll take our money and behead us."

The next morning, they continued on their way, always evaluating what might work as a safe shelter where they could set up camp. Several days passed when, finding a good spot, they settled in for the night. James and Joanna sat quietly at the campsite that still had some greenery, praying that God would show them the way.

Jason was depressed and needed some time alone. He ventured down a nearby path to think, pray, and ask God for forgiveness and help. His mind was chaotic. He worried about the fate of his family, but every time his mind went to his wife, Allie, or his daughter, Sabrina, he tried to refocus. It was too painful. There wasn't anything he could do. He remembered the words of Jesus, *"Let the dead bury their own dead."* He squeezed his eyes tightly against the tears. Hungry, thirsty, weak, and nauseous from lack of food, he sought a quiet spot to pray.

Hearing voices, he stopped short, his heart pounding. He had grown quite adept at sneaking through the woods soundlessly and he didn't expect to hear human voices.

Creeping closer to the sound, he spied a group people on the deck of a dilapidated mobile home, drinking and partying. Jason crouched behind a bush, whipped out his binoculars, and surveyed the group. One man pushed another and a fight ensued until a woman pointed a gun at one of the men's heads and threatened to blow it off if he didn't stop fighting. The man spit at her. She shot him through the head. Brain matter and blood splashed on the bystanders, who all screamed at the gore dripping off their own faces and clothes. Someone vomited. All had *666* on their foreheads.

Jason fell to his knees and swallowed hard. Quietly getting up, he turned and ran back to the campsite.

Barely able to describe what he saw, Joanna interrupted, "They'll kill us!"

"Let's get out of here!" James urged.

They gathered their belongings and, although exhausted and hungry, they moved on. Jason prayed they would find a deserted house to sleep in for the night, protected from the acid rain and constant gloominess of diminished light.

Hours later, still exhausted, they came across a well-hidden overgrown dirt road, where they spied a little cabin. Jason told them to stay, while he scouted to see if it was safe. Shortly he returned, and directed them to follow. The cabin had two furnished rooms and a tiny kitchenette. A short distance from the building was an outhouse. This was an answered prayer!

"Look, there's a hand pump outside. Let's see if there's water!" Joanna squealed in renewed vigor. After several pumps, the spigot coughed out rusty, then clear water. "The Lord is surely with us! Thank you, God!" she yelped, and put her face under the spewing water.

Jason disappeared in the cabin and came back outside beaming. "No kidding, this is crazy, but look!" In his arms Jason had two big cans of beans, a box of dried milk, and canned fruit.

"It isn't crazy! It's the Lord. He's taking care of us!" James laughed. "We'll stay the night, and scope out the area tomorrow. We have some food and now we have water. This could be our shelter for the duration. If we die, we know we go to the Lord. If we survive, then that's what He wants us to do. We depend on Him."

They stayed. Days turned into weeks and the weeks wore on. Always looking for food, they went out searching and came across another abandoned house that looked promising.

"Let's check it out. I'll go first and signal if it's safe," volunteered Joanna.

Through the darkened day, they watched Joanna deftly weave around the bushes of the house, peeking in windows, and scoping doorways. In the diminished light, she signaled back all was okay. Both men sprinted to the house. Wasting no time, they found more canned goods, some first aid items, and stale, but in the wrapper, crackers. They struggled with their knapsacks for the long walk back home.

"I wonder if the lack of light is because of all those explosions and fires." Jason trudged heavily along the dusty path behind James and Joanna.

"It's the fourth trumpet warning from God. Look in Revelation," James answered over his shoulder. "And there's much more to come. Pray God will protect us."

CHAPTER FOURTEEN

THE UNITED STATES

"DISSOLVING THE HOUSE AND THE Senate has had its consequences," Chief of Staff Danny Powell complained to President Sarratt as he scrolled through numerous legal documents on his computer.

"We expected that, Danny. But the governing segments of the Federation have segued smoothly into the overall governmental roles of our country. We have a lot more to be concerned about." He looked at his staff chief and shook his head in concern, "Like assessing the damage from the fire and hailstorm, the tsunamis, the meteors, cleaning up decaying corpses and animal carcasses, and worrying about our economy."

The president looked at a report. Holding it up to Danny, he said, "Because of the meteor that plunged into the ocean, we can't even count the population lost along coastal areas. It's beyond our ability to assess at this time. We aren't even making a dent in clean-up. If anything, it's getting worse. The water is thick with blood and human and animal decomposition. The contamination is severe. It's causing serious illnesses and disease! And what impact did the meteor have on our shipping industry?" he continued without waiting for comment. "For all intents and purposes, it's gone! So trust me, Danny, I'm not worried about lawsuits."

The president tossed the report on his desk and picked up another. Leafing through it he said, "All of these disasters, one after another. It's beyond belief! Just when I think we can move on, bam! We're hit with another catastrophe!" He waved yet another report in the air. "Here's yet another meteor explosion. This one caused acid rain to fall on all exposed fresh water, making it toxic! How many people and livestock have perished from that incident?"

Glumly, Danny answered, "We have no idea. We can't make assessments because we don't have the resources and people to find out. With one calamity after another, it's impossible to keep up."

"Precisely my point." The president sighed. "And to top it all off, we're now dealing with limited daylight. I have never seen such black nights either. It seems like the sun, moon, and stars have been turned off!"

"We're not in this alone. No country is exempt from all of this." Danny sighed as he continued to review the documents on his computer screen. "But I am concerned about the legal ramifications of dissolving the Congress. It's been going on for a long time now without resolution."

"Danny, forget about it. I know you're concerned, but that is for the Federation to deal with now. It's out of our hands. Any correspondence should be forwarded to the Federation's legal ministry." President Sarratt could barely concentrate. He never expected these crazy events to disrupt his own plans for power.

"Your thoughts on Israel?" Danny asked, changing the subject and closing down his screen. He switched on a wall-mounted monitor to watch the clean-up efforts the Jews were undertaking from the attack they suffered under Russia and Iran. For miles and miles bodies, partially eaten by vultures and animals, were strewn across the valley and the lower slopes of the mountains. Small troops of Israelis in protective gear were burying bodies and other small groups with heavy equipment were stocking piles of weaponry for burning. The effort was daunting as the drones and satellite scanned the scene.

Turning from the monitor, the president responded, "The Federation's briefing on the attack was astonishing. These cataclysmic natural events we've been experiencing even impacted war. Have we ever encountered natural events occurring simultaneously that had such a deadly outcome? Never!" He shook his head in disbelief. "Hundreds of thousands of troops killed by an earthquake, hail, sulfurous fires and, in the confusion, by friendly fire. If that didn't get them, they were killed by their own chemical weapons!"

Danny added absentmindedly, "It will take years for the cleanup," then turned back to the screen.

President Sarratt said, "And we can thank the Super Dux we didn't get involved trying to protect Israel. He can pat himself on the back. He made the right decision when he told everyone to hold tight to see what the outcome would be. He never did believe Russia and Iran would use nuclear weapons. To what purpose? Yes, they wanted to annihilate the Jews, but they wanted the land, their goods, businesses, and energy sources."

"Staying on the sidelines was the right call," Danny agreed. "I have to admit, it was alarming the Federation couldn't protect Israel but, as everyone later agreed, there simply was not enough time to mobilize our troops."

The president nodded. "We were actually lucky."

"Yes, we dodged a bullet on that one. Had we gone into war, our collective troops would have been wiped out," Danny pointed out.

"Speaking of Israel," President Sarratt said, "we'll be leaving for the summit there next week to meet with the Super Dux and the other leaders in the Federation. I detect an undercurrent of hostility toward Israel that is building on the part of the Super Dux. Among other things, he believes Israel should have had better intelligence on the Russia and Iran attack. After all, troops were positioning along her borders. How could they have not known?"

"President Sarratt," Danny argued, "he shouldn't care at this juncture. As we said before, had Israel known in advance that they were going to be attacked, and the Federation had to live up to its agreement of protecting the country, all hell would have broken loose. As it is, the outcome of the attempted attack is a huge benefit to all of us and the Super Dux should recognize this. Our troops are intact which can't be said of the Russian, Iranian, and coalition armies."

"True, but I think so many of us in the Federation are weary of Israel. What worth does the country have?" the president asked sarcastically.

Danny was surprised at this question. Everyone knew Israel was worth taking over. "As small as it is, Israel is a very wealthy country. The vast barrels of oil that have been discovered are waiting to be tapped. Those spoils alone are worth going after. And before all of these cataclysmic events, she was enjoying a high gross domestic product. Her monetary value of finished goods and services was more than double most countries her size. Israel might be small, but she is ripe for plucking."

"Yes, I stand corrected. She does have worth, but if we have to protect her in the future, it will be costly," the president said. "And the world is tiring of the Jews clamoring for the right to exist. I know that the Super Dux is and I concur. Alliances are to be made elsewhere with better return on investment. The treaty is a wasted effort and, in reality, I don't think the Federation wants the expense of protecting her."

An alarm went off in the executive offices.

In the Situation Room, monitors flashed to a new high alert. Another aberration of nature beyond imagination was descending upon the nation and the world. A monitor keyed for the top one hundred cities in the country flashed live streaming video at five-second intervals. Views of selective streets were shown, starting with those cities with the greatest population to the least. Another monitor streamed the top one hundred cities of the world in like manner.

"What is it now?" the president asked wearily as he followed Danny to the Situation Room. Analysts, technicians, and aides were glued to the monitors, watching macabre scenes unfold on the city streets as people were relentlessly attacked by what seemed like mutant insects. The president was aghast.

A young analyst stood up from his screen and in a rage screamed as one demon-possessed. "Aha! The fifth trumpet judgment of God! Beware! Let me tell you about it!"

Security ran to stop him, but the president said, "Wait. Hold back. I want to hear what he has to say before we get rid of him."

The young man, with *666* blazoned on his hand, laughed dementedly, climbed a chair, then stood on a desk and shouted, "There are seven trumpet judgments of God during the tribulation."

Quoting from the Bible he bellowed, *"Then the fifth angel sounded: And I saw a star fallen from heaven to the earth. To him was given the key to the bottomless pit. And he opened the bottomless pit, and smoke arose out of the pit like the smoke of a great furnace. So the sun and the air were darkened because of the smoke of the pit. Then out of the smoke locusts came upon the earth. And to them was given power, as the scorpions of the earth have power. They were commanded not to harm the grass of the earth, or any green thing, or any tree, but only those men who do not have the seal of God on their foreheads. And they were not given authority to kill them, but to torment them for five months. Their torment was like the torment of a scorpion when it strikes a man. In those days men will seek death and will not find it; they will desire to die, and death will flee from them.*

"*The shape of the locusts was like horses prepared for battle. On their heads were crowns of something like gold, and their faces were like the faces of men. They had hair like women's hair, and their teeth were like lions' teeth. And they had breastplates like breastplates of iron, and the sound of their wings was like the sound of chariots with many horses running into battle. They had tails like scorpions, and there were stings in their tails. Their power was to hurt men five months. And they had as king over them the angel of the bottomless pit, whose name in Hebrew is Abaddon, but in Greek he has the name Apollyon.*"

The crazed analyst doubled over in laughter and the president gave security the sign to take him away. Everyone in the room was deathly quiet. "Where did that speech come from?" the president coldly asked, looking around at his assembled staff.

Someone googled it and answered, "It's from the last book in the Bible. The book of Revelation, chapter 9, verses 1 through 11. God has some seven judgments he lays on the earth during the so-called seven years of the tribulation. The locust-like insects are the fifth judgment."

A tech asked, "What were the first four? Could everything that's been going on these last years be judgments from . . ." The staffer hesitated.

Before she could finish her sentence, the president proclaimed, "This is some freak of nature that is a result of the unnatural events we have been experiencing since the Vaporization. I will not have any more mention or reference to God! For the record, keep God out of this. We must get a handle on this!" He turned to Danny and instructed, "I want you to oversee the effort of pulling together a task force of scientists, doctors, naturalists, entomologists, and all the necessary personnel you need to find out what these beasts are and how we can fight and eradicate them."

"Got it," Danny said and opened the door to leave.

"Katrina," the president said to another advisor, "I want you to..."

Danny had just cracked the door of the Situation Room when an ominous buzzing was heard in the hallway. Someone screamed, "Close it, close it!" But it was too late. Pandemonium erupted as people tried to swat, duck, or run from the powerful mutant locusts. There was nothing security could do. Mace was ineffective and only damaged the eyes of those nearby trying to escape the attacking insects. They stung and swarmed. Piling through the doorway, the group screamed and ran as the insects followed. It was an awful scene of pain and terror.

There wasn't a room to which they could take the president where there were not several insects, and they dared not take him outside, which was teeming with the creatures. As they scurried from one room to another, insects clung to clothing and to hair, and no amount of plucking or pulling could release their grip. When the staff ripped the jacket off the president to rid him of the insects, several more locusts found purchase on his shirt. He screamed in pain.

Reports were coming in from all levels of staff and security saying that nowhere was safe. Some areas were less infested than others, and they sought to find those shelters. The president, Danny, and some senior staff members made for the president's apartments, but there was no escaping the onslaught. All the security detail could do was stand guard and take the malicious stings of the locusts.

In the surprise attack, the locusts had gained entry into every home, shelter, bunker, or vehicle. They were everywhere: inside and out. No one throughout the world was prepared for this unthinkable assault of insects that attacked continually and viciously. No one knew where they came from or how to kill them.

"It's like closing the barn door after the horse was out," Danny said to the president as they worked in extreme pain from the safest place, the president's apartments. "There's nothing we can do." In his mind he was hoping that this infestation, which no one was able to combat, would indeed end in at least five months as the lunatic analyst had predicted, but he dared not say a word to the president. That would be giving credence to the Christian Bible. He also thought that through this string of horrendous events, no one turned to the Christian God for help. If anything, they cursed that God, claiming if He was real, they hated Him.

There was no respite on the attack of the winged insects. People looked for death, but in truth did not find it. They were unable to commit suicide because, it was almost as if the locust-like insects knew when a person was trying to end their lives, and the locusts prevented any success by attacking more ferociously. The people were better off enduring than trying to outwit their attackers. If everyone wasn't in so much excruciating pain, it would have been worthy to discuss and find out why people were not able to kill themselves. It was surreal.

The media brought to light that all the people who had the mark of the Super Dux were attacked. "Scientists say it is possible the locusts are attracted to the ink in *666* or the metal that is in the chip imbedded under our skin." Many accepted the reasoning, but they dared not rid themselves of the mark, or cut out the chip, because it was the only way to buy and sell. They would rather suffer the pain than die of starvation.

"The only people who are not attacked, according to the media, are the two witnesses who don't have the mark, that no one can attack anyway, and the strange evangelical group of Jewish men who are preaching in Israel and throughout world. They don't have the mark either," Danny informed the president.

"And like the two witnesses, they escape harm not only from the winged beasts, but from anyone wishing to do them injury," the president added. "All of them untouchable."

"The Super Dux and his Prophet haven't been attacked either. Of course, they don't have the mark," Danny reasoned through puffy stung lips. "People argue they weren't attacked because there's something otherworldly about Marcus Junius and his Prophet. If they're so 'otherworldly,' why can't they stop this infestation!" In extreme pain and discomfort, Danny took a call in the president's office in the apartment suite and took the message.

The president, numbed with pain that no narcotic could quell, looked at him questioningly. It hurt to talk.

Steeling himself against his own discomfort, Danny told the president, "The summit is cancelled for five months."

CHAPTER FIFTEEN

THE FEDERATION

"ROBERTO, I WANT YOU IN on this conversation." The Super Dux pointed to a chair. "Please, sit down."

Roberto was just starting to heal from the vicious stings of the mutant locusts. Because neither the Super Dux nor the Prophet had been attacked, they had no idea the pain people suffered and so there was no sympathy on their part toward Roberto or the rest of the staff. It was work as usual.

"Awhile back I told you that I had some unusual power, likened perhaps to the Christian God. We got sidetracked from the conversation, dealing with the attack of the locusts and all the other disasters that came before that. Now that the Prophet has appeared"—the Super Dux nodded to the former Cardinal Giovanni, who was seated to his left—"he will be working with us by exercising his own mystical powers, making my supernatural power complete. Shortly, I'll be viewed as godlike."

Roberto looked at the two men in question. This wasn't exactly a surprise because the amount of work and accomplishment Marcus was able to achieve with little pushback from the Federation and the world was seemingly superhuman. Hearing the words *mystical, supernatural,* and *godlike*, he realized he was in a serious game-changing situation. Agreeable or not, he was a part of a team that was insuperable.

"We are under the direction of the 'prince of this world,'" the Super Dux said simply and without drama. "We are now positioned to move forward achieving total world power."

Roberto knew who the "prince of this world" was. He was thoughtful on the subject. It was one thing not to believe in God, but it was another to believe in Satan. If you believed in one, it stood to reason to believe in the other. He understood wanting to rule the world, and he understood the concept of having people believe the Super Dux was a god. However, Roberto also recognized he was caught up with three demonic personalities waging a spiritual warfare he wasn't sure he wanted to be involved in, although it was intriguing. And he had to admit, the power had been drawing him in for some time.

"All of these extraordinary and cataclysmic events that have occurred has worked to our advantage," the Prophet stated. "The people are tired and fearful of what might happen next. They will welcome a messiah and that would be you, Marcus, a leader they can turn to. Thus, we are now poised to show the world your power, which I will bring about through the authority that has been vested in me to perform miracles on your behalf. The prince of this world is working through us to bring about a new totalitarian reign."

Marcus sat back in his leather chair. "You are likening us to the 'Unholy Trinity.'" He smiled.

"Marcus, I will have the people worshipping you as a god. They will venerate you. You will be raised far higher than the Christian God. We will conquer the world!"

"I like your words, Prophet."

"Now that the attack of the locusts is over, we can commence with the summit, bringing member nations' dignitaries and commissioners together. People are beginning to heal and look forward to comfort and prosperity through the guidance of a supreme leader," the Prophet continued, "We must encourage them in depending upon you for security. This will be done through supernatural wonders. After I am done showing them your greatness through my miracles, they will not only accept your total rule, but *want* your total rule, for there will be no other like you. You will be their god, but rather than a spirit or an idol, you will be flesh and blood."

Marcus realized this was all part of the great plan. The prince of this world had already communicated this to him through his dreams, and he was told it would start with Jerusalem. "That is the plan, Prophet. I want to use the summit in Jerusalem as our venue for the proclamation of my power and your miraculous abilities." Marcus leaned forward to the Prophet and Roberto for emphasis. "Because we will have international coverage, this will give us the opportunity to show the world my supremacy."

"Not to interrupt, Super Dux, but I also suspect there are three nations who are not in alignment with you. They will be at the summit too," Roberto warned.

"I have an idea of how to ferret them out, Roberto. I will require a confirmation of loyalty and we can work out the details. Once it is confirmed that they are not willing to be supportive of me, I want you to set up a kill and I want it done at the summit."

Roberto nodded. "It will be done." Now he knew he was committed. But then again, he had stayed in this for so long, what would be the benefit of walking away? Not that he could anyway. He would be crushed like a cockroach.

"And shortly after the summit, I will break the treaty with Israel. I will gather the military might of all the nations that we have under our control for our own invasion of Israel, which will be successful, unlike the fiasco of Russia and Iran's attack against Israel. It was an auspicious decision I made to wait and see the outcome of that attack." Marcus sat back. "Ultimately, I want to annihilate the men, women, and children of Israel. I'll start there. Then, I'll move across the globe. I want no Jew or Christian on the face of this earth alive. Or, if they want to save their lives, they will worship and give their allegiance only to me."

Roberto was eager to hear the plans of supernatural display of power by Marcus and the Prophet, but the men asked him to leave for the remaining part of their meeting.

"Roberto," Marcus said, smiling as his chief gathered up his gear, "as you know, everything that is discussed between you, the Prophet, and me is highly confidential. Always. At this point there is no need for you to know anything more. Should there be any leaks of anticipation, you'll be blamed and I don't have to tell you what that would mean for your well-being."

Roberto was well aware that if anything ever leaked out concerning any discussions in the executive offices, he would be held responsible and summarily lose his life in probably a most gruesome manner.

The summit opened on schedule. Dignitaries, commissioners of each Federation nation, President Sarratt, and Israel's prime minister, chief of staff, cabinet, and other high-level leaders met on the terrace at the Aish HaTorah World Center for the opening ceremonies of the summit scheduled to begin the next day. Views of the western wall and the Temple Mount were stunning under the setting sun. Telescopes allowed guests to view the Old City, Mount Scopus, the Mount of Olives, the Judean Desert, and the mountains of Moab.

At the moment, all were mingling, enjoying the view, chatting, and sipping wine. Hors d'oeuvres platters of fresh Israeli fruits and vegetables grown in greenhouses were circulated among the crowd eagerly sampling them. There were so few fresh fruits and vegetables in the world now due to the fires, toxic waters, earthquakes, storms, and diminished sun that a slice of an orange was a rare delight.

There were also guests who circled a sculpture of Israel's pride, a model of the new temple. It was set to the side of the podium on a pedestal encased in ballistic glass. During the banquet, the Israeli prime minister was going to speak about the construction and invite the delegates to a private visit of the temple. However, at the last moment, his speech was cancelled.

"Prime Minister Ben-Zion, I'm afraid there won't be time for your speech tonight. The Super Dux regrets the inconvenience, but perhaps at the end of the summit, if there is time, we can schedule a talk for you," Roberto said condescendingly.

The prime minister barely reacted. Graciously he said, "Of course. I understand."

His own senior staff was furious and wanted to lodge a complaint against the decision, but the prime minister insisted they must not challenge the Super Dux. They were, however, free to field questions about the partially constructed temple from reporters who were looking for sidebar stories to the summit.

It wasn't as spectacular a temple as in King Solomon's time, nor was it as humble as the Second Temple built by Ezra and Nehemiah, or as grand as in Herod's rebuilding in 30 BC, but it was a beautiful building. The main structure, which included the holy of holies, the Holy Place, and the courts of the priests, were completed, but the court of women, court of gentiles, and other structures and landscaping were not. The building was incredibly important and of historical magnitude to the Jews, but it was also a trophy held high against the Muslims, who claimed the site for their Dome of the Rock. The Jews readily took back the mount and started construction after the crushing and humiliating defeat of Russia and Iran, along with their Muslim coalition.

Levi turned from his companions, who were complaining quietly about the missed opportunity of speaking about the historic rebuilding of the new temple. "Do you see who are preaching by the Wall?" he asked the prime minister.

"Yes, the 'two witnesses.' We can only keep the crowds back from causing a disturbance, but the press is everywhere. We can't stop the witnesses from preaching or the press from recording. Look. The media is interviewing the Super Dux. I hope they avoid talk of the witnesses." The prime minister nodded toward where TV reporters and a crowd were forming around the Super Dux, listening raptly to his words. "I only hope that there is no disruption from the two men to embarrass us."

"I hope not either," Levi said. He groaned and took a long drink of his wine.

"Sadly," the Super Dux criticized, "the Israeli government has not been able to stop the two witnesses from their detrimental preaching. I've been assessing the damage they've been doing not only to the citizens of Israel, but the world. Their constant harassment must stop, along with their murders of innocent people who are just tired of hearing them preach. They must be held accountable for lack of rain and other disasters for which they're taking credit for as punishment to people such as you and me who do not believe in God, or do not believe in 'sin.'"

The prime minister leaned into Levi. "He's establishing his position. He wants to usurp our power."

"We," the Super Dux said, including the listening crowd with a sweep of his arm, "have no intention of turning from our lifestyles! Who are they, or their God, to judge us? I promise you, I will easily take care of two men the Israeli government seems to have no control over!" The group listening roundly applauded him.

"And did you see where we are sitting?" Levi asked the prime minister, who was keenly listening to the words of the Super Dux.

"Not at the head table, Levi. I would be affronted, if I didn't understand what is to be."

The Super Dux continued to work the crowd of adoring followers. After thanking a large group, he caught the eye of Roberto, who pointed to his watch. With that, he straightened his tie and walked to the podium with his Prophet behind him.

The crowd on the rooftop quieted and all were drawn to the dais. The media was in place, cameras were rolling, and microphones were extended as Marcus Junius held up a hand for everyone's attention.

"Friends of the press and friends of the Federation, we are going to reveal the mystery of my success and consequently the Federation's triumphs, along with the plans for an ultimate worldly nirvana. Please, find your seats."

An excited murmur rippled through the crowd as they searched out their name cards.

After everyone was placed, Marcus eyed the gathering and grandly announced, "I wish to formally introduce you to the Prophet, my closest advisor. You will see why I call him by this esteemed title."

Dressed in a simple suit and tie, Giovanni stood, smiled, and extended his hands to all in a humble gesture. "My dear friends, it has been revealed to me by the prince of this world that we are embarking on a new world order. As the Super Dux proclaimed, a 'worldly nirvana.'

"Some of you might know who the prince of this world is. He is the one who has anointed Marcus Junius, as your Super Dux, designated to rule the world." He smiled broadly at Marcus. "I prophesy we will be traveling on a journey filled with success and mystical profundity." An excited murmur rippled through the crowd as the Prophet continued. "There is no one like him who has the powers that have been bestowed upon him. Some of you might not believe in gods and think that those beliefs are ancient, but I assure you, and will prove to you, he is a new world deity. I will also show you powers that have been granted to me to show you his divinity."

Before anyone could absorb the Prophet's words, he raised his hands and a perfectly round fireball appeared in the air. It stopped in front of all to see, then, at the direction of the Prophet's hands, it whirled to the sculpture of the temple, consumed it with a deafening clap of thunder and flare of red, blue, and gold flame, then disappeared with a cascade of stars. Nothing else was burned. The podium and case that enclosed it were intact. People gaped in awe at the void where the two-meter model had been.

The table of Israelis was aghast, then confounded and angry. This display was a prized model of their ancient and historic landmark that was needlessly and thoughtlessly destroyed for the edification of the summit attendees to show them the power of the Prophet! How dare that man do such a thing! And how did he do it? That fireball was not a robot or drone; it was a real sphere of flames.

The prime minister touched Levi's knee under the table and turned to him. "Do not be distressed." He then directed his remarks to his senior staff sitting nearby. "Let it go. This is not the place for verbal retaliation."

Seething in anger, they stoically sat as the Super Dux smiled and extended his arms.

"I proclaim to you my sovereignty!"

At these words hundreds of uniformed soldiers filled the terrace carrying automatic rifles.

"I will lead you into paths of success," he continued, "but you must give me your total alliance. Yet I do not hold you hostage. Anyone who does not wish to be a part of my rule may leave and come to no harm."

Three of the leaders who did not agree with Marcus abruptly stood and hurried out of the room. All watched in surprise and trepidation as the two men and one woman rushed to the stairs, forsaking the elevator and disappeared from view.

"Ah, the triumphs they will be missing!" Marcus sighed dramatically as the attention of the guests turned back to him.

Suddenly, a sharp crack snapped the air. In shocked surprise, the Super Dux looked at his guests wide-eyed, then crumpled to the floor with a bullet hole in his forehead. Screams and panic ensued. People jumped up, knocking over chairs and pushing one another to escape the sniper. In an unnaturally loud commanding voice, the Prophet shouted to the soldiers to keep everyone in the room. A collective racking of gun barrels froze everyone in place.

"Sit down!" the Prophet ordered.

All sat back down in shock, as lines of guns were aimed at them. When the crowd was under control, the Prophet stooped down and peered closely at Marcus, touching his head. His hand came away bloody and soiled.

"He's dead," Roberto Pertucci said softly and disbelievingly as he knelt by the Super Dux's body. Gently, he closed Marcus' staring blank eyes with his fingertips. All the hopes and dreams were now extinguished in one foul act. The leader of the new world order was dead. It was unfathomable.

"Please, cover the body," demanded the Prophet.

All were craning their necks around the soldiers to get a look at the dead Super Dux. Someone handed Roberto a tablecloth.

Many minutes later, the emergency medical team arrived and took his vitals. They pronounced him dead. Then Mossad, several security officers, and detectives arrived, viewed the body, and began interviewing all the guests. At least an hour passed before the body was allowed to be removed. Guests were still being interviewed as the EMTs put Super Dux Marcus Junius on the stretcher. People were openly crying and pushing toward his body. It was unbelievable that one minute he was vibrant and alive holding a promising future for the world, and the next minute his brains with world-changing ideas were splattered across the wall. As the EMTs pushed his body through the crowd, people reached out to touch the cloth that covered him, sobbing.

Just as the elevator opened to swallow the fallen leader, the cloth was ripped from the body. The Super Dux held the tablecloth in his hands and sat up in bewilderment, then effrontery. "What happened?" he gasped, looking around in confusion.

For a moment there was stunned silence, and then incredulous gasps and cheers arose. Pandemonium erupted.

The Prophet grabbed Marcus' hands and helped him off the gurney. The front of his head showed no entry wound. He gently touched the back of Marcus' head and it came away slightly bloody, but when the Prophet put a white napkin to the wound, there was nothing there. He was completely healed!

The Prophet lifted the white clean napkin. "Behold! The Super Dux has come back from the dead!"

The babble of the crowd reached a frantic crescendo.

"How could this have happened? He was dead for over an hour!" a woman exclaimed.

"I have a piece of his brain in my hand!" another cried. "As a memento!"

"This is a miracle!" another shouted. "Indeed, he is a god! It's true! He was dead and now he's alive!"

People began falling on their knees, calling him a god and worshipping him. The news media couldn't believe their extraordinary good fortune capturing the drama on video. It was shown live around the world. People now truly believed that the Super Dux was a god.

How could anyone survive a bullet to the head and be pronounced dead, only to come back to life?

The medical teams confirmed the assassination was not a staged event. Marcus had truly been shot and killed. People showed the TV commentators gathered bits of Marcus' brains they gleaned from the floor and off the wall to keep as treasures.

After the guests were given the clearance to leave by the security officials, the Israeli contingency left as well. Prime Minister Moshe Ben-Zion and his chief of staff, Levi Gur, stayed behind to see the Super Dux, the Prophet, and Roberto into their limo.

"This has been an astonishing and exemplary evening, Prime Minister Ben-Zion," the Super Dux said magnanimously as he shook the prime minister's hand. "It was a miracle, was it not? I was raised from the dead!" He smiled broadly in wonder, touching his forehead, and looked about him. Video cams were still rolling.

Pulling the prime minister's arm close, and with his back to the cameras, his facial expression changed from warmth to intense iciness. In the prime minister's ear, he hissed, "I'll look forward to seeing you at the summit tomorrow and I expect to hear that your team found the person who shot me. Do you think your Mossad, or whatever you call them, can do this task?"

The prime minister pulled his arm away from Marcus' grip and stepped back, emotionless. He didn't utter a word.

The next morning, the three bodies of the leaders who did not take allegiance with the Super Dux and the Federation were discovered slaughtered in their motel rooms. It was rumored that they were a part of the plot to kill Marcus Junius, but there was no confirmation.

There were also no leads on who assassinated the three or who attempted the plot to kill Marcus Junius. The Israeli government would have no news to give to the Super Dux.

Videos showing the introduction of the Prophet, his fireball miracle, the assassination, and the Super Dux coming back to life went viral. All who viewed the video were solidly convinced the Super Dux was a god and the adoration and worship grew worldwide with those who had taken the mark 666. The murder of the three leaders who disengaged themselves from the Super Dux and the Federation were downplayed. There was so much information to be assimilated that the coming back to life of Marcus Junius was in the forefront of all news media and discussions. A massive manhunt was underway for his assassin. They would never find him.

Throngs of people ran through the streets of Jerusalem, praising the Super Dux and mocking the God of the two witnesses.

"This has worked out to our great benefit, Marcus," the Prophet said before the breakfast meeting of the summit. He looked out the window at the adoring, clamoring crowds. "Now is time to kill the two witnesses. You have been granted the ability to slay them."

"Yes, I know. I've had a vision of that confirmation. I've been told by the prince of this world that I have the power. After last night's miracles, we have the people in our hands—even the hardheaded Jews, but I want to know who shot me!"

"Marcus, it might have well been orchestrated by our dark prince. You don't need to know who shot you. You are alive and a miracle was performed in front of the world. Let it go."

Marcus thought about it. The Prophet was correct. The miracle proved his absolute power. No one could kill him. It was part of the prince of this world's plan. He needed to move on. "I want this evening's cocktail party to be held at the restaurant that is on the street where the two witnesses are preaching. On that building, there is a rooftop terrace and from there, I'll perform the miracle of executing them. The summit will be ending in four days, and I want their bodies left in the streets decomposing as proof of my power."

"How are you going to do this?" asked Roberto, looking at both the Prophet and Marcus.

"I have a plan that was given to me. Sorry, I can't share it with you. It's enough to know that it'll be successful. I promise you this."

That evening on the rooftop, Marcus was surrounded by Federation members, dignitaries, and many influential admirers, who were dumbfounded and reverent over the recent miraculous events. The media was in full force. Marcus had promised them all another spectacular event, one involving the witnesses and one they would never forget. He had asked for the people of the world to watch TV. For those in the streets of Jerusalem he ordered them to stay behind the barriers without exception.

"What can we expect to see that is better than you dying and coming back to life?" a reporter shouted above the din.

"Another fantastic wonder!" the Super Dux answered. "The world will celebrate this occasion too, as all observe my power."

Risers were set up on the terrace, ensuring all of a view of the platform where Marcus Junius and the Prophet were standing, as well as a view of the street below where the two witnesses were preaching. To make sure everyone could see what was going on, monitors were set up on the roof and on the side streets.

The Israeli contingency, along with the prime minister and his chief of staff, arrived. Although they were the host nation for the summit, they were roundly ignored by Marcus, his staff, and other attendees. Sensing a disapproval of the Israelis by the Super Dux, US President Sarratt and his officials ignored them too. The Super Dux stopped the Israeli security detail at the entrance and replaced them with the Federation security force on the rooftop. In the streets, his forces ordered the Israeli Security and police to stand back.

The appointed time for the miracle was at hand. The crowd below on the streets and the guests on the terrace waited impatiently as the Super Dux took the microphone and looked around and down at his adoring audience.

"Do you see those two men below?" the Super Dux asked.

"Of course," someone answered. "They have been preaching for three and a half years. No one can stop them!"

"I can," the Super Dux said simply. The crowd waited in anticipation. He went to the railing of the terrace, stared at the cameras, and shouted, "Watch!"

His right arm came up from his side, his hand extended out, and his finger pointed at the two witnesses, who were preaching repentance and warning of more judgments of God. A deafening thunderclap resounded as the two witnesses collapsed on the street, dead. A stunned silence lasted for a moment before a spontaneous cheer went up from all those on the rooftop and all the hundreds of people standing behind the barriers and those watching on monitors. They clapped, whistled, danced, and shouted.

"This is a miracle! Even the Israeli security forces couldn't kill the men, yet the Super Dux did!" someone shouted.

"How did he do it?" another asked, but no one could answer. How was such an amazing, powerful deed accomplished through thunder?

"No one is to touch those men," the Super Dux ordered. "They are to be left to rot!"

Cell phones and cameras flashed. TV reporters and videographers jostled one another to get the best coverage of the two dead bodies lying on the ground. The media was frenzied.

The people on the streets were ecstatic, partying well into the night and early hours. The men who were constantly telling them to turn to God through salvation in Jesus were dead. Hallelujah! The men who pointed out the people's so-called sins were rotting in front of everyone's eyes! It was a delight to see. Finally, the people didn't have to hear about judgment and the coming wrath of God! They were free of criticism and threats.

"God? What God? Our god is Super Dux Marcus Junius!" they chanted, waving the flag of the Federation. "He will save us! He will bring the nations back to greatness!"

The Israeli contingency, led by the prime minister, left the rooftop stunned and frightened. The Super Dux had powers beyond their understanding and was sustained by a spiritual entity they could not comprehend. The act of killing the witnesses that the Israelis had failed to do proved that their country was in serious jeopardy. Was this an omen of being swallowed up by the Super Dux and his Federation?

On the last day of the summit, the attendees, with the exception of the Israeli prime minister and his leaders, met up on the terrace roof again to celebrate the end of a successful meeting and the inauguration of absolute rule by the Super Dux.

"The Jews aren't here," Roberto pointed out to Marcus.

"Are you surprised?" Marcus answered. "It was on their watch that an assassination attempt was made on me, that three country leaders were killed in their hotel rooms, and that the two witnesses whom the Israelis, with all their might could not kill, yet I did, by merely pointing my finger."

"But it goes beyond that, Marcus. For the last two days, they said they have come across some 'spiritual' information and have been warning all those who are in Jerusalem to leave the city. They claim an earthquake of enormous magnitude will hit the city today."

"They are proving to be crazy. No one is listening to their hysterical warnings. Neither am I. They're obviously trying to make mischief by upsetting the last day of the summit, and I think they're trying to match me with their own brand of 'supernatural' powers or knowledge," he said to his chief of staff. "Please! None of our seismologists concurred, otherwise I would not be here, Roberto."

The guests made toasts to the Super Dux and to the success of the Federation. Gourmet food, at the expense of the Israelis, was eaten in great quantities, and attendees exchanged gifts with one another. Member nations of the Federation, important private citizens, and hopeful new members presented Marcus with lavish gifts of gold and gems.

President Sarratt, along with Danny, enjoyed the camaraderie of the Super Dux, the Prophet, and Chief of Staff Roberto. As the US President looked around at the contented crowd, he inwardly congratulated himself for aligning the US with the Federation. It was the winning team, because regardless of all the disasters the world was enduring, the Super Dux would lead them to success. Imagine! He had the power to come back to life! He thrilled the world by killing the two witnesses who even now lie rotting in the street. Only Marcus Junius proved to have the power to put to death two men that no one, not even the highly skilled forces of Israel, could eliminate. Could it get any better?

CHAPTER SIXTEEN

ISRAEL

HAVING NOT ATTENDED THE CLOSING ceremonies of the summit, the prime minister and his chief of staff, along with other officials, agreed to meet together in the Command and Control room in the bunker north of Jerusalem, not knowing when the earthquake could hit.

"I don't know what to think," Levi said to the prime minister as they sat in the executive suite of the bunker. "We have our team working the forensics of the murder, or attempted murder, of the Super Dux. We just have to sit tight for the results. We have no clue who shot him or who killed the three country leaders that chose to leave the summit, nor do we understand how he could be dead, then alive."

"It's immaterial, Levi. It's all in prophesy. See here in the book of Revelation, chapter 13?" The prime minister pointed to the text. *And I saw a beast coming out of the sea. It had ten horns and seven heads, with ten crowns on its horns, and on each head a blasphemous name. The beast I saw resembled a leopard, but had feet like those of a bear and a mouth like that of a lion. The dragon gave the beast his power and his throne and great authority. One of the heads of the beast seemed to have had a fatal wound, but the fatal wound had been healed. The whole world was filled with wonder and followed the beast.*

"We can't control the outcome, Moshe, my friend. At the moment, we must brace ourselves for more tragedy before the end. Again, I refer to prophesies written in both the Jewish and Christian books. It's been nearly four days since the two witnesses were killed. More calamities will come today."

"Yes, and although you and I will be saved, there will be great suffering and loss of our people. I've been teaching my granddaughter about Jesus Christ and she has come to believe in the Lord, so I know that we'll be saved. What about your wife and family?" Moshe asked his friend. He knew soon he would lose his title of prime minister.

"They, too, have come to believe. I told them we might be killed, but we know we have final victory in Jesus. It's the truth. We're afraid of course, but at the same time we're not. Does that make sense?"

"Yes. Fear is in the flesh, hope is in the Spirit," Moshe answered, putting down the Bible.

The prime minister addressed the small group, "As you have been briefed by Levi, after three and a half days the two witnesses who have been lying dead in the street will rise and when they do, there will be a great earthquake in Jerusalem and a significant amount of our citizens will be killed, according to Scripture. I've repeatedly told our leaders and staff, who refuse to listen. For those of you who have chosen to heed my words, you come here at peril for your own careers and maybe lives, but at least for this day, you'll be safe. I also hope that your families are somewhere safe. We have no idea how the Super Dux will respond once the earthquake hits, if he and those in Jerusalem will even survive, but he has been forewarned; nonetheless, he is going on with the closing ceremony."

"And I've called the media to alert them of the impending disaster, but they are all covering the Super Dux. No one is listening!" replied an anguished press secretary.

"Keep the staff on all the monitors and activate the drone cams," the prime minister said to an aide.

The minister of defense, the minister of internal security, the head of Mossad, and a few other staff members and aides hurried in looking worn and apprehensive. Worried that this might be a false alarm, and worried that it might be for real.

The prime minister was surprised, and greeted them somberly. Earlier when he told them of the impending disaster, they brushed him off as irrational and blustered that his newfound faith was interfering with governing Israel in these trying times of disasters and interfering oversight of the Super Dux. Their words highlighted their lack of confidence in their leader.

"I hope all of your families are safe," the prime minister said without reaction.

"Yes. Just in case you're right," the minister of defense said grudgingly. "But we want to see for ourselves where you got your information."

Prime Minister Moshe Ben-Zion opened the last book of the Christian Bible, Revelation 11 and read aloud verses 7 through 13, written by the apostle John: *When they finish their testimony, the beast that ascends out of the bottomless pit will make war against them, overcome them, and kill them.* He stopped and said, "'They' that are referred to are the two witnesses and the beast is Satan, working through the Antichrist, that is the Super Dux." He continued, *And their dead bodies will lie in the street of the great city which spiritually is called Sodom and*

Egypt, where also our Lord was crucified. He looked up and said, "We know this is Jerusalem."

Continuing, he read, *Then those from the peoples, tribes, tongues, and nations will see their dead bodies three-and-a-half days, and not allow their dead bodies to be put into graves. And those who dwell on the earth will rejoice over them, make merry, and send gifts to one another, because these two prophets tormented those who dwell on the earth.* He stopped and looked at all seated around the table. "Have we not witnessed this already?"

Levi answered, "Indeed we have."

Adjusting his glasses, the prime minister went on, *Now after the three-and-a-half days the breath of life from God entered them, and they stood on their feet, and great fear fell on those who saw them. And they heard a loud voice from heaven saying to them, "Come up here." And they ascended to heaven in a cloud, and their enemies saw them. In the same hour there was a great earthquake, and a tenth of the city fell. In the earthquake seven thousand people were killed, and the rest were afraid and gave glory to the God of heaven.*

"Did you hear that?" a wide-eyed adviser loudly interrupted. A TV station, with the audio turned down low, was broadcasting the closing festivities of the summit. A loud commanding voice interrupted the broadcaster's coverage. The videographer turned his camera from the Super Dux to the streets below.

All eyes in the Command and Control bunker went from the prime minister to the TV as they watched in shock as the two witnesses came to life, got to their feet, and ascended into the air while shouts, cries, screams of disbelief, and fear filled the atmosphere.

The streets broke out into chaos. No one knew how to react. No one had ever seen such a thing! The TV producer cut back to the Super

Dux to catch his reaction, but Marcus Junius and his Prophet were nowhere to be found. The camera panned the guests craning their necks and pointing in stupefaction. It was an unbelievable sight! For several minutes, the guests stood in awe and wonder, continuing to look up in the sky.

As so many were talking excitedly and pointing to the sky and others were shouting in disbelief, a low ominous groan rumbled from the depths of the earth. The people's eyes went wide in collective terror. With little warning, the earth shook and heaved violently. A videographer, trying to catch the confusion and terror of the guests on the terrace roof, dropped his camera when the floor began to cave in. The TV monitor went black.

As the shockwaves found their way north of the city, all eyes in the bunker were focused now on the other monitors receiving feed from the drones and satellites hovering over Israel. Live video showed buildings shaking violently and collapsing in rubble. Another camera picked up roads breaking apart, and smoke and dust filling the air of Jerusalem. Explosions resounded throughout the city.

In three minutes it was all over. Everyone in the bunker held their breath. Some prayed, and of those praying, they believed. The truth was right before their eyes the entire time. They had been too blind to see!

More live videos showed massive damage and appalling destruction. Later, loss of life would be confirmed as predicted: seven thousand people perished. A quarter of the city was destroyed, but the temple remained.

"Colleagues, I think you will now agree that what we have been saying to you is true," the prime minister said in a shaking voice. "In the short time we have left, I ask you all to study our Holy Book and the Christian New Testament. You don't have time to go through it all to pick out what you need to know, but I will tell you one thing: Jesus the Christ is Lord and Savior. Our book has been pointing to a Savior all along, and He is Jesus. I'll put it simply, but you must read and study for yourselves. Then you must have faith and believe. If you refuse to believe, you will be the object of God's anger and I pity anyone who turns his back on the living God."

Levi broke in. "God has promised a homeland to the Jews. He will not go back on His covenant that He made with our patriarch Abraham. We'll run into great anguish, but in the end when Jesus our Lord returns to destroy the Antichrist, Super Dux Marcus Junius, and his false prophet, we who hold steadfast will be saved and will see the land promised to us."

"Yes, we have more trials to endure," the prime minister agreed. "As Levi has said, hold steadfast and, I add, be of good courage and wait on the Lord. As Joshua, second in command to Moses said, *'But as for me and my house, we will serve the Lord!'* That, ladies and gentlemen, is what my household and I are doing from now on. We are serving the Lord Jesus. Think about it."

Hours later, they made their way back to Jerusalem, encountering many roads that were blocked with rubble, but when they arrived at the governmental offices, they were still in place. Upon entering his office, the prime minister ordered his staff to begin enacting the country's emergency response plan. Levi held a message out to his leader. The Super Dux had escaped the carnage and was now en route to Rome with his entourage.

"It was predictable, Levi," the prime minister said. "The Super Dux will have his day though. His time has not yet come."

Days later, the Israeli prime minister's personal cell phone rang. "Prime Minister Moshe Ben-Zion, I will be back," a calm Super Dux proclaimed. "We must talk one-on-one. As you have witnessed, I am the one true powerful god. I admire your own 'spiritual' information, but it is just information. You, personally, haven't any power. We've seen that your leadership is weak, and like the great United States that is in shambles and useless, your country, too, will soon be rendered useless. You certainly don't have the mighty military or security forces that you once had. You were unable to kill *two men* that I alone could kill, and the results of this latest massive earthquake will hit your economy harder than you ever dreamed. If that is not enough, the entire Federation—the world—holds Israel in contempt due to the incompetency of defending yourselves and or me at the summit. I was shot and killed on your watch! Fortunately, it proved to be so beneficial. I came back to life. Who can do that but a god?"

The prime minister quietly said, "You are not a god."

"And let's take it to the max, Mr. Prime Minister. Well over half of your people have pledged their allegiance to me by bearing my mark 666. It will only be a matter of time before you lose complete control!" he exclaimed harshly. "Therefore, before civil war breaks out, shortly, I am sending a contingency of Federation Security Defense Forces to protect Jerusalem and the temple from rioters and looters. Yes, I will be defending the temple. The symbol of the Jewish people who will be conquered once again."

"Super Dux, you cannot do this! We are still an independent country!"

"Prime Minister Ben-Zion," the Super Dux acidly cut in, "I can do whatever I want. I am poised to take over the world. You and your little country have absolutely no strength to stand up to my command."

"What of the witnesses?" the prime minister challenged. "They, too, arose from the dead!"

"What of them? I killed them and they disappeared. People were surprised, but those who believe in me trust that I was the one who got them off the face of this earth. You will soon read the papers. Listen to the commentators. I am coming out on top. I love the media and the media loves me."

"Many believe it was God!" the prime minister spat out.

"It hardly matters. I will overpower all," the Super Dux said. "My forces will be coming back!"

The Super Dux lived up to his word. A worried advisor hurried to meet with the prime minister and his staff. "Prime Minister, several aircraft have landed and soldiers from the Federation are disembarking. They're going to occupy Jerusalem and guard the temple!"

"Where is our Minister of Defense?" demanded the prime minister.

"Dead," Levi said entering the office, and throwing his jacket on a chair. "He confronted the troops, they took him prisoner and later killed him. Made him an example to the troops and our Security Cabinet. Mossad and Internal Security are scrambling, but the Federation has made it clear we are not to retaliate. We are not totally crippled, but we're a close to it. Our real problem is lack of unity. So many of our people have taken the mark since the witnesses were killed and have put their loyalties with the Super Dux."

"Get all the staff who believe in prophecy and who do not have the mark to the conference room now."

As the senior staff, advisors, and aides entered the conference room, many had the mark *666* on either their foreheads or hands.

The prime minister raised his voice. "I am still in charge and I do not want anyone in here who has the mark!"

"Prime Minister, you can't stop us from being here! We're staying. Our allegiance is to the Super Dux. You're a puppet now who must follow the Super Dux's orders!" Benjamin, a young staffer, held out an official document claiming the prime minister's new status.

"Not yet. The Super Dux has not spoken to me personally. I said out!"

The guards that were chosen by the prime minister and who did not take the mark *666* hastily ushered the protesting staff out.

The phone rang. "The Super Dux is on the line," an aide said nervously.

The prime minister clicked it on speaker as his loyal senior staff circled around the conference table.

The Super Dux's voice boomed, "I'm sure by now you know the seriousness of my intent to occupy Jerusalem and protect the temple. This Saturday at six o'clock, I personally will occupy the holy of holies in the temple."

Angry murmurs erupted in the room.

"Why, Super Dux?" the prime minister asked coldly, waving his hand to quiet his people.

"Because, the Prophet will be presenting a game-changing event that will solidify my rule. The world, particularly the Jews, need to hear and see it. All media worldwide have been alerted to cover the events at the temple. Do not interfere. Am I making myself clear?"

Most in the room knew what event he was referring to. It was part of prophesy they had come to believe. The shattering event would be televised and many more would come to believe in the Super Dux's powers.

After he hung up with the Super Dux, the prime minister called the meeting to order. "As you know, we are hurtling toward the end of the world as we know it. I am not expecting any of you to continue to work, particularly when it really doesn't matter anymore. It will only be a matter of time and whim when the Super Dux decides to exercise his authority to kill you. I expect he will start his persecution shortly after his display of power. Too many of our people have joined his side and we don't have the forces to protect those without the mark. Only God can according to His will. This is the time you should spend in prayer with your families. I appreciate your support and I ask that God protect you. For those of you who wish, be at my home Saturday. We can watch the horror together, then I urge you to find shelter. We still have some time before the end."

As they left the room, those with the mark were standing outside glaring at them.

"You cannot continue to exclude us from your meetings, Prime Minister," Benjamin warned. "I have been directed to keep the Super Dux informed of all of your activities."

"Benjamin," the prime minister answered, "I don't care what the Super Dux wants." Moshe Ben-Zion left the room. There was no point in continuing the charade of government.

That Saturday, Israel and the world were waiting with excited anticipation for the evening news. With great fanfare, a large crate had been forklifted into the holy of holies earlier in the day amid violent protests from practicing Jews and counterprotests from those who had the mark 666. Many were injured in the melee, but the Federation security forces quickly controlled the crowds.

Inside the temple, crews were feverishly running cables and setting up lights. One wall of the holy of holies had been knocked down to accommodate seating for dignitaries, VIPs, and Federation leaders that survived the earthquake.

Giant monitors were set outside the temple and enormous crowds filled the area. TV trucks and commentators were sprinkled throughout the throng, and only a handful of important reporters with their crews were allowed inside coverage.

The guests, fortunate enough to be invited inside, walked the red carpet to the entrance of the temple as photographers jostled one another for the perfect shot. Inside they chatted excitedly, drinking rare champagne while waiting for the moment that would shake the world.

The time had arrived. The Prophet walked to the center of the holy of holies where, in place of the Mercy Seat, stood a tall object covered in a drape.

The room quieted to silence.

"Greetings from our leader, Super Dux Marcus Junius, who was killed yet came back to life. What you are about to witness, will change your world, and give you the ultimate understanding of the power of our leader. You will know that he is worthy to be worshipped and venerated. Only he will save this world!" The Prophet spread his arms to the towering form. "People of the world, I give you the power of the Super Dux!"

With that, the drape was snatched up high without human effort and hovered in the air like a billowing cloud. The audience in the temple, those outside on the streets watching giant monitors, and the people around the world watching TV were smitten dumb as they gazed at the ten-foot statue in the exact likeness of Marcus Junius. To the great fear and awe of all, the statue was a fluid form of human flesh and bronze-like material. It stretched out its arms, spread its hands wide, and smiled benevolently upon the camera lenses and the people. Then the kind stare turned hard and piercing as a reptile's unblinking eyes. There was no doubt the image was Marcus Junius, Super Dux, in supernatural form.

People fell to their knees and cowered in fear and in reverence as light danced off his fingertips and swirled around the room, landing on people and dissolving into many colors and shapes.

"I am your god," he boomed. "You will have no other god before me. I will satisfy all of your needs, but I command complete and total worship. You will all bow down before me now!"

Inside, men in tuxedos, women in gowns dropped to their knees and cowered, sneaking peeks at the talking and moving statue. Outside, the people fell to their knees and in fear bowed their heads as the Federation guards aimed their weapons at the crowd. One woman, without the mark, continued to stand. A sharp report of a rifle brought her down. The crowd did not move.

"Anyone who does not obey will be killed, for I am all powerful and knowing. I am the sovereign ruler of the planet!" The statue spread its legs, put its hands on its hips, and turned to survey the crowd with laser-like eyes. Those who stole a glance at the creature were mesmerized. Whatever the being was, it was not a hologram, robot, or human-constructed wonder. It was a miracle!

The prime minister, Chief of Staff Levi Gur, and others who elected to meet together in the prime minister's home watched in stunned silence. Levi picked up the Bible and read, *"He ordered the people to make a great statue of the first beast, who was fatally wounded and then came back to life. He was then permitted to give life to this statue so that it could speak. Then the statue of the beast commanded that anyone refusing to worship it must die."* Holding the book open he said softly, "Friends, this is directly from the book of Revelation 13, verses 14 and 15. There's more." He flipped to the book of Matthew 24:16–22, and began, *"Jesus was telling his disciples, 'Then those in Judea must flee to the hills. A person out on the deck of a roof must not go down into the house to pack. A person out in the field must not return even to get a coat. How terrible it will be for pregnant women and for nursing mothers in those days. And pray that your flight will not be in winter or on the Sabbath. For there will be greater anguish than at any time since the world began. And it will never be so great again. In fact, unless that time of calamity is shortened, not a single person will survive. But it will be shortened for the sake of God's chosen ones.'* Some say Jesus was referring to the destruction of the temple by the Romans nearly forty years after His death, but many say that Jesus was referring to what is happening now," Levi said as he closed the Bible.

"What shall we do?" one of the younger women cried in deep distress. "I have little ones!"

"I don't know," the prime minister answered. "Get out of the city. Try to find a safe place, but do not go north. In the near, very near future, that will be where the last battle will be fought, but armies will come from all sides. I hope the Lord will keep us all safe, according to His will." He sighed greatly. "Run all of you, and hide! But first, let's pray: Father God, we come before your throne in the name of Jesus, and recognize you as the triune God of Father, Son, and Holy Spirit. We have sinned by not believing and going against your commands that are perfect and just. Now, in these end times, we see the error of our own imaginations. We were wrong. We humbly ask to be forgiven of our many, many sins. We know that Jesus died for us on the cross as a perfect sacrifice beyond lambs, bulls, and rams of our ancient heritage."

Moshe Ben-Zion, the man who would soon be deposed, held out his hands, tears running down his cheeks. "Lord, we are so grateful for your work in redeeming those who believe and those who ask for forgiveness. We know you love us. In that knowledge and confidence, we ask you to give us courage as we soon face persecution and even death. We pray that your Holy Spirit will guide us and give us strength. For we know you, Jesus, are our Savior, Messiah, King of Kings, and Lord of Lords!"

"Maranatha." Levi wept too.

Before they left the room, they hugged and kissed one another, praying for God's blessings and protection. They would all see each other sooner than later, someone softly joked.

Monday, Benjamin looked disdainfully through the papers strewn across the prime minister's desk. "You traitor!" he spit out as he looked through a synopsis about end-times prophecy. Not bothering to read it, he crumpled it up and threw it in the wastebasket. He had been promoted into the prime minister's place to oversee what was left of the governing powers and to reorganize the staff, aides, cabinet, and ministries. It was time to get the Israeli house in order according to the Super Dux and the Federation's directives. Many Jews were going to be persecuted, particularly those without the mark and those sympathetic and loyal to Prime Minister Moshe Ben-Zion's government. They were dead men, women, and families.

It was going to be an enormous task, but Benjamin was young and ambitious. Turning on his computer to create a new organizational chart, he suddenly winced and touched the side of his face. Aghast, he looked at his fingertips coated in blood. Horrified, he went into the prime minister's private bathroom and looked at himself in the mirror. In his shock, he backed out of the room and stumbled into the outer offices where others were gasping in their own horror and pain. Erupting on all who had the mark *666* were rancid oozing sores. The smell was intense; many gagged at their own stench.

Benjamin didn't read the Bible verse that stated, *Ugly, festering sores broke out on the people who had the mark of the beast and worshiped its image.* It was crumpled up in the wastebasket.

"We must get to a hospital!" someone pleaded, not able to even dab at the blood dripping down their exposed skin. The sores were that painful.

Another cried out, "Please, call the house doctor to come to our offices!" Frightened and in pain, people ran from the room and jammed the hallways to get to the infirmary.

Benjamin, also dealing with the painful oozing sores, kept a clear head and hastened to call the Super Dux. Something was dreadfully wrong. Maybe there was a contagion that permeated the government offices. Was this a plot by prime minister's supporters? The Super Dux must be informed of what was happening in Israel's high offices.

"Benjamin, what is going on?" Roberto demanded. "We expected a report from you by now."

"I . . . I don't know where to begin! We have an outbreak of sores of some kind and—"

Marcus jumped on the speaker phone. "I'm not interested in your health, Benjamin. I want to know about the prime minister and his followers. What happened when they saw the miracle of my likeness talking and moving like a god?"

"I don't know how they reacted. They never showed up at the unveiling."

"They didn't? Where are they?" the Super Dux demanded.

"I don't know. At an earlier meeting, those with your mark were not allowed in, so we don't know what was said or what they have planned."

"You don't know?" screamed Marcus. "You let them conduct a meeting without you?"

Benjamin gasped in pain. "We had no choice. We . . . " He didn't know what to say. He didn't have a proper excuse. The pain was spreading across his body, hindering his concentration and focus. "But, Super Dux, something—"

"Stop, Benjamin. I'm putting you on hold."

As Benjamin waited, he worried about the sores that were affecting everyone.

The Super Dux came back on the line. "Turn on the TV."

As Benjamin went into the meeting room, the monitors were already on and running including various TV stations. He clicked on the speaker phone.

"Benjamin, I want a press release sent to all media based on the words of the major network news commentators," the Super Dux demanded. "The media are calling me a god! Everyone in Israel and the world must be made aware of this!"

Benjamin could hear the Super Dux clapping his hands in joy. He also heard him say, "Roberto, what's on your face?"

"I'm not sure," came an answer. "It just started to happen. They're erupting on everyone in our office."

"Maybe it's from all the dust from the meteor that exploded," the Super Dux said absently, concentrating on his victory of being acknowledged as a god.

"That's what I've been trying to tell you!" Benjamin interjected over the phone. "We all have these disgusting painful sores. Can you heal us?" he asked desperately.

"I'll get back with you on that, but in the meantime get the press release to all media, and find out who is with or against me in the Israeli government!" The Super Dux hung up.

A few hours later, Benjamin came back from the doctor's office.

"What's happening to us, Benjamin?" a coworker said miserably, touching his face.

"I called the Federation physicians and they don't know what causes the sores. Then I went to the doctor at our own clinic. He took a biopsy, but he has several on his face and hands too. They're so painful and drugs help little!" He could barely think he was in so much pain. "So far no one knows what's causing the outbreaks. It's happening all over." Under his breath he added, "To everyone who has the mark."

CHAPTER SEVENTEEN
THE FAMILY

"OWE, YOU'RE HURTING ME! STOP!" a man wailed.

"No, I've got to clean these up or they'll get infected! Look what happened to Linda. She can't walk she's such a mess!"

Jason spied four ragged people in a small field. One man was slowly and painfully building a fire beside a rusty, dented trailer, one woman was standing over a man, and a third—he couldn't tell if it was a man or woman—was sitting deathly still in a chair. The woman was dabbing something on the man's face and he screamed out in excruciating pain each time she touched him. Jason got out his binoculars. Crouching behind thick bushes, he found an opening and peered closely at the foursome.

The woman's hand was partially wrapped in a dirty white bandage that was stained with blood and was gently wiping the face of a man covered with oozing sores. He was moaning in pain, but she persisted. He looked over at the other two. The one who was trying to build the fire had sores on his face and hands too. The other one, a woman Jason discovered, was propped up in a low lawn chair. She too was covered with sores and her exposed legs were wrapped in sticky, bloody bandages. He was downwind from them and he could smell them from where he was hiding. Through the bloodied sores, he could just make out the marks of *666*, on each one's forehead. They had taken the mark of the Beast. He remembered in the book of Revelation that sores would erupt on everyone who took the mark.

Backing away, he hurried along a dirt road. Many miles and hours later, he came to another double-wide trailer. He heard the sound of whimpering, and deftly picked through trash to get closer to the sound. Underneath the trailer by a nearly empty bowl of stagnant water was a skinny little dog. When she saw Jason, she crawled on her belly, grousing at his feet.

The door to the double-wide was closed, but he could smell the unmistakable scent of death. He and his friends had come across this so often in their travels. Sadly, it was the main way they were now getting their food: from the homes of dead people. Gingerly he opened the door and to his dismay, he saw a man and woman, in the early stages of decomposition sitting on a coach, dead from gunshot wounds. It looked like a murder-suicide. Each had the mark of *666*, and was covered with sores.

Jason covered his mouth and looked around. The dog whimpered and backed off the little porch and down the steps. She trembled on the walkway.

Looking back at the dog, he thought how hungry and thirsty she must be. Skirting the bodies, he walked into the small dirty kitchen and rummaged through the cabinets. He hated going into homes where people were lying rotting, but it was the only way they could survive. They each took turns daily to widen the circle of homes they could safely target for food. But lately, they were coming across more and more people who were either murdered, or who killed themselves, or who were just plain dead.

Today he came across a treasure trove of canned goods, bottled water, and some old newspapers. He would bring his friends back to load up, but in the meanwhile, he gave the dog some kibble and water and put as much as he could into his sack. Grabbing all he could carry, he made his way to the walkway. The dog followed him. What could he do? They would either eat, or all starve together. "C'mon, pooch."

Back at the little cabin, Joanna was working in the garden. The seeds they collected had yielded a small crop that wasn't ready for harvest yet, but they were looking forward to fresh tomatoes. She stood up as Jason approached and James, who was fixing the roof, saw him lugging a heavy satchel with a little black dog following at his heels.

Climbing down from the roof, he went to meet Jason and help take his load of bounty. "Where did you find the dog? We haven't seen animals for so long!"

It was true. They had been on the run for what seemed like forever.

"This little one was hiding under a house, half-starved and thirsty. I didn't have the heart to leave her. It was another house with dead people."

"Well, I could complain we don't have enough to feed ourselves, but at the moment we do and God put her in our path, so she's welcome." James smiled sadly while patting the little dog that was wagging her tail wildly.

"Ooooh! A dog! How wonderful!" cried Joanna as she ran from her garden. "Oh, how I've missed seeing animals. Look at this little one! What a doll!" Joanna hugged and kissed the dog, not able to hide her tears. "I would never have imagined missing animals so much!"

Jason said, "I've found a jackpot. We need to go back and get the rest of the food. There's lots of it. They were probably prepping. We should go before someone else finds it."

"Should we go now? Or wait 'til tomorrow?" Joanna asked.

"Guys, I'm really tired. I walked miles and hours," replied Jason. "How 'bout we go tomorrow?"

"Sure. Let's hide this in the cellar." They had dug one shortly after deciding to use the cabin as a permanent home.

"Hey, James, I came across more people with the mark in a small clearing in the woods and they have sores all over their bodies! I don't think they're going to be around long either. They were really sick. I found this too." Jason laid a newspaper down. The headlines screamed, *Two Witnesses Dead!* "This is an old paper, but it's still good news. It's all falling into place just as prophesied."

"If you discovered people with sores, that means that the false prophet erected a statue of the Antichrist in the temple in Jerusalem. It means that those people, who worshipped it and have the mark of the Beast, will get awful, painful, gross sores. It is happening now!" exclaimed Joanna.

Jason said quietly, "Yes, and there are other prophesies that yet need to be fulfilled. Pray we can make it 'til Jesus comes!"

A distant series of booms went off. Nervously, they looked at one another.

"We've been hearing that for a couple of days now," Joanna whispered.

"Don't worry. Whatever it is, it's very far away," James said confidently.

The next day, with Pooch safe in the cabin, Jason took Joanna and James to the double-wide trailer. They didn't get there until the afternoon because Pooch got out in the morning and disappeared. They dared not call too loudly, but she didn't respond. Jason refused to leave until she came back. She wandered back before noon, exhausted.

"She must have been on a scent. Maybe the animals are coming back," Joanna said hopefully as she put the dog in the cabin.

"Maybe, but we need to keep an eye on her. We can't have her wandering off," Jason said. "I don't want to lose her after all we've been through."

Once they arrived at the trailer, they pulled scarves over their noses and mouths to combat the smell. By this time maggots and flies were all over the bodies.

Joanna tried not to look. "Guys, we've got to get as many supplies as we can carry and leave. We can come back tomorrow for the rest."

The three knew they had to come back and get as much as they could, but they were always afraid of being discovered. The people in the trailer were probably dead for a several days and others might come looking for them. Jason wondered, was it worth the risk?

"Maybe it's worth the risk," James said, as if reading Jason's mind. "But I think we need to bury the bodies."

"Yes," Jason said. "And if we bury the bodies and camouflage the graves, then whoever might come looking for them will think they're gone, particularly if the dog is gone too."

"Okay. Let's do it, but I'm not sure we should this late in the afternoon. We can't see a thing out there now," Joanna pointed out.

"I agree," James said. "The late morning will be better and give us enough light to bury the bodies and hide the graves."

Walking through the woods on the way back was difficult because the moon and stars gave weak light. Jason had a lantern, but they hesitated to use it in case someone saw them. But after tripping and falling over broken limbs and rocks, James finally said, "We'll have to take the chance. I can't see a thing. Maybe we should camp in the woods. Otherwise one of us is going to get hurt and it's probably going to be me!"

"We've left Pooch alone long enough. We've got to get back home. Let's take our chances and use the lantern," Joanna argued.

Jason lit the lantern and turned it down low. "It looks like a giant firefly," he said. "Do you remember them as a kid? I do. They were so cool. We would try and catch them, but one of my aunts wouldn't let us. She said they needed to be free."

Suddenly, they felt the ground shudder beneath their feet and they heard muffled booms in the distance. "There are the booms again, the ones we've been hearing for days," Joanna whispered to herself, trying to contain her fear. Aloud she said, "Is it possible our cities are being attacked?"

"I don't know. We're too far away from any large city to be threatened, but with weaponry as sophisticated as it is, anything is possible," Jason said, thinking how afraid they were when they first started to hear the distant explosions.

Later, they agreed that they were safe, provided no one was using nuclear or chemical weapons. Then ear-shattering roars filled the sky as fighter jets raced across the sky.

"Where did they come from?" Joanna cried in alarm and instinctively ducked.

"Don't worry, we're safe," Jason said comfortingly, patting her shoulder and helping her to straighten up.

"I hope," added James as he looked up at the black sky.

They made it home safely, but each had their own prayers for safety, deliverance, and hope.

Back at the trailer the next morning, they covered themselves in coats from the deceased, put on gloves they found in a closet, and wrapped towels around their heads. They smeared gobs of Vicks VapoRub under their noses and tied clean cloth napkins around their mouths. Trying not to retch, they wrapped the bodies, now flaccid, in blankets and bedspreads, and dragged them out of the house.

Outside, away from the trailer, the two men found shovels and dug two shallow graves while Joanna kept watch. Carefully dragging the bodies through the tall grass, avoiding tossed-out trash, they dumped them in the holes and covered them with dirt, trash, and brush. The graves blended in with the terrain.

"Should we say a prayer?" Joanna asked tentatively.

"Let's say a prayer for ourselves. These two poor souls are lost. They have the mark of the Beast. Let's pray," James said and bowed his head. "Father God, we ask forgiveness for not believing, for doing things that were against Your will, and for thinking sin was all a part of life. Even now we still sin because we are only human. In this we ask forgiveness. We try to do better with Your help and guidance from Your Holy Spirit. Father God, we beg You to send Jesus soon to rescue His remnant here on earth. We so look forward to a new earth and new heaven! Please protect us while we wait for His return. We are eager to see Him in the sky coming to destroy the prince of this world, the Antichrist and his false prophet! We wait for Him to rescue us, His prodigal children. Father, we pray this all in Jesus' name!"

"Amen."

Quickly, they made their way back to the trailer to continue to pack up supplies. Joanna saw a TV in the kitchen and wished there was electricity. She wanted to know what was going on. The muffled explosions they were hearing indicated something was happening. Jason and James left her to pack and went outside.

Minutes later, Jason poked his head into the kitchen and said, "Joanna, come quick!"

Outside, James was fiddling with a generator. "I've gassed 'er up and want to see if she runs. If so, we can get some electricity and see if we can get the TV going."

"Oh, man, I don't know. These things are so loud. Suppose someone hears?" Jason worried.

They both looked to Joanna. "I'm concerned too," she said. "But we've covered miles of this area and found no one. And even those people Jason saw, that were covered with sores, were hours away and are in no shape to walk through the woods to find out where the sound is coming from. I don't think they can hear it." Looking closely at the generator, Joanna asked, "If it works, maybe we could turn it on just for five or ten minutes?"

It worked. They ran into the kitchen and switched on the TV. It came to life, but the images frequently pixilated or froze and the sound was scratchy. After minutes of straining to follow the sound and images, Joanna shouted in frustration, "I can't make out what's going on!"

"I think we were in a war. It sounds like a world war, and there's been global destruction," Jason said. The commentator's report was confusing and fragmented, but the gist was, vast numbers of the population had perished.

"God's sixth trumpet judgment says that a third of mankind will be killed," exclaimed James as he struggled to hear the reporter's words drowning in static.

The video went to a street in New York City and showed a reporter shoving a microphone under the nose of a man hurrying down a smoky roadway, arms full of packages.

"Sir, sir, can you tell me what you are doing?" the reporter screamed.

The man gaped at him and shouted, "Can't you see we've been bombed? Are you crazy you don't know our desperation?"

The reporter continued to interview people on the street, who were blatantly looting stores and filling their arms, bags, and children's wagons with goods.

"We need food! We need clothing! We need water!" they howled and rushed from the camera.

One man stopped and said, "It's every man for himself. Can't you see we've had enough? We've had to deal with a polluted atmosphere, horrible sores, toxic water, no fresh food. Now our cities have been bombed! Look, this was once a huge city!" the man opened his arms expansively. "Now it's rubble! And we don't even know who's attacking us! The Super Dux has done nothing to help or protect us!" He ran away, dragging a nearly empty cart.

"After all the horrors that have occurred over these many years, no one thought to guess that these disastrous events were warnings from God," James said quietly, then told Jason to shut off the generator. Joanna wanted to hear more, but James said, "Why? It looks like cities have been attacked including New York. The great Babylon." He sighed. "Why listen? It's getting close to the end of the world. We knew this from the start, Joanna. This is the sixth trumpet judgment. One more to go before the Lord comes."

In fear, but elation, they looked at one another.

"Can it be?" whispered Joanna.

Before the TV went dead, a woman screamed to the reporter, "If God is hearing me, I curse Him for bringing so much anguish on the face of the earth! We deserve to be treated better!" The screen froze and faded out. The noise of the generator stopped.

Jason wandered back in. "It doesn't make sense. You think the people would understand what's been going on by now. How can so many awful things occur in nearly the seven years since their so-named Vaporization happened, and the people don't relate that maybe, just maybe, the disappearances were in fact the rapture? And maybe these crazy disasters happening could be God's judgments? Don't they see the hand of God in all this? Why don't they see it?"

"Jason, you know better than to ask that question. So many people, including us and your own family, didn't get what God was all about," Joanna said gently.

"They're probably dead by now," he answered, thinking of his family. "They would never have been able to survive the smallest disaster, let alone a major catastrophe."

"It's sad, but you can't dwell on events or people you can't change. You can tell them about the Lord, but you can't make them believe," Joanna replied.

"Yes, I know. The only person we can depend upon is Jesus and He's coming soon to rescue us. And you know what? It doesn't matter if we don't make it. One way or the other we'll be with Him."

"And I'm looking forward to it!" Joanna smiled. "The three of us have been given a second chance."

James chuckled. "I remember a Christian friend of mine named Jerome said, 'You can't kill a Christian. You can only change his address!'"

This was why they weren't rooted in fear. Indeed, they were scared, many times hungry, and sometimes sick and weak, but knowing they were going to be saved and live eternally with the King of Kings was the only assurance they needed.

"Let's go," Joanna said. "There's still more stuff we can use, but we can come back. Let's get out of here and go home."

CHAPTER EIGHTEEN

THE UNITED STATES

DANNY POWELL, STILL CHIEF OF staff, looked out the window as he flew to Dover, Delaware, one of the few areas that was still intact after the horrific Asian coalition attack. Years ago, Dover was designated as an emergency second executive office and residence for the president and his senior staff in the event of an attack on the White House. Who cared about Dover? It was hardly strategic.

The president, his staff, and senior aides had barely escaped the attack on Washington, DC, by hiding in a deep subterranean bunker designed specifically in the event of an emergency. It also housed a small heliport. They were not able to escape the White House grounds in time, but once the fighting stopped, they emerged from the bunker and were now traveling to Dover via helicopter.

Looking down through the haze, Danny was stunned at the absolute destruction. DC and New York City had been attacked at the same time. The nation's capital and its massive, ornate buildings were reduced to rubble. The Lincoln Memorial, the Washington Monument, the Vietnam Memorial, on and on, were destroyed, along with the White House. The buildings of the Smithsonian, the precious artifacts, documents, art, jewels—anything and everything—were in ruins, gone forever, never to be replaced. The airports were bombed, as was the Pentagon.

A dense gray fog hung over the city. It was to be hushed and insignificant for ever more. It was pitiful. Thankfully, no nuclear weaponry was used in the United States.

"I can't believe what I'm seeing." Danny's voice cracked.

"It's beyond comprehension," President Sarratt said, barely audible, looking out over vast miles of smoking destruction. All he had hoped for, all he had attained, was wiped out. A city of immeasurable power was no longer.

Danny turned to his president. "What will happen? The seat of power is gone. All federal government is extinguished. And New York . . . gone too. I can't grasp it all." He sat in shock, staring out over the ruins.

"We have some redundant systems in Dover, but only those crucial to immediate command, control, and communication systems," the president said with shaky reassurance. "I'm waiting for an update on our military losses and will brief the Super Dux on Washington's destruction. He also wants to know about New York City. We can't give him that info until we assess it." President Sarratt, too, was in shock. The United States for all practical purposes now held little value. The Super Dux demanded to know the condition of New York City and the state of the US military. He didn't care about Washington.

The attack against the Federation, to include the United States, was swift but brief. As in Washington, DC, most of New York City was pulverized. And like DC, the significance and importance of the city was to be no more. Wall Street and the American Stock Exchange were bombed out. Times Square with all her vibrancy and flashing marquees was in shards. Infrastructure was destroyed, the Holland Tunnel collapsed, and the fanciful colors of the Metropolitan Life Insurance Company Tower would never be lit again. The Statue of Liberty rested in pieces in the harbor; the Trump Tower was wreckage; the Empire State Building, a memory—all the landmarks of the city, decimated. People were scattered, wounded, and dying. A great city once known for its power, fame, wealth, and trade was now a starving commoner looking for a crust of bread. All hope and joy of gaining wealth and power were extinguished as bombs dropped and rockets were fired.

The president's entourage made it safely to their Dover compound, but it wasn't until weeks later when roads were semicleared around New Jersey and New York that the president and his minimal staff could make their way to New York City to assess the wreckage for the Super Dux. It was impossible to get a helicopter landing where they needed to go. They had to travel by armored SUV. The president and his chief of staff sat quietly in physical and mental pain as their driver circumvented crashed cars, toppled buildings, and twisted debris littering the roadways.

President Sarratt's first stop was to visit the mayor of New York City, who lay critically injured in a hospital in New Jersey. "We have no resources to rebuild the city," the president told the mayor, who remained semiconscious. "Our country relies on the Super Dux and the unity of the Federation countries, and although the Federation military stopped the attackers by detonating two nuclear devices in Syria and Iraq, the Asia coalition was still able to strike us with a deadly blow. The other Federation nations were hit hard too, but they will rebuild and restructure those nations. As for us? We must rethink how our nation can survive."

The mayor could barely talk. Sores covered his face. He had been buried under debris of City Hall for twenty-four hours. With multiple broken bones, a punctured lung, and a concussion, there was little he could add or discuss with the president. He was in far too much pain. There was nothing to say anyway. His city was never to be again. He was unlikely to survive.

Danny lightly touched President Sarratt's sleeve. "The TV crews are outside. They're looking for a statement."

Leaving the room, the president smoothed his hair, looked into a hand mirror to be sure no sores were oozing through his bandages, and followed Danny to the media room in the hospital. This was the moment he was dreading. Without the support of the Super Dux and the Federation, the United States was impotent. A sea of lights was directed at his face, a wall of microphones was set up on the podium, and before him were scores of reporters wrapped in their own bandages and drugged with painkillers.

"The attack is over. The nuclear devices the Federation exploded in Syria and Iraq put the brakes on the aggressors. Until we get full reports, I can only say some Far Eastern and Middle Eastern countries formed the Asian coalition that attacked the United States and the Federation nations." Adjusting a bandage on his hand, he continued, "The United States is in a place it has never been before." He paused, quickly thinking how his dream of power and alignment with the Super Dux was now in jeopardy. Without New York, the United States was nothing. "We are entering a new age. No longer are powerful and influential people living in major cities that are able to lead and mold the country. With California, and now New York, fallen we must restructure with the resources we have left. However, it doesn't mean we can't rise from the ashes. After the terrorist attack of 9-11, another leader said, *'The bricks have fallen, but we will build with dressed stones; the sycamores have been cut down, but we will put cedars in their place.'*"

A female reporter nudged a male reporter and whispered, "That quote is from the book of Isaiah in the Bible. Odd, wouldn't you say? Do you think our dear president, or the previous leader, had any clue who they were quoting and the context? Do you know what the following verses are?"

The male reporter shook his head no, not interested.

At that moment Danny whispered into the president's ear.

The female reporter took the opportunity to further her conversation. "I carry this around with me all the time." She dug a well-worn piece of paper from the side pocket of her purse and gave it to the man to read. He still wasn't interested, but he read it anyway.

"*The bricks have fallen down,*
But we will rebuild with hewn stones;
The sycamores are cut down,
But we will replace them with cedars."
Therefore the Lord shall set up
The adversaries of Rezin against him,
And spur his enemies on,
The Syrians before and the Philistines behind;
And they shall devour Israel with an open mouth.
For all this His anger is not turned away,
But His hand is stretched out still.
For the people do not turn to Him who strikes them,
Nor do they seek the Lord of hosts.
Therefore the Lord will cut off head and tail from Israel,
Palm branch and bulrush in one day."

"What does it mean? I don't understand it." The male reporter shoved the piece of paper back to her.

Before she could answer, the president spoke up. "The mayor of New York has succumbed to his injuries."

There was a polite groan from the press corps. "Another good story," chirped the reporter with a camera. "If it bleeds, it leads." Overall, they were delighted to be getting a treasure trove of reports, for they had an abundance of news for nearly seven years, since the Vaporization and the recent events were just getting more dramatic and intense. Some were starting to think that all of these disasters might mean something, but the majority thought them cyclical or an anomaly. Commentators swathed in bandages and gloves to hide the nasty sores filled the radio and television stations, which were now few and far between, but of those, they were intent and gleeful in spouting their views of the ongoing crises. In all this, with the exception of those in hiding without the mark, they wouldn't attribute the events to the power of God. And if they did, they cursed Him for either sending these calamities to earth, or cursed Him for not helping to stop them. No one with the mark looked to these horrors as warnings or judgments. Their sights were all set on the Super Dux, his power, and how he, their new god, would lead them.

President Sarratt continued, lying, "The Federation and the great and awesome power of the Super Dux will save us. It might seem like an overwhelming task to reorganize, but with the supernatural power of our god Marcus Junius, whom we all worship, we will be strong again!"

Great cheers rose from the reporters and spectators as the telecast was seen around the country by those who still had access to the limited networks and internet.

Danny led the president and his entourage to waiting armored SUVs in the dusky light of day for their trip back to Dover. Haze filled the foreboding sky, along with oily particles and thick dust that swirled about. The damage the bombs and missiles made was tremendous. Bodies were being pulled from the wreckages only to be piled together to be burned. There were so few able workers left. Those that were, worked in the half-light of the day, plodding painfully around huge chunks of broken buildings, their faces and hands wrapped in filthy cloth.

"It's like watching a zombie movie," Danny commented to the president. "We're all covered in bandages, emaciated, and sick. We're the living dead." His phone rang. Answering it, he turned to the president, who was lying back against the seat cushions willing the pain from the sores on his body to quiet. "Mr. President?" Danny said in defeat. "It's being reported that the oceans have been hit with red tide." He shook his head in disbelief. "It's a mass kill of fish. It's happening globally."

"The food chain is slowly being destroyed. We have little produce because of the lack of sun and clean air. To irrigate, we must use polluted water. Our herds have starved from lack of pasture or supplemental feed, or they've died from poisoned water and disease. Wildlife has all but disappeared because of the wild fires and other disasters that have happened, and now we've lost our salt water fish. You watch. Next the fresh water fish will be killed off." President Sarratt took a pill without water, grimacing as he swallowed it. "As if this helps. Even morphine doesn't work!"

Danny knew that not many would continue to survive under these ongoing conditions. "What's to become of us Mr. President?" he asked hopelessly.

"I don't know," President Sarratt answered truthfully. "The Super Dux has made it clear that New York, while important at one time, is not now. He has no intention to rebuild, and why should he with so many dead? The shakers of the city have been extinguished. Trading, selling, buying, celebrating—all a thing of the past."

A phone buzzed. The president fumbled in his pocket. Cell phone capability was sporadic. He had special communications throughout his vehicles and offices, but was only able to occasionally link up to satellite communications since so many had been shot out of the sky. "President Sarratt, an update. We didn't have enough firepower to successfully mobilize against the air attacks . . . as you know," the secretary of defense reported. "And the Federation forces weren't able to help because of the attacks on their side of the pond."

"Tell me something I don't know," the president uttered. He knew the military had been in decline since President Foster was assassinated. When he agreed to disband the House and the Senate along with the cabinet and other departments, the Federation took direct control over the Department of Defense to keep the military from becoming a threat to the Super Dux's rule. They barely kept it functional with meager funding. So before the attack, the United States military was a shell of what it once was. The president was surprised they were as successful as they were defending the country in this unprecedented violent aggression. "Secretary, I am on my way now to Dover. I would like you and your staff to get there as soon as possible. We have much to discuss." He clicked off.

Danny said, "If there is a God, where is He in all of this? Why would He do this to people? Clearly, the nations won't be able to recover their economies with what's left of people and resources if these wars and natural disasters don't stop. Starvation and disease are claiming the few that are left."

"I think you've answered your own question, Danny. There's no God. There's only the Super Dux."

"What will he do for the world now?" Danny demanded. "How will he deal with the vestiges of war throughout most of the country? He can't control nature. The days are depressingly dark, and the nights are without even scant light. How long could the human race continue under these conditions?"

President Sarratt gave Danny a long look. In another place and time, he would severely reprimand Danny for traitorous talk, but he had his own thoughts and questions to deal with. He needed to get to Europe, become a permanent member of the Super Dux's inner circle. He would have food, shelter, and a piece of power, of that he was sure. He would find a place in Rome and leave the United States to fend for itself. There was nothing worth ruling here, now. There was nothing to stay for. His wife and son died from drinking deadly water, and over half his staff were dead from one thing or another. It was time to leave a country that in short order would implode. If he could, he would take Danny. He owed him that much.

As the group arrived at Dover and entered the governmental offices, an aide hurried up to the president. "We have drastic news concerning fresh water."

"Again! I knew it!" The president turned away in disgust to Danny. "I called it, didn't I? Did I not say that the next disaster would probably be on fresh water? We were already hit once, when the meteor exploded over the earth and contaminated open water! Now, just when the water is getting a bit clean, it's happened again! Well, at least we had the forethought to be prepared! We have collected and stored billions of gallons of water in our warehouses."

"I doubt many others are prepared unless they have a covered cistern or a supply of prebottled water," Danny said, thinking of the already dwindling supplies of bottled water. Even now, rogue groups of citizens were combing the more rural areas for wells and cisterns.

"There's nothing we can do, Danny. We've got to get guards all around the perimeter of the property and protect what little supplies we have, particularly the water." The president's residence and that of his staff was part of a mansion that was used for their governmental offices. Because of destroyed homes, offices, and loss of life, the president decided to consolidate living and working accommodations with those that were still able to work.

As he sat on the balcony, waiting for the rest of his staff to arrive, to include the secretary of defense, he began planning his flight to Rome when Danny came through the open doorway.

"Do you see what I see?" Danny asked the president with excitement in his voice. The sun was poking through the gloom.

"Yes, it's the sun!" the president responded in delight, closing down his notebook. Until he knew he could take Danny with him, he didn't want his chief of staff to know he was planning on leaving the US permanently as soon as he could. "Finally! Maybe things are changing and turning around. We won't be living in constant gloom and darkness. We'll finally have our days back!"

As they watched the day brighten, they welcomed the warmth of the sun. The guards looked around in happiness and turned their gray faces to the sky. The gloom of the days had plunged every human being into despair and ultimately, severe depression. The sun now hung like a fiery orb in the sky, sending out its light and warmth.

Like the guards, the people on the streets basked in the sun's rays, enjoying this amazing event, but as the minutes wore on, the heat became increasingly warm.

"It's like the days of summer," Danny said to the president. "Remember when the cold and bleak winter days were far behind and spring and summer were upon us? The sun would come out and the days would get hotter."

"I remember it well," the president answered. "Everyone would ultimately complain about the heat and humidity! We humans don't like it too hot or too cold. Just right!"

Danny didn't want to admit concern, but the heat was getting increasingly uncomfortable, maybe because they weren't used to it. They hadn't seen a sunny day in a few years.

"I don't know, Danny. This is getting extreme." The president took off his tie and unbuttoned his shirt. He looked below at the guards, who were now seeking shade.

"Something's not right. This is scorching!" Danny made for the doorway.

They couldn't look toward the sun now. It was searing. Quickly they went inside. Minutes later they were surrounded by staff that were already severely burned, complaining loudly in their pain as blisters erupted on their exposed skin. The remaining sores that so many still had were burned black.

"It wasn't enough we had to endure these awful sores, and now we are being burned alive!" A staffer hurried to find first aid cream for everyone.

"Turn on the news if we can get a signal. It seems we get more information from TV than our own intelligence groups," another staff member said. The TV came on as a newscaster was urging everyone to stay indoors. The welcome sight of the sun, after the extended period of time of reduced light, had taken a deadly turn. The weather forecaster was at a loss to explain.

As the staff closed windows, drapes, and doors of the president's office and turned on the air conditioner, they railed against yet another awful situation. In their frustration and discomfort, they openly spoke harshly about a supreme being who would do this to the human race. Even the president had to agree. If there was a God, why was He allowing these awful events to continue? What they had expected as a blessing by seeing the sun, turned into a curse! How much more could anyone take?

"God!" an aide shouted in the air. "If You are even there!" he said derisively, "I, for one, want nothing to do with You! You have tormented us for years now. When will it all end?"

Danny left the executive offices to go to the communications' suite. The remaining staff monitoring the few satellites and communication stations dotted throughout the Federation were tracking this latest disaster. "Chief, this is another devastating situation," an analyst moaned. "The sun's intensity is affecting the world. There's no night. Only intense, constant, burning sunshine. We have reports here of people getting third-degree burns. No one has an explanation." He turned back to his monitor as he handed his chief a handful of printouts.

Danny came back with news. "This is mostly anecdotal, because so many of our communications networks are down, but people who were caught outside and unable to get to shelter quickly, were badly burned.

Likely, because of the little available health care we have left, if the burns are severe, they're going to be in trouble. There's no one to help."

"How can anyone control the sun?" the president asked rhetorically. Could the Super Dux? So far he hadn't been able to foresee, let alone control, any of these supernatural events.

An aide came in with a folder and handed it to Danny who slowly opened what he knew was just more bad news. He scanned the one-page document, then mechanically read aloud the concluding paragraph. "The radical shortage of health care workers will only lead to ongoing deaths as time goes on. Plant and animal life that has been exposed will certainly succumb. There are no resources to provide a solution to address the problem." He tossed it in the trash. When the aide left and they were alone, Danny said, "Mr. President, we don't need reports about what we already know. We need to think about our own survival."

"Yes. You're right. I'm not sure how long we can sustain the staff, but we need to take care of ourselves. I'll make arrangements for you and me to get to Rome and join the Super Dux's inner circle."

"How do you expect that to happen? We have nothing the Super Dux would want now that New York is gone."

"We still have our military to barter with and I think that the Federation would see the strategic benefit of having our troops in Europe. The secretary of defense will be here shortly. We'll work out a plan and an attractive package for the secretary's cooperation. Whether Marcus believes it or not, his adversaries will rise again. He's going to need our help coordinating the effort of getting troops mobilized."

He peeked through the drapes. The sun was blazing and heat shimmered off the ground. Night did not come. The sun continued to shine, emitting fierce heat.

CHAPTER NINETEEN

THE FEDERATION

"PRESIDENT SARRATT HAS ASKED TO join our staff here in Rome," Roberto said to Marcus Junius after reading a document on his cell phone, one of the few being served by the Federation's communications satellites. "He also wants Danny, chief of staff, and their secretary of defense to join us too."

"Yes, I know. We had a long talk an hour ago about the condition of the United States, loss of important cities, and with this intense heat and burning rays of the sun, they will not be able to maintain themselves much longer. The country doesn't have much of what we need anymore, other than what's left of the military and, apparently, that's not much. But it's better than nothing. Over half of the population is dead, and any goods or services they had, have dried up. In fact, it's a land of desperate people who are sick, hungry, corrupt, and now burned.

"We are better positioned than the United States to cope with the results from the recent attack by the Asian coalition, but admittedly, we've lost substantial military strength, and with the skirmishes that are ongoing in our own backyard, we could use additional resources," Marcus acknowledged.

He knew some countries of Asia had been rallying against him for some time and were preparing another assault. At least this time the Federation was in better shape to fend off aggression; the United States not so lucky. The detonation of the nuclear weapons by the Federation in the Middle East put a quick end to further aggression, and it was now time to strike Israel when all those against him were in a state of military disarray.

He broke from his inner thoughts and said to Roberto, "The United States has been known for good warriors and President Sarratt is supportive of a program to recruit Americans to the Federation that can still walk and carry a gun. I want what's left of the US Air Force, Army, Navy, National Guard, and Coast Guard—"

"The US Coast Guard was nearly wiped out," Roberto broke in. "And the US Navy was heavily damaged from the massive tsunamis, but anyone who survived and any equipment we can use, we will."

"Gathering the United States forces for our needs is a good job for President Sarratt before he comes here with his chief of staff," the Super Dux said. "I want him to start immediately recruiting able-bodied men from America to Italy. If he needs resources, give it to him. And I want the US armed forces here as soon as possible."

After Roberto left to begin coordinating the task of amassing United States troops for the Federation, the Prophet entered the room.

"Sit down, my Prophet." The Super Dux smiled. "Now is the time we conquer Israel. We will use the consequences of the recent debacle of the Asian coalition attack. What were they thinking? That someone who had nuclear power wouldn't use it to stop them? It's to our advantage this whole situation happened. We can now march through Syria, Lebanon, and Jordan without resistance. We have the strength and the means with new reinforcements from the United States."

"Yes," the Prophet agreed. "It is time to crush the Jews and make our move to rid the world of a population that should have been decimated years ago during the Holocaust!"

"My friend, I have been aiming to wipe them out of existence since I attained power. Between you, me, and our prince of this world, we'll finally reach our goals." He poured himself a brandy and lifted it to the light, appreciating its color. He took a sip and put down the cut crystal goblet. Turning his attention to the Prophet, he admitted, "I've had a few setbacks. The Federation has gone through a lot of distress, but I believe now we're in a position to achieve greatness. We'll place our troops along the mountain range bordering Northern Israel. The plain spread before us will be a perfect area to launch the battle to end all battles! We will annihilate the Jews and anyone who comes against us! We won't fail like Russia and Iran did when they attacked Israel."

"Absolutely," the Prophet heartily agreed, pouring himself a drink too. "The plain is historically significant. So many battles won and lost there. Perfect for the plain of Armageddon!"

Weeks later, the Federation's minister of defense met with the Super Dux and the Prophet. After a communal toast to success he said, "Super Dux, your plan of conscripting men from the United States and using what's left of their armed forces is proving invaluable. They're well-trained and we were able to transport substantial ground and air weaponry. Our own Federation Security Defense Forces have ramped up drafting new soldiers from other nations in the Federation as well. In addition, we've been conducting highly classified talks with some of the Muslim organizations who are only too happy to join the effort."

"But don't they have their own agendas?" the Super Dux asked with suspicion. "Ideologically they're a fractured group. I think there are something like seventy-two factions? Will they work for or against us?"

"I am assured the Taliban, ISIS, the Muslim Brotherhood, Al-Qaeda, and nearly six other groups will help us, for they all have one thing in common—wipe Israel off the face of the earth."

"And establish Islam," the Super Dux said in disgust.

"That will not happen," the minister of defense assured him. "At present, they're focused on one thing: destroy the Jews. Once that is done, you can be assured they'll start quarreling among themselves, then they'll start killing each other. It will be the head biting the tail. They cannot possibly get along with each other, but while they are agreeable in fighting for us, let's use their forces. Once we prevail, we turn on our Muslim brothers in their own confusion and wipe them out too. We'll enjoy immense wealth, limitless energy products, and be able to create an economy where we can sustain our empire."

"Yes, I like that. Wealth and power. The two go hand in hand. These past several years have been challenging," the Super Dux said, shaking his head. "The war against Israel, which the Russians and Iranians lost, ultimately worked for us, but constant pockets of upheaval across the globe have achieved nothing but more poverty. Poor nations can't pay taxes and tariffs. Fortunately, terrorism has yet to attain Islamic goals, but the war against the United States and the Federation was devastating to us until we ended it by using nuclear weaponry, but even that came at a cost. An oil rich area now polluted. We need to regain a hold on our financial system and authority."

The Prophet added, "I regret the loss of New York. We could have used the city for its wealth and trading capabilities."

"Wiping out New York was a surprisingly successful feat. I didn't think the aggressors had the talent or range," the Super Dux added, clearly impressed. "But, we can't mourn a resource that will never be. We seek out a new resource, Israel, and move forward with our plans."

The Prophet was deep in thought for several moments. He finally cautioned, "We must not get too complacent thinking that by conquering Israel we can relax. We must continue to control unrest in our own Federation. We know some members are becoming disillusioned over our rule. They complain they're not receiving the benefits that they have been promised."

"What do they expect?" the Super Dux snapped. "Look at the enormity of the calamities we've had to endure. And we know who is behind those powerful blows. It's not like we can solve their problems overnight or stop the supernatural from happening."

"Unlike them," the Prophet added, "we know the reason for all of these events and, I assure you, we are going to win this contest of wills! In the meantime, be aware of your detractors."

The Super Dux sighed. "They want to fight me, yet they want me to feed them. They don't see the big picture of an ultimate global empire. They have only their narrow interests at heart, they desire creature comforts, and they're not willing to sacrifice. At this juncture, I have no intention to deliver what I have promised. How can I? We don't have the resources."

"I agree, Marcus. We're dealing with a group of contemptuous leaders and their people who want more, regardless of the circumstances we're in. But I caution you, it is well to watch your back."

Marcus smiled. "I promise you they'll think the last seven years were a picnic after I conclude my triumphant invasion of Israel. I'll remember them. I'll have them on their knees begging for mercy and will show them none!"

Hours later, Roberto came back to the Super Dux's office. "We just got news that a great army in Africa is forming," he began.

"Is it Africa's Joint Multinational Force?" the Super Dux asked in surprise. "I thought they split up long ago. Many of the African nations are in the Federation. Are they going to join us?"

"No, no. We're hearing word that they're against us, and there's more." Roberto stopped speaking to swallow the pain permeating his face.

"Spit it out, Roberto!"

"It looks like Russia is mobilizing again too. We're not sure who is with her."

The Super Dux flew into a rage. "Armies from the north and south are planning on attacking us? We must move quickly! No way will I let my prize get away from me this time. I will subdue the subversives, then I will destroy Israel and leave Jerusalem in pieces!"

The battle began.

Days passed into weeks. The Super Dux, through great loss of yet more life, was able to put down the rebellion from the limping armies of the north who were not as powerful as they once were, and the African nations from the south, who were no match for the skill and firepower of the combined American and Federation Security Defense Forces.

"That was a job well done," the Super Dux told his defense minister. "Your efforts in pushing back our enemies will be rewarded."

"Timing, talent, and weapons worked in conjunction with the leaders of the battles. We lost men and equipment, but our enemies lost more and we gained much spoil to replace the weaponry we lost," the minister boasted.

"What of the troops? How did they handle the blazing sun?" asked a curious Roberto. The sun was still an issue of relentless heat and searing rays. Daylight was twenty-four hours and there was no respite.

"Those who were not protected with sunglasses and protective gear were badly burned and those who lost their gloves, well, their hands are now useless," the minister answered. "Even those who did have protection still had to contend with the heat that was overwhelming. Many died from heat exhaustion. But that's the price of war. Such is cannon fodder."

"Get rid of those who cannot fight anymore. We can't afford to feed and water them," Marcus instructed his defense minister.

"Yes, Super Dux, I will do so." The man bowed to his leader, then left the room.

"We will now move forward with our plans to take and destroy the Jews!" the Super Dux exclaimed to Roberto and the Prophet.

The Federation Security Defense troops, along with the United States military, regrouped after the attacks from the armies from the northern and southern armies. Though there were casualties, the combined militaries were strong and focused. Once again organized and refitted, the minister of defense soon mobilized them to the mountain range bordering Northern Israel.

Shortly after the armies settled in place after putting up protective tarps and tents, the inferno of the sun was abruptly smothered. Darkness consumed the land and, immediately, coolness fell across the earth as the sun was hidden from view.

The troops cautiously came out from tents and shelters, looking around in utter amazement. Taking off sunglasses and gloves, they looked up into the black sky. "What's happened?" a young soldier asked of no one. "The sun and its terrible heat has been extinguished. No more burning pain!"

The men, who were struggling with readiness under the searing rays and suffocating heat, now shouted with joy, and took down their shelters and peeled off their protective gear. Congregating in the outdoors, they lit lanterns and celebrated the cool darkness. Clapping one another on the back and sighing in great relief, their attitudes and resolve to fight for the Super Dux and destroy Israel were strengthened. Finally, the heat and the burning rays were gone. Finally, they could maneuver freely without fear of being burned! They rejoiced throughout the day and night. Once in bed, they slept in cool comfort.

But their relief was short-lived as soldiers woke up crying in pain. An unknown infection rapidly spread among the troops. It also infected the population of the world. Once again, all those with *666* on their hands or foreheads were stricken with sores so severe the people gnawed their tongues in agony.

Those who thought the Christian God might be responsible for this latest disaster loudly cursed Him. If this and past horrific events were judgments, no one admitted any responsibility of sinful behavior. No one had any intention of changing their ways. And they refused to ask God for help. They believed "the Beast," as the Super Dux was now proudly called by the troops, to be their true god.

While Super Dux was in his modular Command and Control center being briefed by his officers about the latest plague of sores, an astounding notification came in through the lines. The Euphrates River was dried up. Puzzled, the commanders looked at one another silently. What could this possibly mean? Another episode of disaster? The Super Dux asked an officer to explain.

"The Euphrates River, which originates in Turkey and flows through Syria and Iraq, joins the Tigris and empties into the Persian Gulf." The officer pointed on the map. "Iran, Pakistan, Afghanistan, and four other 'Stan' nations—see these nations here?" He pointed with a stick. "They, along with China, Russia, Georgia, and several other nations, can now literally walk across the dried-up waters and easily march through Syria, Lebanon, Iraq, and Jordan."

An officer jumped up from his module, whipping off his headset, and spoke to the commanders crowding around the map. "Troops are moving toward us," he said in fright.

"Specifically what troops?" asked President Sarratt in anxiety and dread. All eyes turned to him. As pseudo commander-in-chief of the US forces he, along with Danny, had been allowed to be present in the Command and Control center along with the Super Dux, the Prophet, officers, and executive staff. While his ranking was least among the men, he was respected for his country's armed forces.

"I, that is, we are not sure, sir," the confused officer said. "Our satellites show a number of different standards, and we can't be certain, but it looks like it could be another coalition of nations."

"Can you get a read on the numbers of troops, and are they ground infantry?" demanded a senior officer.

"We're trying to ascertain that as we speak. We just can't get updated information. The satellites just went down."

The Super Dux stood and looked around the room, angrily focused and intent. His hands on his hips was so reminiscent of his godlike statue in the Jewish temple. "Whoever they are, they're not for us. They will fight us. They will fight Israel. For those of you who know the ancient history of the Jews, you will know what a landmark opportunity this is to destroy a people who for thousands of years avoided extinction. It's a supernatural game of chess, and he who captures this queen wins."

"The plain of Armageddon can't hold such numbers," the minister of defense said.

"That's why we're here first," boasted the Beast. "Get ready."

CHAPTER TWENTY

ISRAEL

EX-PRIME MINISTER MOSHE BEN-ZION MADE a decision to return to his office after getting intelligence that not only was the Super Dux preparing to attack Israel, but there were other armies marching toward Israel. It was time to put an end to the charade of Marcus Junius as world leader and conqueror. He was compelled to reason with those that had thrown their allegiance to the Super Dux and maybe save those before it was too late. He had nothing to lose. They had their very eternal lives to lose.

As he walked through his offices, Benjamin came hurrying over to him. He stopped Moshe with his hand and said, "We, that is the remainder of your staff that hasn't left, need to speak with you."

"Benjamin, all, please come into the conference room. I wish to speak with you too."

As they filed into the large room and sat down, Moshe stood and with his hand up he said, "I wish to speak first. In a speech many years ago, Prime Minister Netanyahu addressed the United States Congress much to the chagrin of President Barak Obama and many in the Democratic Party, who at the time were delusional about the intent of Iran and its 'nuclear program.'" Moshe paused. "Even then, I felt the words of Netanyahu to be prophetic. So I've carried this portion of his speech around with me to keep me always cognizant of the fragile state between Israel and the world. I should have paid attention to his words and not have accepted Marcus Junius' seven-year treaty." He shook his head at his own stupidity. "But at the time we all felt the desire for protection and peace, only to be gravely misled."

"Get on with it, old man. We don't have all day!" groused a mean-spirited administrator.

"Yes, getting back to Netanyahu's speech. I keep it in my wallet." Moshe pulled out a folded piece of paper and adjusted his reading glasses. "Netanyahu said, and I read, 'In this deadly game of thrones, there's no place for America or for Israel, no peace for Christians, Jews, or Muslims who don't share the Islamist medieval creed, no rights for women, no freedom for anyone. So when it comes to Iran and ISIS, the enemy of your enemy is your enemy.'" He let the words of a much-admired prime minister sink in.

"I don't get it," the administrator said with scorn.

Moshe fixed him with a hard look. "This is poignant because our immediate threat is not isolated to radical Islamists who want to annihilate Israel. Rather, it includes many other enemies of Israel, particularly the Super Dux. We are at this moment witnessing the many troops positioning themselves along our borders to include the Super Dux's and we know of hordes of warriors who are already on their way from the East who can now easily cross over the Euphrates and attack us. We see that these kingdoms and principalities are in fact playing a very deadly game of thrones." He spread out his hands. "You are merely pawns in this game. Take heed of the saying 'The enemy of our enemy is our enemy.'"

He walked about the room. "Marcus Junius, called Super Dux, is also called the Antichrist and the Beast by Scripture. He is marching in to kill the Jews and take Israel for his kingdom. He will not win. And this is not because of our might, or the other aggressors' might, but it is by the might of God, whom I now trust."

The staff sat silent and fearful; they had not been informed of this latest news of a double invasion and a double cross. They were told that the Super Dux was bringing troops into Israel to enforce his coup; they didn't expect aggression from their new leader towards them; it was unthinkable. They had aligned themselves with the Federation. And to learn that more warring nations were on their way was incomprehensible. They were rooted in fear, with nowhere to turn. Who was fighting whom?

What will happen to us? Benjamin thought. *Will the Super Dux save his supporters?*

"We know how the story ends," Moshe said confidently. "We who believe will be saved. We Jews will finally get our land, the land promised to Abraham, and we will be ruled by our King David, who will be led by Jesus the Christ. Many inside this room do not believe this. But there are many Jews who do. Having said that, there is no point in your even being here. Go home to your families. There is nothing you can do now except turn to the living God before it's too late." He looked carefully at those listening, some with contempt but many in alarm. "Jesus will win this war for us for He is the King of Kings and the Lord of Lords. I have no more to say. Benjamin, you have the floor."

The staff sat in uneasy silence as they watched Benjamin. Seething with betrayal and fear, they didn't know how to react. Would they, too, die a violent death due to the onslaught of troops descending on Israel like a swarm of bees? Would they be protected by the Super Dux or cut down by him? Israel was rendered helpless now.

"Old man," Benjamin hissed, "we know whom we can trust and rely on and it isn't your God. We pledged our allegiance to the Super Dux. He will not forsake us! What you have said is nothing but a lie. The Super Dux would never turn on his people!"

"Benjamin," Moshe responded quietly and with dignity, "you are not 'his people.' He hates you and every Jew. He will turn on you and all who put their trust in him. You will miss wonderful light, love, and eternal salvation and be doomed to darkness and pain worse than those sores oozing over your body. And it will be for eternity. It breaks my heart. You and those with the mark, along with the Beast, this Super Dux. His false prophet and Satan will not be successful. You will all lose! There is no more discussion."

Benjamin stood to face the prime minister. Those marked with *666* waited expectantly. The tension in the room was thick with hostility and smelled of fear. It was as if demons were dancing in glee at their soon to achieve success. "I will vacate Beit Rosh HaMemshala immediately." Moshe walked past Benjamin.

"You . . . you," Benjamin stammered. "You will be swatted like a fly!" He shouted to Moshe's retreating back.

On the street, Moshe said to Levi, who was waiting in the car, "Come to my house and take Sarah with you and your family when you go south. I pray you will be able to wait in safety. The battles are going to happen very soon. I am going to make my way to Armageddon. I want to be there to see Jesus destroy the Antichrist and the troops of demons!"

"Moshe, I think we will all see it, but I understand your need to be there, feet on the ground."

"*Saba*, no! You can't leave me!" Sarah wrapped her arms around her grandfather's waist.

"Sarah, *ahuvi*, we've talked about this. This might be a scary time, but it's going to be only for a very short time. Remember that no matter what happens, we will be together even if we both die, because we will live again!"

"Nooooo! I don't want to die to live again. I don't want you to die or *dod* Levi!" Sara sobbed.

"If it even happens, it will be only for a moment and then you will be with the Messiah and me, and *dod* Levi." It was a comforting thought Moshe held deep in his heart. He didn't want his Sarah to experience terror even for a moment. "If we have to die, it will be just like walking through a door from one room, into a far more beautiful room. It's possible we might not even have to die. We might be untouched in all of this, *ahuvi*."

Sarah gathered a few belongings and after tearful hugs, she got in the back seat of Levi's car.

Moshe's ex-chief of staff hugged him but not in sadness; it was with excitement. True, they all could die very soon, but they would be resurrected and be with Jesus. They held firmly onto the belief that God's promises in the Old Testament to Israel for land, many descendants, and blessings would now be fulfilled with Jesus' coming. The excitement was electric.

"I will see you soon, my friend! Shalom!"

EPILOGUE

MARANATHA

THE CAMPFIRE SPUTTERED, AND SMALL bright sparks drifted lazily up into the sky. Jason, Joanna, James, and Pooch gathered close to it. It was a calm night. They were taking a chance of having an outside campfire, but the act of making a fire, sitting by its warmth, heartened them and tonight they were willing to enjoy this small pleasure at the risk of being discovered by intruders. They were anxious and wondering when Christ was going to return. They knew He would come, they just didn't know when, and they were uncertain how they were going to continue to live here. Their supplies would eventually get low again, and they might have to move on from their little cabin to find food, but for now, they had what they needed to last for a little while longer.

"What do you think?" Jason asked his two friends as he poked a stick into the fire.

Joanna didn't say anything, just petted Pooch and stared into the fire.

Softly, James spoke, "I don't know. We can't overlook prayer and I'm confident God will keep us alive until Jesus comes, but even if He doesn't, we'll still be with Him."

"I know," Jason responded. "But it's the uncertainty of it all."

"It's too bad we're so human!" Joanna sighed.

"Yeah. That's why we worry, right?" James added. "But we need to have faith that God is going to take care of us one way or another."

"Well, I sure hope He comes soon," Jason said.

Joanna leaned forward. "James, tell us the story about the Valley of Meggido, where the last battle—Armageddon—will be fought."

James leaned back in his lawn chair. "Meggido is called the Mount of Slaughter and has been significant throughout Jewish history. Not only did the ancient Jews fight battles there, but so did the Crusaders, the Greeks, the Egyptians, and many other nations. It's in Northern Israel and is only about fifty-five miles from Jerusalem and really close to Nazareth and Haifa. The Valley of Meggido, or Jezreel Valley where the battle of Armageddon will take place, was the area where God, in the Old Testament, gave Barak, commander of the Israelites, and Deborah, Prophetess and Judge, victory over the Canaanites. It was also where God gave Gideon victory over the Midianites." He paused. "The story of Gideon is really interesting. He asked proof of God's will by having God perform three miracles for him, which God did. Later, God gave him victory over the huge army of the Midianites while Gideon only had three hundred men. Needless to say, it was God's victory."

"And Joshua, Moses' second in command, killed the king of Megiddo there," Jason added. "And it was also where King Saul and his sons, notably Jonathan, died. And King Josiah died there too."

"The battle of Armageddon won't just be contained to the valley," James explained. "It will affect all of Israel and probably some neighboring nations. The Antichrist will lead his troops against Israel, but another surprise will happen that the Antichrist won't expect.

Massive troops under the 'kings of the East'—China maybe? I don't know—will fight against the Antichrist, who might think he's in control, but from what I've read in the Bible, his grip on world domination is weakened. There are many nations grating against his power and are willing to fight him. But we know what will happen and how it will end. Christ, as warrior and king, will appear and extinguish all battlefield chaos and finally put an end to the Beast, or Antichrist."

They sat quietly visualizing a great battle.

"And you know these dark days we now have?" James asked. "The dark is a signal of Christ's return." He looked to the sky.

"Yes, it's a welcome relief from that scorching heat," Joanna admitted. She remembered for so long they had to contend with limited daylight and blackened nights, and when the sun finally came out, they were ecstatic only to have it build into an intense heat they couldn't endure. They had to protect themselves and Pooch from getting badly burned by the blistering sun. Now it was dark again.

Jason nodded. "And the battle of Armageddon will be of epic proportions."

"Honestly," Joanna said, "I so want Him to come, but I'm scared!"

"We all are," James agreed. "We look forward to being with our Lord, but it's going to be an experience like no other."

"Be thankful we're not in Israel!" James smiled. "That's where the fireworks are really going to happen."

"Read to us again from the book of Matthew," Joanna said. "That part in chapter 24."

James flipped open his Bible and read, *"For as lightning that comes from the east is visible even in the west, so will be the coming of the Son of Man. Wherever there is a carcass, there the vultures will gather. Immediately after the distress of those days the sun will be darkened, and the moon will not give its light; the stars will fall from the sky, and the heavenly bodies will be shaken. Then will appear the sign of the Son of Man in heaven. And then all the peoples of the earth will mourn when they see the Son of Man coming on the clouds of heaven, with power and great glory. And he will send his angels with a loud trumpet call, and they will gather his elect from the four winds, from one end of the heavens to the other."*

"Yeah, I'm more than a little scared," Joanna whispered, holding Pooch tightly.

"Me too," Jason said. For a fleeting moment, he thought about the loss of his wife, Allie, and daughter, Sabrina. He wondered what happened to them. It was tragic that they had refused to listen to him. But it was their choice. Now, he was looking forward to eternal life with the Lord Jesus! Where would they be? Did they come to belief or not? There was little gain in going over the situation. While the loss of his family still gently tugged on his heart, he had let it go. He was ready for his new life!

James turned to them both as the night got even darker. "This is going to be so amazing. And yet, I'm scared too. This is the time we have been waiting and praying for! Come, Lord Jesus! I hope it's tonight!"

They looked steadfastly up into the sky.

"So many kings have marched through this valley," the Super Dux said as he readied himself for battle. "I wouldn't miss this for the world."

The Prophet laughed heartily. "Of course you wouldn't miss this for the world! Because for all intents and purposes, you already have the world!"

"Most of it. But I want all of it and my prize is Israel! We will beat those that are coming to attack us, and we will conquer Israel!" He raised his fist high. President Sarratt, his chief of staff, Danny, and the Super Dux's chief of staff, Roberto, smiled. The time had come for the spoils of war. They were all to be a part of this historical conquest! It was immensely exciting. They would be part of the new world order.

The Beast turned to the False Prophet with a delighted gleam in his eye. "This victory is what we were created for. We will strangle Daughter Zion! She will not be able to lose the garrote. We will choke her to death. There will never, ever be a remnant of Israel! And her God will be rendered subservient to us. For *we* are the unholy trinity! We will be the power and glory!" He deeply laughed as he admired himself in the mirror. His uniform was crisp, his hat was jauntily placed on his handsome head, and his boots were gleaming black. Standing regally, he turned to show off to the Prophet. His signet ring flashed in the light.

"Super Dux, I have something for you to complete your look." From a hand-painted box, the Prophet pulled out a purple velvet bag. "I think you should wear this as you direct your troops." Out of the bag he gently pulled the finely hewn golden crown made in Caesar-like fashion. Gold leaves wrapped around the finest pearls, rubies, emeralds, and diamonds. The Prophet took off his commander's cap and replaced it with the crown.

"Ah yes, my crown!" the Super Dux joyfully exclaimed. "You are right, now being the time to wear my crown." He admired himself in the mirror. "A shame my designer, Allie, isn't here to see me wear the best piece she ever created. She would be so proud to see her work acknowledged as a statement of my power. Her death and her daughter's were unfortunate, but I'm delighted you had her create this before the tainted water took her!"

The Prophet ignored the reference to Allie. He flicked his hand. "When the kings and leaders from the East arrive with their troops, they will know who the true king of this world is! You! Come let's make ready for you to lead your troops. Our helicopter is waiting."

The coalition of troops under the "kings of the East" were marching from Asia toward Israel. They had recently passed over the Euphrates River. The thrill of victory was in their hearts and savagery was on their minds as they imagined easy defeat of the Super Dux's troops and the destruction of Jewish lives.

"Once we ravage the vineyard, destroy the vine, and drink from the press, we will plow Israel into a field!" a commander promised, mocking biblical imagery.

Someone from the coalition of troops shouted joyfully, "We will also defeat the Super Dux and his armies. He will not be the victor! The path will be clear to obliterate the Jews!"

"We will cut off their heads and feed their bodies to the carrion birds!" cried the commander. "And when they have had their fill, we will burn their bones. No God of the Jews will ever protect them from our might!"

An earsplitting roar arose from the countless troops as they continued their march with their ferocious weaponry. "We will be known as the formidable coalition that beat the tyranny of the Super Dux and quenched the power of a God that protects Israel. We will wipe Israel off the face of the map, take her spoil, and create the most powerful kingdom on earth!"

Moshe Ben-Zion stood on a small knoll overlooking the Megiddo Valley, about twelve miles from Nazareth. Even in the distance he could see the clouds of dust raised by the vast number of troops assembling at the bases of the distant mountain range. Aircraft hovered in the air and a deep rumbling of armored vehicles and tanks could be heard across the plain. From his view, he could see fires and lights situated in two different locations. There were the two armies—that of the Super Dux and that of the kings of the East. An odd thought popped into his head as he viewed the troops moving in across the vast valley. He shook his head as he remembered years ago when Zion Oil had a drilling license for approximately 98,000 acres in the Megiddo and Jezreel Valley. Life looked so promising for Israel under the treaty. It was all about profitable energy sources, individual wealth, and huge economic growth to the country. And now? Moshe shook his head.

Their dreams had turned into nightmares. Wars, earthquakes, fire, hail, poisoned water, sores, locust attacks, and so many other judgments fell on them and, still, they did not believe those judgments were from God! Even he didn't until the last moment. God spared him.

Now, those that grudgingly gave credence to God for the supernatural catastrophes cursed him and didn't turn from their blind path, but there were some who did come to believe and didn't take the 'mark of the Beast.' A small group, but they would be saved.

He bowed his head with immense thanks. "Father God, thank You for opening my eyes. I humbly wait for our King and Messiah, Jesus Christ. I might be killed in the chaos, but I know that my granddaughter and I are saved. I thank You for forgiving all my sins, for redeeming my life! As I look out to the terrors on every side of this valley, I know You will save Your remnant, Your chosen, which have their hope in You and in Your Son, Jesus Christ."

The noise became deafening. The smells pungent, oily, and bitter as dust devils swirled manically in thousands of red clouds. Troops from both sides were moving forward under the banners of death and destruction. A small army of Israeli military that was still tragically loyal to the country was gathered to face the onslaught, but were vastly outnumbered. Aircraft was useless in the valley itself, but enemy fighter jets screamed towards Jerusalem and Haifa. The Iron Dome was activated to fend off incoming missiles, but how long it could be effective with this onslaught was unknown.

This is the last chapter of Israel's defense, Moshe mused. He was very afraid, but hopeful. Quietly he waited for his King of Kings.

Like waves of fire ants, soldiers under the kings of the East marched into the Valley of Mediggo from the bases of the mountains to attack the inadequate army of Israel and the Super Dux's military. Troop after troop poured over and into the land with two goals in mind: defeat the Federation's armies and capture Israel, the queen, then put her in checkmate.

But the Super Dux's soldiers were also on the move and fought against the attacking kings' troops. The conquest of Israel was to be the prize of the Super Dux, not anyone else's. He would fight all of his adversaries including God. He had the power. He was in the unity of the unholy trinity. With Satan, how could he and his prophet be defeated? Confident and arrogant, he would prove his might and destroy anyone in his path who would try to take away his victory!

Confusion reigned. Acrid smells of smoke and blood perfumed the air while heart—rendering cries and ear-shattering blasts bombarded the senses. The ground was drenched in blood and slippery with body parts. Who was fighting whom? The common goals of the two armies were to beat each other and destroy Israel. They were also ready to fight the God of Israel if he came to Israel's rescue. Both armies tasted victory, and with hatred in their hearts, they blindly moved forward, slaughtering each other in trying to be first to get to the Jews.

Super Dux Marcus Junius readjusted his crown as he listened to his commanders' positive reports. It seemed the Federation's army was pushing back their adversaries and easily pummeling the frail Israeli military. Smiling, he left the confines of his Command and Control center on the side of the mountain and, protected from the melee below, he viewed the action spread before him, but it was impossible to discern between the three different armies. Pandemonium reigned. He climbed atop a Humvee to get a better view.

As men and armored vehicles were clashing, guns reporting and rockets soaring, an unexpected burst of lightening of enormous proportions split the sky open, overshadowing all turmoil on land. A great earthquake shook the ground, and, equally startling, stars of all sizes tumbled from the sky! In a violent wind, hail of mammoth sizes was hurled to the earth.

Marcus Junius—the Antichrist, the Beast, and the Super Dux—grabbed the roll bar to steady himself and frantically looked around. His golden crown flew off his head and wrapped itself around a twisted, bare tree. No title or crown could protect him now as he gasped in total astonishment and great fear. Before him, the firmament of the sky split apart like a dark cloth being torn. In all directions, hundreds of thousands of soldiers who were still alive had been thrown to the ground and were frozen in terror as they were pummeled by sharp chunks of hail. Those that struggled to their knees reeled in confusion and shock as the earth violently trembled. In terror and disbelief, they watched as their tanks and other armored vehicles were swallowed up by the hungry black earth.

Moshe Ben-Zion was drenched in fearful sweat as he watched the battles rage. The smell of his own fear washed over him, souring his stomach. His face was smeared with tears and soot from the distant explosions and fires. The Israeli army didn't have a chance. The scene spread before him was unlike any he could imagine. It was total heartbreak and devastation. Corpses were strewn everywhere. Even from his point on the knoll, he could see puddles of blood pooled under the heads and bodies of the slain. Pathetic wails of pain and loss of hope filled the air.

Without warning, he was brutally thrown to the ground, hitting his head hard on the rocky ground. Groaning, he touched his hand to his bloody head and rolled over to see giant hail bouncing off the ground around him. The sound of screaming from the battlefield rose to a sharp keening. Grappling the ground with bruised hands, he sidled to the protection of a tossed tree. Protecting himself with his arm from the falling hail, and leaning close into the broken branches, he looked skyward and blinked.

There, there! That was what he was waiting for! Trembling with joy, Moshe crawled from the base of the tree, blood from the wound on his head pouring into one eye. Wiping it away, he raised his arms smiling. He shouted, he laughed, he cried, he sang! He opened his eyes wide in delight. The light was awesome!

The Antichrist howled in abject bitterness! He knew! It was over! He lost! He, the Beast, was conquered!

The false Prophet cried out in abject disbelief. How could they have lost? In desperation he grabbed the arm of the Antichrist.

Marcus Junius whirled on him, snarled, and pushed him away. He then looked to the sky. The light was blinding.

The Bible flew from James' hand as his chair lurched and collapsed. He tumbled hard to the ground. Instinctively Jason, James, and Joanna reached for one another as the earth jumped and rolled fiercely beneath them. The campfire fell apart and tongues of flame danced along the ground, igniting the dry, dead leaves and sticks. The fire continued to spread at a rapid pace. Giant-sized hail peppered the ground but missed the three friends and their dog. Pooch, at first surprised by the moving earth, stood wagging her tail wildly and barked a happy I'm-so-excited-to-see-you bark once the quaking stopped. She had no fear. Stars tumbled from the sky and the three looked at each other with eyes wide and mouths open. They were too stunned to be afraid. Just as suddenly, the sky ripped open.

"Look! Look!" they screamed in unison. They jumped from the ground and danced for joy with arms outstretched.

"He's here! He's here!" Joanna shouted as they hugged each other, crying and laughing. Pooch ran around them, happily barking and pawing the air.

Laughing and dancing, they were wrapped up in the most amazing light. Pooch too.

The Bible lay not too far from where James had been sitting. It was opened to the book of Revelation 19:11–21:

> "Now I saw heaven opened, and behold, a white horse. And He who sat on him was called Faithful and True, and in righteousness He judges and makes war. His eyes were like a flame of fire, and on His head were many crowns. He had a name written that no one knew except Himself. He was clothed with a robe dipped in blood, and His name is called The Word of God. And the armies in heaven, clothed in fine linen, white and clean, followed Him on white horses. Now out of His mouth goes a sharp sword, that with it He should strike the nations. And He Himself will rule them with a rod of iron. He Himself treads the winepress of the fierceness and wrath of Almighty God. And He has on His robe and on His thigh a name written:
>
> KING OF KINGS AND LORD OF LORDS
>
> Then I saw an angel standing in the sun; and he cried with a loud voice, saying to all the birds that fly in the midst of heaven, 'Come and gather together for the supper of the great God, that you may eat the flesh of kings, the flesh of captains, the flesh of mighty men, the flesh of horses and of those who sit on them, and the flesh of all people, free and slave, both small and great.'
>
> And I saw the beast, the kings of the earth, and their armies, gathered together to make war against Him who sat on the horse and against His army. Then the beast was captured, and with him the false prophet who worked signs in his presence, by which he deceived those who received the mark of the beast and those who worshiped his image. These two were cast alive into the lake of fire burning with brimstone. And the rest were killed with the sword which proceeded from the mouth of Him who sat on the horse. And all the birds were filled with their flesh."

Also By S.A. Jewell:
Visit From a Shepherd Boy
a Young Adult Fiction
Available Now!

CHAPTER ONE

JOEY RETURNS

SOMETHING WAS NAGGING HIM. A memory? In a state of drowsiness, Josh blinked, yawned mightily, and slowly woke up. With a start he realized, *oh my, it's Christmas!* Half asleep, he looked at his clock. Staring at the hands in shock, he realized that it was nearly noon. He rubbed his eyes several times, confused.

Aloud he said, "I thought it was just about dawn! The room is so dark." But as he looked out the window, he saw thick snow squalls blocking the weak daylight. He involuntarily shivered.

Then the morning's events returned to him in slow motion. His memory came back. He was still in bed because he had tried to find Mr. George, the snowman he had made for his mom and aunt for Christmas. Yes, that was it. Through half-closed eyes, he looked back out the window again and could hear the snow being driven so hard against the pane that it sounded like sand blasting the window. Yes, the blizzard. It was all about getting lost in the blizzard.

A week ago, he had built this very cool snowman on an old sled he found leaning up against the wall in their dusty, cluttered garage. He dragged the rusted sled to the back of the yard where a small white shed stood surrounded by overgrown bushes and saplings. Behind the building was a small clearing, and there he built his snowman, whom he called Mr. George for no other reason than he liked the name. It was a perfect hiding place because no one ever walked to the back of the large wooded lot, and he could work without anyone seeing him.

His plan had been to slide Mr. George to the bottom of the porch stairs Christmas morning to surprise his mom and aunt. The snow man was way too heavy to lift and bring up to the porch, but he would make a perfect sentry for the foot of the stairs. Josh was very proud of his work, and he knew his mom and aunt would love their present.

As Josh made his way toward the shed this morning to get Mr. George, it was snowing so hard that every bush was covered in deep drifts. Even the white shed was barely visible in the storm. To his dismay, he couldn't find the little clearing where Mr. George quietly sat and waited. Everything looked different as he trudged past the shed. The drifts were everywhere, and the snow was swirling in his eyes, making it difficult to see. The yard covered more than an acre of woods, and as he leaned into the howling wind and gusts of snow, he became confused. In what direction was he going? He kept walking, trying to find his way back to the shed and home, but instead he found himself dreadfully lost. So lost, he feared he might freeze to death before anyone could find him. As he lurched through the ever deepening snow, he realized his only hope was to find shelter. Miraculously, he saw a towering pine straight ahead of him.

Now lying in bed, he pulled the covers up to his chin. He silently thanked God he had been found—unconscious—but alive. His neighbor Dave said the reason they found him was because of Josh's little toy dinosaur—something he always carried with him. It had fallen out of his pocket as he crawled and scratched his way under the giant evergreen tree. When Dave and his mom were frantically searching for him, they noticed the little toy poking out of a snow drift in front of the tree. They then knew where to find him—under its snow-laden boughs. Sure enough, when Dave dug his way through the snow and pushed under the heavy branches, there was Josh leaning against the trunk of the tall evergreen. Josh didn't remember a thing about being found. He was in a state of frozen slumber.

Remembering all this, he closed his eyes to the bedroom and the fearful events of the morning. He settled deeper under the warm covers, not wanting to think about his early morning ordeal, but his mind didn't want to let it go. Finally, he slipped into sleep again, where images appeared in his mind. The sky was gray with fat, lazy snowflakes quietly drifting in front of him. He turned his face upward and opened his mouth to catch the delicate flakes on his tongue, but the gentle wind tossed the flakes around like feathers, just out of his tongue's reach. He watched the flakes, one by one, dance around his face, teasing him. Suddenly, without reason, they turned into sharp, icy crystals that swirled dangerously close to him. He batted them away and tried to run, but his legs were too heavy. The wind hurled the beautiful but jagged crystals at Josh like tiny spears. He ducked and swatted at them, but they managed to hit him. He was surprised they didn't hurt. They melted harmlessly on his cheeks like tears and curiously, when he wiped them away, they didn't feel wet at all.

He held his hands in front of his face. No mittens. Where were his mittens? He squinted because the storm was in full fury, and he looked around to get his bearings. Snow pelted him. He couldn't tell where he was. Up ahead, he saw a majestic pine tree soaring to the sky. Its boughs, like arms, were beckoning to him, "Come, come," it whispered. "Find safety under me!"

With great effort he tried to reach the tree, but the storm intensified. His legs became as heavy as lead. He couldn't move them. He panicked. Would he ever be safe?

Blinking away sleep and the dream, Josh opened his eyes. He was back in his bedroom! Safe. His heart was pounding like a hammer, but he knew it was only a bad dream brought on by the morning's events. He took a couple of deep breaths to calm himself and pulled the covers closer to his chin. Yes, he was safe! Protected in the room he shared with his two little sisters, who were somewhere off in the house playing with their Christmas presents. Although groggy, he decided he should be out there too opening his presents, but he was still too sleepy and weak.

Lying quietly, he enjoyed the luxury of being in his sisters' bed. There wasn't much space in the small room, so as the oldest, he was stuck with the mattress on the floor while they got the bed. But because he nearly froze to death, his mom tucked him in the warmth of the girls' bed.

Josh smiled as he remembered the discussion his mom and aunt had over the room. His mom thought that even though it was a closet, it would make a great kids' bedroom.

"But it couldn't have been a closet," his aunt had reasoned when she first saw it. "It has a window."

"I think it was a big walk-in closet. Look, it has shelves and hooks."

His mom and aunt had argued about this for a while because the apartment they were renting together was once part of a farmhouse, and it had lots of weird nooks and crannies. The owners had created three apartments with different layouts, and this one had either one large walk-in closet or one tiny bedroom.

"Well, no matter," his mom had said with a wave of her hand. "We'll have to use the room as a bedroom for the kids. Josh will just have to sleep on the floor. We can't get two beds and a desk in here at the same time, but there are some long shelves here we can use to put their clothes on."

"Oh, it will work out fine," Aunt Katherine had said. "It may be a little drafty for ol' Josh though." She messed his hair and laughed. "I'll make sure you have plenty of blankets!"

He checked the floor by the side of the bed for his mattress. Somebody had slid it and the blankets under his sisters' bed. He hoped he could stay in their bed for the night and wondered briefly if his sisters would have to sleep on the couch.

When he looked back up, he gaped in astonishment at the end of the bed. There, sitting at the desk that was jammed between the foot of the bed and the wall, was a small figure. This small person was fiddling with Josh's little toy dinosaur and watching him. Already rattled from the morning events and his bad dream, Josh didn't know what to think.

"Hey, it's about time! I thought you'd be stuck in that snowstorm forever!"

Josh could only stare as the young boy hopped off the chair and dragged it around the end of the bed. He carefully positioned the chair beside Josh and perched on the edge of the seat. With eyes as big as a baby owl's, he stared at Josh intently, appraising him. "Whew. You're okay. You had me worried there for a minute."

Josh looked closely at the boy. Was he dreaming still? It couldn't be Joey, could it? When his mom put him to bed earlier, the doctor had given her some kind of medicine that she poured in a little plastic cup for him to drink. It tasted like sweet, purple grapes. The taste made him gag. His mom pleaded with him to swallow, which he finally did. It made him bleary and finally put him to sleep. Maybe that was why he was having odd dreams about snowflakes attacking him. Was this vision of Joey a result of the medicine too? Was Joey a hallucination? Was he for real, or was Josh dreaming?

"Of course I'm okay," Josh said defensively. He was still confused. "When did you get here?"

The boy leaned back, tilted the chair on its back legs, and put his feet up on Josh's bed. He crossed his arms snuggly over his sheep wool vest and giggled like a demented elf. Joey was here again! This was just too strange. Josh wanted to rub his eyes to make sure he was seeing straight.

"So, when did you get here?" Josh asked again. He propped himself up on his elbow to get a better look.

"I've been here awhile, but I didn't want to wake you up, so I waited for you to come around. I think that medicine was pretty strong." Almost as an afterthought, Joey added, "That was some weird storm you were in."

How did Joey know about that awful medicine, and how did he know about Josh being in the snowstorm? Was he talking about his dream, or was he talking about him actually getting lost in the blizzard earlier this morning? Josh opened his mouth to ask, but a strong odor of wet dog wafted around him like a damp cloud. Only Joey smelled like that. It was a combination of the lamb wool vest he wore, those strange leggings, and raggedy shirt. Tentatively, Josh stretched his hand out from under the covers and grabbed Joey's foot. The boy yelped in surprise.

"Sorry, Joey. I . . . I thought I might still be dreaming."

This really was Joey, who popped in last night—Christmas Eve—to visit Josh in this same bedroom while his sisters slept soundly in bed and he was on his mattress on the drafty, cold floor, and his mom and aunt sang Christmas carols in the kitchen. Joey was the one who spent hours with Josh, telling him all about the first Christmas because he claimed he was there! This young boy literally appeared in his room without anyone knowing he was in the apartment. Josh couldn't figure it out. Joey seemed to know so much about the past and the present. He was a kid he'd never met before, but Joey seemed to know all there was to know about him. And here he was again, grinning at him like a little crazy monkey.

"Hey, Josh," Joey whispered and snapped the chair forward. His eyes grew bigger and rounder than they already were. "I know where Mr. George is hiding."

Leaning in close to Josh, Joey continued to smile. "You know that short, round bush that's beside the pine tree to the left of the shed? That's where he is!" Joey uncrossed his arms and smoothed his wild, black curls, pleased with himself.

Josh groaned. He even knew about Mr. George! "It's because of Mr. George that I'm in bed in the first place!"

"And in the second place?"

"In the second place," Josh said, sighing, "it wasn't such a bright idea to hide him with a snowstorm coming. I should've known I'd never find him."

"Yeah," agreed Joey. "It *was* kinda stupid. Who hides a snowman during a snowstorm?"

Josh felt embarrassed that Joey knew he'd gotten lost in his own backyard, but the snow was so thick in the whipping wind, it was blinding.

Joey nodded. "It must have been pretty scary for everyone, but God took care of you, for sure."

Josh nodded in agreement as he recalled the events of the morning. It didn't seem real. He remembered while he was hiding under the tree from the battering snow, he prayed to Jesus. His fear almost got the best of him. But he had faith that God would take care of everything. And so He had. One minute he was almost dead, and the next minute, he was safe. Now, it was late afternoon, and Joey was happily talking with Josh once again like nothing had happened.

"Does my mom know you're here?" Josh asked with concern.

Joey shook his head, with a smile a mile wide. How did he sneak in under Mom's nose again? Josh remembered how shocked he was last night when he rolled over on his mattress and saw a young boy sitting on the floor under the windowsill. How did this little kid with no hat, no gloves, and only a wool vest over a threadbare shirt, and sandals with wool socks get around in snowstorms? How was he able to get in and out of the house to Josh's bedroom, past his mom, aunt, and sisters? Two times, no less?

Josh narrowed his eyes and pursed his lips in deep thought. Was this boy a ghost or an angel? He wanted to ask but was afraid of what the answer might be. Josh was tempted to touch him again but decided not to. He already learned that Joey's foot was real.

Returning to the present, Josh sat up, leaned against the wall, and asked a little apprehensively, "So, you know what happened to me this morning?"

"Yes, and like I said, it was pretty dumb going out in a snowstorm!"

"Yeah," Josh admitted. "I guess I got caught up in the excitement." He plopped back down on his back. "But I'm feeling better now, just a little tired. I'm glad you came by. I must have fallen asleep on you last night. I remember your telling me the story of the first Christmas and about your shepherd friends, David and Luke, and you started to tell me how you all were going to follow Jesus and His parents to Egypt—" Josh began sheepishly. "I guess I fell asleep while you were talking. When I woke up this morning, I wondered what happened to you. I didn't mean to be rude—"

Knowing Joey, he could have gone anywhere. He was like a spirit or something. He had an uncanny way of appearing, disappearing, and appearing again.

"Oh, no problem. I know it was late and all," Joey said with a shrug. "After you fell asleep, I decided I'd better get home to my Father. But I came back today to see how you were doing. If you want, I can finish my story from last night."

Josh snuggled back under his covers. He was still a little drowsy, probably from the medication. He would always remember the story Joey told him about the very first Christmas.

"I have to stay in bed before they let me up again anyway, and there's no TV in here, so yes, I'd like to hear your story."

Joey smiled. "Okay, so you remember my shepherd friends David, Luke, and I were in the fields with our sheep, when the angel appeared in the sky and told us that Jesus, our Savior, was born in Bethlehem?

After we got over our fright of seeing thousands of angels hovering above, I left my sleeping sheep in the fields and went down the path to the stable in the cave. I left without David and Luke—they were taking too much time checking on their sheep! I just took off; I was so excited. And when I got there, I saw the baby Jesus with His mother, Mary, and her husband, Joseph."

Josh nodded, recalling the whole scene as it had been told last night. Mary invited Joey in to see the baby, and he'd been thrilled to see the newborn Jesus sleeping peacefully in His mother's arms. A little later, Joey's two shepherd friends, David and Luke, arrived, but already a group of poor people were gathered around the front of the stable, looking in at Mary and her baby. Joseph allowed them to come closer to see the baby, and it was wonderful. David and Luke played their flutes, and everyone enjoyed the night. It became a party to welcome the newborn King!

While Josh relished hearing the story, he still found it confusing. After all, here was Joey, a kid his own age who appeared from nowhere to visit him, telling Josh all about the first Christmas as if he had been there! Joey had seen and heard the angels, touched little Jesus' face, and talked with Mary and Joseph. He was a shepherd, and his friends were shepherds, he said. He knew everything because he was there! Joey was there, and now he was here in Josh's bedroom! How could this be? This was all too strange.

As soon as Joey finishes his story, Josh told himself, *I've got to ask him what he is. A ghost? An angel?* The thing was, if he was an angel, where were his wings? But, maybe they didn't all have wings.

Joey interrupted Josh's thoughts. "Remember how I told you that a couple of years later, an angel appeared in a dream to tell the wise men who visited Jesus to go home a different way? They had to take a different route from the way they came so that Herod, the crazy king who wanted to kill Jesus, wouldn't catch them and force them to tell him where to find Jesus. Well, they didn't have to be told twice. They knew that King Herod was a vicious murderer and liar, so after the angel warned them, they took off on their camels with their servants and left gold, spices, and other gifts with Mary and Joseph."

Joey emphasized that not only did an angel warn the wise men to leave in a hurry, but the angel also spoke to Joseph in a dream too. The angel directed Joseph, "Rise, take the child and his mother and flee to Egypt, and remain there until I tell you, for Herod is about to search for the child, to destroy Him."

"See," Joey explained, "what the angel said is written right here in the Book of Matthew, chapter 2, verse 13."

Joey pointed to the words in the Bible he was holding. Josh followed Joey's finger to the printed paragraph. Another surprise! He hadn't seen Joey with a Bible a moment ago. Where did that come from? His curiosity got the best of him, and he reached for the book spread open on Joey's lap. Joey handed it to him. It was heavy. Thumbing to the place where Joey had pointed, he read that sure enough, an angel did tell Joseph to leave with his family and escape Herod by going to Egypt. Josh handed the book back to Joey, who put it on the floor by his chair.

Sitting straighter, Joey became more animated as he talked. "Remember how I told you that King Herod was a mental case, a mad, blood-thirsty ruler? This is what I found out. He was so crazy that he even killed some of his own family! Can you imagine that? He was just awful. The Romans made him king of Judea, which was sort of like a state or region in the Middle East. Bethlehem was a city in Judea, and he had power to do whatever he wanted in that town, so he sent his soldiers to Bethlehem to find Jesus. He was afraid that Jesus would grow up to take over as king, and he didn't want that to happen. Jesus was a threat to him and his royal family, so he wanted to get rid of Him."

Josh went pale. Herod was like a serial killer, only he didn't have to hide. He could kill whomever he wanted. No wonder the wise men and Jesus' family ran! The man was evil!

"The good news is that when he died, he died in a really bad way. I won't give you all the details because it's too gross, but an ancient historian named Josephus said worms killed him!"

"Worms?" Josh asked incredulously.

"Yeah. They were eating him from the inside." Joey pointed to his stomach and grimaced.

"Eew," groaned Josh. "How gross! Worms in his belly? Nibbling his guts?" Josh put his hand to his mouth and laughed nervously. It would take him awhile to get rid of that picture of the evil king, disintegrating like one of those creatures in the mummy movies.

Worms and all, this story was getting interesting. Leaning on one elbow, head in hand, the pillow snuggled behind his back, Josh urged Joey to continue.

For more information about

S.A. Jewell
and
Blink
please visit:

www.teamofGod.org
www.SaraJewell.com
teamofGod@earthlink.net
www.facebook.com/sarasantosjewell
www.facebook.com/teamofGod

For more information about
AMBASSADOR INTERNATIONAL
please visit:

www.ambassador-international.com
@AmbassadorIntl
www.facebook.com/AmbassadorIntl

If you enjoyed this book, please consider leaving us a review on Amazon, Goodreads, or our website.

www.ingramcontent.com/pod-product-compliance
Lightning Source LLC
Chambersburg PA
CBHW070048080526
44586CB00013B/957